D1237121

THE ULTIMATE
Mountain Bike
BOOK

The definitive illustrated guide to bikes, components, technique, thrills and trails

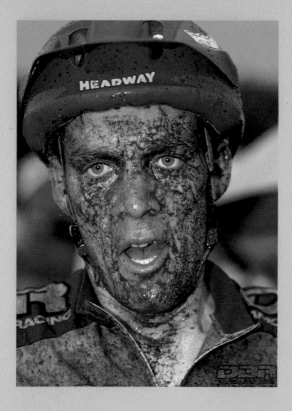

This edition first published in 1996 by

Motorbooks International Publishers & Wholesalers

729 Prospect Avenue

PO Box 1

Osceola

WI 54020

USA

THIS IS A CARLTON BOOK

Text and design copyright © 1996 Carlton Books Limited

All rights reserved. With the exception of quoting brief passages for the purpose of review no
part of this publication may be reproduced without prior written permission from the Publisher.
Motorbooks International is a certified trademark, registered with the United States Patent
Office. The information in this book is true and complete to the best of our knowledge. All
recommendations are made without any guarantee on the part of the author or publisher,
who disclaim any liability incurred in connection with the use of this data for specific details.
We recognize that some words, model names and designations, for example, mentioned
herin are the property of the trademark holder, We use them for identification purposes only.
This is not an official publication.

Motobooks International books are available in discounts in bulk quantity for industrial and
sales-promotional use. For special details write to the Special Sales Manager at the
Publisher's address.

Library of Congress Cataloging-in-Publication Data available.

ISBN 0-7603-0333-9

Project Editors: Liz Wheeler/Sarah Larter

Art Editor: Zoë Maggs

Designer: Carol Wright

Picture research: Ruth Darby

Production: Garry Lewis

Printed and bound in Dubai

THE ULTIMATE
Mountain Bike
BOOK

The definitive illustrated guide to bikes, components, technique, thrills and trails

Nicky Crowther
Maintenance section by Melanie Allwood

Motorbooks International
Publishers & Wholesalers

contents

welcome to the world of the
knobbly
bike!

In the late 1970s, after one group of riders climbed a high pass in Colorado and another descended a high-speed fire-road near San Francisco, "mountain" got hitched to "bike". The sport spread like wildfire. The number of mountain bikes (MTBs) in the world quickly rose from one – Joe Breeze's first *Breezer*, produced in 1977, to millions. In fact, half the bikes now sold around the world are mountain bikes, of which a third are the genuine off-road article. Anyone who wonders why this is so has never been in a mountain bike saddle. It only takes 10 minutes for off-road fever to take over, and there is no known cure for the advanced condition. Mountain biking can mean different things to different people, but once infected you can't shake it off. For enthusiasts, the sport is more than a game – it becomes a way of life.

Perhaps the most surprising thing about the mountain bike is that it took so long to invent. It is by far the most versatile of all bikes – MTB and rider can go on-road and off-road at speeds of up to 80 km/h (50 mph) for adventure, commuting, holidaying and training. It is a passport to the alternative pedal-power movement and a guaranteed introduction to the renowned *joie de vivre* of a society of bike lovers. Many people assume that sunshine and dust are the ideal conditions for mountain biking, but when the temperature drops you can adjust your clothing, grit your teeth and keep on riding. Unlike sports such as football and tennis, mountain biking is a sport that can be enjoyed all the year round.

Today we live in the most mechanized society in history. We need temptations like the mountain bike to keep us active and to stay in touch with the world we live in. On our bikes we give the passive entertainment of screen and car the slip, saving our legs and hearts from certain redundancy, keeping our minds alert and the planet alive. City dwellers can lose themselves in maps and wildwoods, teenage spots are treated with organic mud-packs, and night-clubbers can find natural highs from exploiting nature's obstacles for the ultimate natural thrill.

Mountain biking is simply the best way to get off your backside and get fit. Cycling will improve your health and increase your energy levels as well as giving you the opportunity to explore and revel in nature's adventure park – you just can't beat it.

in the beginning –
the USA

A match made in heaven – the terrain of the USA and the mountain bike.

Unlike compact discs and personal computers, two other inventions of the 1970s, the mountain bike owes less to the advance of science than to the pursuit of pleasure. That was how a now legendary bunch of Californian hippie cyclists discovered a great new way to wreck old bikes, and went on to spread the off-road word far and wide.

Of course, cross-country biking is as old as the bicycle itself. Who didn't do it on their local tracks as a kid? However, in 1976, when these guys in Marin County were likewise obeying their natural instincts, they innocently tripped the wire of a new worldwide sport. First, they decided to compete against the clock hurtling down a short, steep piece of track. Then, they sprinkled the ancient *Schwinn* cruiser bikes or "klunkers" they were using with new home-tooled parts to do so.

Daredevil descent

This humble affair was the first Repack Downhill race on Mount Tamalpais above San Francisco and was attended by just a fistful of people. 2.9 km (1.8 miles) long with a 366 m (1,200 ft) descent, the course record stands at 4 minutes, 22 seconds. The event is held, appropriately, by Gary Fisher, whose name has since adorned hundreds of thousands of bikes.

Fisher's Repack rivals included Joe Breeze and Tom Ritchey who are attributed with designing and building the first modern mountain bikes. The event's organizer was the wordsmith Charlie Kelly, who edited the long-running mountain bike fanzine *Fat Tyre Flyer* from 1980 to 1987 and who wrote the first magazine articles to touch the wider world, which were published by the American magazine *Outside*. *Harley-Davison* motorcycle factory rider Mert Lawwill, who was later to collaborate with Fisher in designing the first specialist MTB rear suspension, was another Repacker. The event was to run intermittently from 1976 until 1984, when riding rights to the trail were lost and the fire track on Repack Hill was closed by the authorities.

Not only does today's bike bear the Repack legacy, but so does the biker's delight in speed. This is officially evident at the bone-busting big-bucks downhill events of the world series and championships. Unofficially, it is found in the subversive tradition that is relived every time a grown-up kid survives a pant-spoiling descent to ride another day. The bikes the pioneers used were extraordinary beasts compared to today's machines. For a start they were up to 40 years old and weighed up to 23 kg (50 lb). They had *BMX* cowhorn handlebars, no gears and a single rear coaster brake, operated by back-pedalling. The speed of the Repack descent meant that on every ride the grease inside would burn off and begin to seize. The innards had to be repacked every go – hence the event's name and the idea of "smokin" downhills.

Although great fun, the gear-less bikes were too heavy to be much good at climbing – they were only estimable even at descending – so pretty soon the little adaptations that would eventually become standard were flowing out of the backyard workshops and on to the bikes thick and fast. Along came a front brake and seat post quick release, to make it easier to lower the ill-fitting posts and save them from bending.

Gary Fisher is attributed with fixing the first 5-speed gear on a klunker, which also had the first thumbshifter gear levers. The other major advance was the supply from 1978 of the right diameter aluminium rims and tyres, which instantly knocked 2 kg (4.4 lb) off the bike's weight and a lot more off the rolling resistance. No longer was a strength of hulk-like proportions necessary to get one moving uphill.

The first MTB

The honour of creating the first purpose-built frame for a mountain bike goes to Joe Breeze, who was also the rider to win the most Repack races. Breeze was a pedigree road man, holder of a first-category license with the local Velo Club Mount Tamalpais and the five-time winner of a 320 km (200 mile) tandem race, partnered by fellow off-roader Otis Guy. It was partly to escape the pressures of road racing that he and many of his clubmates used to truck up Mount Tam with their klunkers.

In 1977, with a little frame-making experience picked up partly from his engineering father and partly from a traditionalist local bike builder, Breeze conceived and constructed the mark one *Breezer* – the most sophisticated off-road bike then in existence. He followed it up the following year with ten more, built, or so he thought, for his personal circle of friends. The bikes took the best from the klunkers – the fat tyres and handlebars – but had different drivetrain geometry for wider clearance, with thumbshifters that operated derailleur gears, and *Weinmann* cantilevers to replace the old drum brakes, which were operated by *Magura* levers. Although the cruiser-style central tube that ran like a bow from the head tube of the bike to the rear hub is long gone, these first bikes certainly forged the path still followed by rigid mountain bikes.

The originals – including Charlie Kelly and Gary Fisher.

The mountain bike evolves

Now a series of events unravelled, which led to factory production, cheaper prices and high street sales. In 1979 21-year-old Tom Ritchey, a former US national junior team rider and member of the klunker clan, began to apply Breeze's ideas to his own bikes. Gary Fisher bought one of Ritchey's first three models, and then in 1979 linked up with Charlie Kelly to form the first regular bike-selling company, *Mountainbikes*, which operated until 1983. The next step from small-town birthplace to the global off-road village came thanks to Mike Sinyard of fledging company *Specialized*. In 1980, he bought four *Ritcheys* and took the Californian design across the waters to the factories of Taiwan. In 1981 Sinyard

Fat tire bike week in Crested Butte.

Its all downhill for Gary Fisher.

returned with the first model in a line of mass-production mountain bikes – the *Stumpjumpe*r. Along with the business associations of Gary Fisher and Tom Ritchey, Sinyard's *Specialized* has survived the industry's numerous growing pains and is still trading.

Rocky Mountain high

The coincidence of mechanical curiosity and dexterity in the Californian riders is what grabs most of the limelight in retrospectives, but no MTB history is complete without mentioning the Rocky Mountain bikers. In 1976 a thousand miles east in the Rockies, a parallel off-road movement was stirring. In Crested Butte, an isolated little mountain town in Colorado where even the main street was not surfaced, cyclists with lesser machines but with snow-capped peaks outside every window tackled the ride over the mountains to nearby Aspen.

The cyclists' high-altitude route, with its peak at the 3,870 m (12,700 ft) Pearl Pass, dated back to the nineteenth century, when it was used for hauling ore by mule from Aspen to the railway line at Crested Butte. The inaugural Pearl Pass Klunker Tour took place with 15 riders – seven rode the whole way up, eight took rides in a 4-wheel drive vehicle. The report of the ride in the *Crested Butte Pilot* of September 17, 1976 records that at the overnight camp 4,8 km (3 miles) below the pass the riders "consumed one keg of beer, seven more cases of beer, three bottles of Schnapps, two gallons of wine and three bottles of champagne. Then ... everyone got drunk and passed out on the pass." Richard Ullery, the *Pilot* continues, became famous on the ride as "the first man in history to cross Pearl Pass in a bathtub." Unlike the fat-tyred bike, it never caught on.

In 1978 there were 13 riders on the Pearl Pass Tour, among them by invitation several of the Californian names, including Wende Cragg, the only woman who rode regularly in the bunch and whose photographs of what was going on in both California and Colorado at the time make up a substantial amount of the pictorial records. The Pass is still open to anyone who wants to ride it, and the Tour has become a highlight of the annual Crested Butte Fat Tire Bike Week, which was established in 1981 not long after those first intrepid trips. Throughout the 1980s, as the fledging racing scene got earnest in the USA and Europe, this festival and the Canyonlands bike week in Moab, Utah organized for hundreds of people to explore the beautiful areas just for the buzz.

Here to stay...

Mountain biking may be young, but, in terms of personal and environmental freedom and the living it provides to so many people it has earned its own archive within a decade. In 1988 the Mountain Bike Hall of Fame and Museum was established as a non-profit corporation in a humble shack in Crested Butte to preserve the history of the sport and recognize its founding parents. Inside the museum retired machines from the early days are displayed on stands on wooden floorboards. There are three *Schwinns* from 1937, 1949 and 1955, an original 1977 *Breezer*, a 1979 *Lawwill-Knight Pro-Cruiser*, a 1982 *Stumpjumper* and the *Fisher* ridden to US national victory by Joe Murray in 1985. These are supplemented by memora-

Tom Ritchey at speed.

bilia; hand-sewn rosettes, the Repack start sheet and classic photos.

By 1995 there were 51 Hall of Fame inductees including bike builders, racers, organizers and trailmakers.

As well as all the aforementioned pioneers, they include racers Joe Murray and Jaquie Phelan (both inducted in 1988), Cindy Whitehead and Ned Overend (both

1990), and John Tomac (1991) and Sara Ballantyne (1992). There is trailmapper Chuck Bodfish Elliot (1991), Andean MTB explorer Dr Al Farrell (1991) and a large group of entrepreneurial metalworkers including Chris "Fat" Chance (1990), Ross "Shafer" (1991), Gary "Klein" (1992), Gary "Merlin" Helfrich (1993), Keith "Bontrager" (1994) and not forgetting Ignaz and Frank Schwinn (1994).

Honourable scribes include Zapata Espinoza, the editor (1986–1993) of the largest US magazine devoted to the sport *Mountain Bike Action*. The curator of the Hall of Fame Carole Bauer-Romanik was entered in 1991, Kay Peterson-Cook, the driving force behind the Crested Butte Fat Tyre festival, was added in 1995, as was Steve Ready who has organized the InterBike trade show since 1982 and Junzo Kawai, who brought together Japanese component manufacturers and US backyard designers to create mountain biking equipment. Although it is US based, nominations to the Hall of Fame are taken worldwide.

The honourable *Schwinn*.

British beginnings

The wildly successful Muddy Fox Courier.

The urban mountain biker

The UK mountain bike revolution was stimulated less by Californian terrain than by the flair of London cycle despatch riders. The mountain bike was funky. They were great for urban posing, worked brilliantly on pot-holed city streets and contrasted wickedly with the output from the stuffy cycling establishment. Boosted by their association with radicalism and fun – windsurfers supposedly turned to mountain biking when there was no breeze – the fashion press pushed the bikes into the limelight. They were aided by *Muddy Fox*'s advertising flair, which had boxer Frank Bruno astride one model and employed American Jaquie Phelan to crouch beside a stream with paw-prints up her bare back in another. *Courier* sales hit 300,000 annually, the total of today's annual sales of all quality MTBs in the UK – the mountain bike had colonized Britain.

Until the early 1980s touring was the most popular form of recreational cycling in Britain, with a hardcore of serious road racers. A small off-road branch movement was formed in 1955 called the Rough Stuff Fellowship, but although they preferred tracks to tarmac, they rode, and indeed still ride on tourers. Most bikes in Britain then were made by long-established domestic factories such as Claud Butler, Dawes and Raleigh, with individual craftsmen providing the high-end, bespoke market. The touring market was buoyant when the first MTBs hit Britain in 1983. The handful of costly *Specialized Stumpjumpers* which made their appearance at the main trade show that year were dismissed out of hand by the traditional cycling trade as toys.

The fringe builders and the adventure sportspeople disagreed, and the first dirty dozen were snapped up by shops mainly in Edinburgh and London. The first hand-built British mountain bike also appeared. Geoff Apps' *Cleland Range Rider*, which sold 20 models, was short and high and had a sloping top tube with extra front end bracing. That was followed by the *High Path* from David Wrath-Sharman, who fitted an extra long head tube and long cross-braces, also for a very strong front end.

From 1984 onward, sales of imported mountain bike sales multiplied so fast that they caught the suppliers by surprise and activated new British producers. While *Specialized*, boosted by the cheaper *Rockhopper*, sold 600 bikes, *Ridgeback* stepped in with their first models and *Muddy Fox* put the wildly popular *Courier* on sale. Soon another British touring marque, *Saracen*, spotted the trend and launched what was to become another fondly remembered British mountain bike, the *Tufftrax*.

Shimano Biopace chainset.

Early *SunTour* gear shifter.

Early components

U-BRAKES

For a couple of years in the late 1980s, the rear brake was fitted not on the seat stays below the saddle, but underneath the bike on the chain stays behind the pedal spindle. Called a U-brake, because of the long, arcing arms that replaced the straddle wire triangle in what was a very cramped space, their design and position supposedly meant more powerful braking. At this time MTB design was obsessed with strength rather than weight and anything that distinguished the new bikes from road bikes. However, the U-brake had a major disadvantage – it was too close to the ground. The callipers clogged, the cable clogged and the chainring teeth often gouged knuckles when the brake was being fastened – for which the bike had to be standing on its head. They were discontinued in the early 1990s.

BIOPACE CHAINRINGS

This theory said that misshapen elliptical chainrings from *Shimano*, tradenamed *BioPace* and later emulated by *SunTour*, got more power out of the pedalstroke than circular rings. The leg is at its strongest at the start of the downstroke at 3 O'Clock, so here the ring should be flatter to give

increased leverage. 90° further on, at about 8 O'clock, the curve on the ring is sharper, to decrease the leverage and give the leg an easier time as it pulls back up. *BioPace* was claimed to be efficient and knee-saving for beginners and climbing, and was plugged as a pure-breed mountain bike part. However, riders felt though as if they were lurching with each rotation and *Biopace* gradually fell from grace. The road rider's creed of pedalling in smooth rotations regained favour and the offset around the chainrings disappeared. These *Shimano* chainrings are now tradenamed *BioPace Pro*.

HITE RITE

Patented by Joe Breeze and his partner Josh Angell this was a canny sprung clip device that fixed on at the seat post cluster and gripped the seat post. It allowed the rider to lower the saddle for descents, then reset it automatically at the right height. The gadget sold in the hundreds of thousands in the early days so that riders could get right over the back of the bike.

   In the end people got fed up with dismounting to do what became an unnecessary manoeuvre as they learned to bow their legs around the saddle to drop behind it, without changing the saddle height. The *Hite Rite* is now rarely spotted on the trails.

bikes ar

d equipment

ountain bikers have introduced a new language to cycling – one that takes a little practice to understand. This chapter translates the technical jargon and teaches the principles of the equipment. It will help you to find the right bike, and the ultimate kit to go with it. Once fluent in mountain bike-speak, you should be able to read and assess reviews and pieces of equipment independently. You should have the confidence to keep the bike and yourself going, and the ability to realize the right time to upgrade. You will able to avoid the clothing mistakes that can ruin a winter ride, and, with luck, you will even learn enough about mechanics to save yourself huge maintenance bills.

The idea that mountain bikes are slow in design is long dead. With frames built from high-tech metals such as titanium, aluminium, steel and carbon fibre, and with specialized shock absorbers, the top off-road models can match the speed of the fastest road-racing bikes. However, you don't need to be rich to ride off-road. At the other end of the price scale, even the simplest genuine mountain bike, with a sturdy frame, up to two dozen gears, powerful brakes and of course the knobbly tyres, is kitted out ready for a day's trail action.

A lot of mountain bikers get hooked on the sport after having had a go on a friend's MTB. They then go on to develop their own taste in equipment. Restricted by cost, the majority equip themselves with the basics – a decent bike, helmet, shorts and perhaps SPD pedals, upgrading or customizing when significant advances in materials, safety or mechanics roll off the production lines. After all, riding just once a week will get the bike dirty enough and cause enough breakdowns, to keep you busy maintaining it, never mind keeping up with all the upgrades that appear on the market.

There is no compulsion to use the latest equipment, but the rate of new production is so high that you could, if you really wanted to, upgrade your bike's components and kit annually in the name of style, and to take advantage of any small improvements in performance. Bikes and equipment are improving, although not at the speed that advertisers would like us to believe. Gradually, the advances trickle down to even the most basic models and equipment. Watch out for advances in materials and technology that will form the mountain bike of the future. New applications currently being applied include, for example, the use of carbon fibre for frames, computer-programmed metal-working, and new weaves and dyeing processes in the vibrantly coloured world of fleece.

Yet without human energy to transform it into an adventure tool, the mountain bike is a lifeless hulk leaning against a wall. It's a cliché, but however smooth the kit, it's the thighs that count.

what makes a mountain bike

While the visual differences between a mountain bike and a road bike are striking, the structural differences are a matter of adaptation rather than radical invention. A mountain bike (MTB) is built to be stronger because its environment constantly subjects it to stresses that would destroy a road bike. Also proportionally smaller than a road bike, a mountain bike is more manoeuvrable on its uneven home ground. And there are those tyres – chunky, knobbly beasts with superb gripping ability – fitted onto smaller wheels with a 26 in diameter. A mountain bike is easier to ride too – you can brake, change gear and steer simultaneously – without even taking a hand off the handlebars. You can get astride without the flexibility of a gymnast and once on board, you will find a mountain bike more comfortable and upright, so you can laugh at pot-holes and traffic-jams when you sail on it to school, work or the shops.

The Mountain Bike Frame

A cyclist's mountain bike is ideally about 7.5–10 cm (3–4 in) smaller than their equivalent road bike frame. For a full explanation and details about how to achieve the correct frame size see pp. 22–23.

FRONT END

The place on a mountain bike frame that takes the most stress is the area where the down tube and the top tube join the head tube. This is a region where a head-on impact can cause damage – either cracking in the welds or a fold showing on the underside of the down tube. Manufacturers reinforce the area with extra jointing material, gussetting or with a thicker internal wall or external width in the tube. Ensure that you survey and feel the tubes periodically to check for any damage.

DOWN TUBE

The down tube is the backbone of a bicycle. The longest tube on the frame, it carries more stress than the others and is strengthened accordingly – either by fattening and gussetting in the case of aluminium, by butting (thickening the wall at stress points) in the case of steel, or by directional layering of the fibres in the case of carbon fibre.

TOP TUBE

Instantly recognizable in an off-road bike is the low and sloping top tube. Good MTBs have longer top tubes to ensure a crouched, aerodynamic position and to balance the bike between the front and back when climbing mean gradients. The distance between the top tube and the ground is the standover height, and is the central measurement in sizing (see pp. 22–23).

SEAT CLUSTER

Early MTB frames were weak around the seat cluster because the seat post extends much further from the frame than on road bikes. The unforeseen extra leverage in the post would cause it to fold, or for cracking to appear around seat cluster joints. These days frame builders reinforce this area with butting and over-sizing.

THE MAIN TRIANGLE AND REAR TRIANGLE

A bike's strength is concentrated in the main triangle. This means that on budget

Road bikes are proportionally larger than mountain bikes.

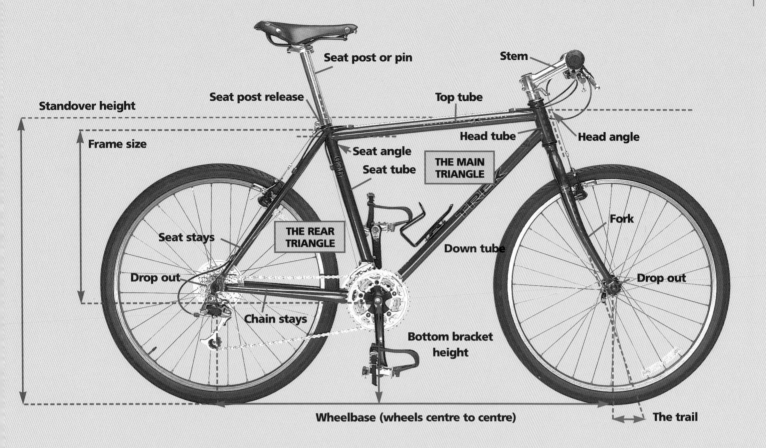

Standover height
Frame size
Seat post or pin
Seat post release
Top tube
Head tube
Head angle
Stem
Seat angle
Seat tube
THE MAIN TRIANGLE
Seat stays
THE REAR TRIANGLE
Fork
Drop out
Down tube
Drop out
Chain stays
Bottom bracket height
Wheelbase (wheels centre to centre)
The trail

bikes the rear triangle may be constructed from lower-grade tubing than the main triangle. When choosing a MTB, try to maximize the quality of tubing throughout. The rear triangle will be constructed from thinner tubing, as stress is shared between the chain stays and seat stays. This allows room for mud to build up on the tyres without clogging.

THE FORK

As the first thing to bend in an impact, MTB forks, both of suspension and rigid design, are incredibly strong. If they break they contribute greatly to the absorption of a crash, and they are easily replaced should they become damaged, or you wish to upgrade them.

SEAT POST (PIN)

Easily interchangeable, the seat post (pin) should be kept lubricated for easy adjustment. It is measured in diameter to sit flush inside the seat tube.

DROPOUTS

The wheel sockets are part of the fork at the front and the frame at the rear. Safety dropouts are sometimes put on the front to stop the wheel falling away if the release comes undone accidentally. On the rear wheel it is advantageous to have a replaceable dropout, so that if it bends in a crash, the frame is still usable.

STEERING-HEAD ANGLE AND SEAT ANGLE

Both measured against the horizontal, the steering-head angle and the seat angle decide the handling feel of the frame as they influence the relative lengths of the tubes, the angle of the rider over the pedals and the steering. The steeper the angle the stiffer and racier the handling. After early experimentation, MTB angles have settled at between 72°–74° for the seat angle and 70°–71.5° for the steering-head angle. The steering is right

when it will ride easily with no hands, without flopping to either side, or holding too firmly in the neutral straight-ahead position. The measurement that decides this is the trail, which is optimal at around 6–8 cm (2.5–3 in).

WHEELBASE

This is the distance between the centre of each wheel – around 102 cm (40 in). Again, the shorter this is, the racier the bike.

CHAIN STAY LENGTH

The average length of the lower stay is 40–43 cm (16–17 in). Off-road, cut-down stays improve traction on the rear wheel and make accelerating and climbing easier; however, they will exaggerate the bike's friskiness on descents.

BOTTOM BRACKET HEIGHT

On a mountain bike, this is typically 2.5 cm (1 in) higher than it is on a road bike.

mountain bike
components

GROUPSET

A complete set of components from one manufacturer, the groupset consists of the brakes, hubs, headset, gearing and levers. Each piece is of a similar grade, compatible with the other pieces, and is adapted according to the type of bike. Most new bikes, regardless of manufacturer, come ready-specified with one groupset or another. It is an area monopolized by the Japanese company *Shimano*, which has a dozen or so smooth and efficient groupsets

for all budgets and types of bike. Other manufacturers are *Campagnolo* and *Sachs*.

BRAKES

Brakes, a vital control on any bike, are all the more important on mountain bikes because of the trickier nature of off-roading and the high downhill speeds. Top-pull cantilever brakes have become the mountain bike standard, as opposed to side-pull calliper brakes, which are standard on road bikes with drop handlebars. A top-pull cantilever brake,

unlike side-pull brakes, can straddle the width of MTB tyres, providing the stronger braking force necessary for powerful deceleration. In the early days of mountain bikes rear brakes were commonly calliper-type "U-brakes" fixed to the underside of the chain stays. Now they are cantilevers, and live at the top of the seat stays as far away as possible from trail muck.

Another type of brake is the hub brake, on which the braking surfaces are sealed inside the hub housing, protecting them from

Seat post release

Gear lever

Stem

Brake lever

Headset top race

Headset bottom race

Back brake

Front derailleur

Rim

Sprockets (6, 7 or 8)

Rim

Front brake

Rear derailleur

Triple chainrings

Front hub (behind)

Crank

Rear hub (behind)

Bottom bracket (inside)

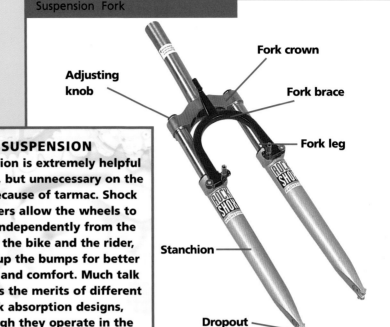

Suspension Fork

Fork crown

Adjusting knob

Fork brace

Fork leg

Stanchion

Dropout

mud. Disc brakes, a motorbike adaptation, are also located at the hub. These types of brake are good in wet weather and on frames that have no place for rim-mounted brakes, such as one-piece moulded bikes, for example, the *Lotus* Carbon Fibre MTB.

GEARS

Most mountain bikes have 21 or 24 gears, three on the front at the chainrings, and seven or eight at the back at the sprockets. They are needed to provide diverse pedalling speeds for the variety of off-road terrain. MTB gears also have a concentration of easier gears for slow or steep ground. The gear controls consist of the front and rear derailleurs, which are the arms that move the chain across the rings and sprockets, the gear cables, and the gear levers, which are top-mounted, under-bar mounted or revolvers (see pp. 68–69).

WHEELS

After the frame, the most important parts of a bike are the wheels, which need surprisingly little maintenance thanks to good hubs, rims, spokes and tyres. Mountain bike wheels are 26 inches in diameter, rather than the 27-inch road wheels. This allows for the fatter tyres necessary for off-road handling.

Hubs are relatively simple items; they contain the axle and bearings and should never be allowed to come loose. Wheel rims should be made of strong, lightweight alloy with a good braking surface. The laws of

SUSPENSION

Suspension is extremely helpful off-road, but unnecessary on the road because of tarmac. Shock absorbers allow the wheels to move independently from the rest of the bike and the rider, taking up the bumps for better control and comfort. Much talk concerns the merits of different shock absorption designs, although they operate in the same basic way. Proper shock absorption, whether elastomer (bumpers) or hydraulic (fluid), works by swallowing the bump in two steps. First, the spring gives way to allow the independent movement; second, the damper soaks up the spring energy and allows a clean return.

physics behind an efficient wheel dictate that the tension in the spokes is evenly maintained, keeping the wheel straight and strong as it is compressed by the terrain. Also, the rotating mass on the outside of the wheel should be as kept as low as possible. This is the part of the bike that moves the most and so it is here that weight is hardest for the rider to overcome. Finally, the width and pattern of the tyres should minimize rolling resistance and maximize grip.

The best wheels come from specialist wheel-builders, but the factory-assembled wheels found on most bikes sold in the shops, roll and last well. Some mechanically minded cyclists even build their own wheels. Maintaining a wheel is mostly about truing it

by tightening and loosening the spokes with a spoke key. This takes out the minor kinks in the rim and returns the tension to equilibrium all the way round the wheel (see pp. 58–59).

STEERING

The head tube of the bike contains a stacked pair of steering bearings, called the headset. This is fairly standard across all types of bike, although a new small-scale development for mountain bikes, called an "Aheadset", is easier to tighten and slightly reduces weight.

PEDALS AND BOTTOM BRACKET

The pedals turn on axles, which are screwed into the cranks and turn in the frame on the bottom bracket or pedal spindle. This is a unit containing a double set of bearings, one on each side of the frame's bottom bracket shell. Performance developments include lighter weight axles and sealed fit-and-forget bearings, to end the chore of having to strip and clean them regularly.

frame
materials

The majority of bicycle frames are made from different grades of steel, aluminium and titanium alloys, with carbon fibre gaining mainstream ground.

TITANIUM

Lighter than steel, longer-lasting than aluminium, resistant and beautiful in the raw, titanium is highly suitable for bicycles. Titanium's ride quality is precision, and as it is corrosion resistant, it needs neither painting nor anodizing (the application of a protective layer of oxides), so can be safely left bare to the elements in its natural dull silver-coloured state. All of which justify its downside – its high cost.

It has taken 40 years for titanium to catch on as a regular bicycle material. Although the first frame, which weighed only 1.5 kg (2¾ lb), was displayed in 1956 at the London Cycle Show, it has only become common in the 1990s, having proved itself in the aerospace and marine industries. The person credited with integrating titanium into cycling society is Gary Helfrich of *Merlin*, USA, a company that builds a small number of exclusively titanium frames. Now most major manufacturers have at least one titanium bike in their range. Not only holding a position at the forefront of bike design, titanium fulfills the demands of cyclists. Little low-quality titanium tubing is found in the bicycle trade. Most of it is a top-quality titanium alloy called 3Al/2.5V, which contains 3% aluminium and 2.5%

vanadium added, or 6Al/4V which has 6% aluminium and 4% vanadium. Aluminium improves the alloy's weld-ability, while the vanadium improves its ability to bend without breaking.

ALUMINIUM

Aluminium built up a fan club in the bike trade in the 1980s because it is light, is great at shock absorption and is resistant to corrosion. Less favourable is the fact that it has the least fatigue resistance of the frame materials. A cube of aluminium weighs less than a cube of steel, because it is less dense. Aluminium's tensile strength

Titanium as viewed through an electron microscope.

Welding together the bottom bracket cluster on an aluminium bike by *Pace*.

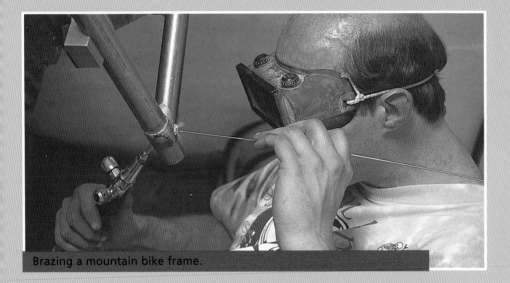
Brazing a mountain bike frame.

CARBON FIBRE

50 years from now we may all be pedalling bikes constructed from carbon fibre, a cheap raw material derived from crude oil. The qualities of a carbon-fibre frame are stiffness, strength and low weight; however, its labour-intensive manufacture means that it will be a long time before bikes made from the stuff can be mass-produced on the scale of steel. *Giant*, a Taiwanese company, is pumping large amounts of money into development, and already produces a range of carbon-fibre bikes for both committed road and off-road riding.

– the point at which it breaks – and yield strength – the point at which it permanently deforms – are both lower than steel, therefore aluminium tubing is made fatter. When you double the diameter of a tube you quadruple its rigidity, so the tube's thickness can be slimmed down to just a couple of millimetres, bringing the volume of material used back into line with weight targets.

Raw aluminium is a weak element and must be mixed with other metals and then heat-treated for strength. A simple six-figure code, for example 6061–T1, describes these metallurgical processes and tells you which grade of aluminium has been used to construct the bike. The first figure refers to the chief alloy, the following three numerals refer to the added alloys in diminishing proportion, and the letter and number after the hyphen define the heat process. 2XXX has copper as the main strengthening element, 3XXX uses manganese, 4XXX silicon, 5XXX magnesium, 6XXX magnesium and silicon and 7XXX uses zinc. Only the 2-, 6- and 7-series alloys can be heat-treated; T6 is the most common form of heat treatment, where the tubing has undergone solution heat treatment and artificial ageing.

STEEL

Steel is the standard material for bicycle frames, with good yield and tensile strength providing rigidity and durability. It is easy to work and, when strengthened by heat-treatment, which is how British-made *Reynolds* 531 tubing becomes *Reynolds* 753 tubing, it can be used sparingly enough to match the light weight of both titanium and aluminium.

Cheap steel bicycle tubing is 'high-tensile', and found on bikes in the lower price range. Among more expensive bikes the most common steel used is "cromoly" – cro-mo or chromoly – with added chromium and molybdenum, which can be butted.

In competition with the new materials, steel has not lost its reputation for performance, and is still the first choice for many racers, who seek its familiar rigidity, good handling and low weight.

The threat to steel's life, however, is rust, so bikes need to be kept well painted and dried. Water must never be allowed to sit inside a frame, particularly around the bottom bracket as it will eat away at the structure. Conversely, frames which have been broken or been badly dented can, unlike other bicycle materials, be repaired cheaply and easily by a frame builder.

The unique advantage of carbon fibre is that, unlike other metals, the direction of rigidity in the tubes can be controlled, depending on how you layer the fibres. A tube with helical (spiral) fibres will resist bending better than one with lengthways-laid fibres. This means that strength can be achieved without extra volume of material, and weight can be saved where stress is less. Layers of resin-impregnated carbon fibre are laid together according to the position of stress points and then cured to create a rigid, light structure with top fatigue resistance. Carbon fibre can be produced in tubes or a single moulded shape.

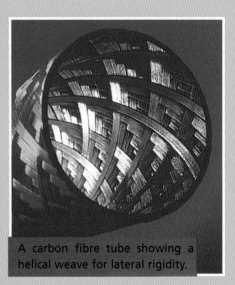
A carbon fibre tube showing a helical weave for lateral rigidity.

buying
a mountain bike

Sizing up

Getting the right size bike is easy if you follow a few simple rules.

SIZE

With the exception of a few manufacturers, who use the terms "small, medium and large", bike size is given in centimetres or inches and is based on leg length. It is the distance from the centre of the bottom bracket up the seat tube to the centre of where the seat tube meets the top tube, assuming that the top tube is horizontal. From this measurement is decided the second most critical dimension of bike fit – reach. This is the distance from the seat to the handlebars. Manufacturers' sizes vary slightly, but not enough to matter, so this central measurement, like shoe sizes, is a reliable estimate of fit that suits the majority of riders. Most ranges will have models to suit adults between 1.47 m (4 ft 10 in) and 1.93 m (6 ft 2 in).

SIZING BY EYE

When you stand astride a mountain bike there should be a gap between your crotch and the top tube, of about 7–13 cm (2½– 5 in). This is more than is necessary on a road bike, where all the gap need be is trustworthy. A larger amount of clearance is needed off-road as MTB frames are smaller for better manoeuvrability and stability. Rocks and hummocks throw the rider about too – and the last place you want to unintentionally

MOUNTAIN BIKE SIZING CHART	
A quick reference guide to MTB frame size	
HEIGHT	**FRAME SIZE**
1.47–1.52 m	33–38 cm
(4 ft 10 in–5 ft)	(12–15 in)
1.57–1.62 m	38–43 cm
(5 ft 2 in–5 ft 4 in)	(14–17 in)
1.69–1.72 m	41–48 cm
(5 ft 6 in–5 ft 8 in)	(16–19 in)
1.77–1.83 m	46–51 cm
(5 ft 10 in–6 ft)	(18–21 in)
1.88–1.93 m	51–56 cm
(6 ft 2 in–6 ft 4 in)	(20–22 in)

straddle is an overly intimate top tube. If you know your size in road bikes, calculate your mountain bike size by subtracting four inches from it. As well as the bigger crotch safety net, this takes in the extra 2.5–5 cm (1–2 in) height a mountain bike bottom bracket is above the ground.

Allow a gap between the top tube and your body.

REACH ▶

One dimension that varies between makes and models is the reach from the saddle to the handlebars. This is derived, rather approximately, from the size of the bike and according to its purpose. Racers prefer a longer, lower reach, with the handlebars a few centimetres below the saddle, in imitation of the rear-in-the-air position of a road racing bike. Beginners find reassurance in sitting more upright and might prefer handlebars which are on a level with the saddle, or slightly higher – although that is slightly less stable.

The reach is decided by a combination of top tube length, stem length, saddle position and head angle. Getting it right can be a little tricky, although there is a degree of leeway. There is no ideal bike-to-body ratio as there is with size, and stems vary in length and angle. People's dimensions are disproportionate too. A rider with long legs and short upper-body might be more stretched with a standard reach than is comfortable. Your rear, shoulders and wrists will

Setting the saddle to the right height.

TAILORED BIKES

For a reasonable price, you can have a bike hand-built to fit your own unique dimensions and achieve the best fit. Craftshops will measure you as if for an expensive suit and build a bike to your choice of tubing, angles, components and colours.

SHE'LL GROW INTO IT!

It's fine to buy a young child a bike at the bigger end of his or her limits but take care that it does not handicap their riding. Wheel diameters gradually increase up to the full-sized 26 in wheels, to fit people from around 1.47 m (4 ft 10 in). Below that, 24 in wheeled bikes with proper off-road componentry are available from *Cannondale, Scott* and *GT,* but their full cost means you may be happier waiting until the child can ride a full-size bike.

let you know if you are too stretched-out – it is a major cause of saddle soreness.

Think about the reach on your test rides: arms should be slightly bent, and you should be able to see the front hub behind the handlebars. If after having ridden the bike for a while you are unhappy with the reach, there are two ways to fine-tune it; either with a different length stem, or by sliding the saddle forward or backward on the rails.

Setting your saddle height

THE PERCH

For easy pedalling and healthy knees the saddle height must be right. Just as you straighten your leg every time you walk a step, so your leg should extend naturally with every stroke, without being stretched.

■ To find the correct measurement work out $\%_{0}$ your inside leg measurement, then set the

saddle that far above the bottom bracket.

■ To set the saddle height by eye, get someone to hold the bike while you sit on it and pedal, with the ball of your foot over the pedal axle. Hop on and off to adjust the height – do not rush it – until your foot is horizontal at the bottom of the pedal stroke.

■ Take the saddle adjusting tool on your first few rides, until the height is right – then you can forget about it.

■ If you are a new cyclist you may want to keep the saddle low enough to put your feet down without dismounting when you stop. This is fine for irregular or short rides, but put it up once you've got some balance and confidence.

SADDLE ANGLE AND FORWARD SETTING

The saddle angle should be horizontal, or tilted slightly downward for comfort. Moving the saddle forward and backward along the rails will alter your reach.

a beginner's bike

A real mountain bike does not come cheaper than about £300. This may seem to be a lot of money, even though it sits at the bottom of a ladder of prices that finishes somewhere in the thousands. A very cheap lookalike mountain bike may seem like a bargain, but it will handle badly, be too weak to withstand the battering of rough ground and will be heavy. More critically though, its braking will be soft and wobbly. A decent road-grade bike for transport and weekend country park fun can be purchased cheaply, but will not guarantee satisfactory, safe off-road riding. Mountain biking is already hard work if you are unfit, so you need to be given a head-start by your equipment.

As their wares are driven by a human engine, the builders of cheaper bikes know that it is not gimmicks that count but a bike's physical performance. Rest assured that you get what you pay for and a quality bike is a guaranteed, complete piece of inspiring equipment that will open up a new world of play, thrills and fitness. Most of the bikes in the lower price bracket have standard characteristics. Individuality comes more into play as the price rises.

A reasonably priced ride

For a relatively cheap mountain bike the *Kona Hahanna* weighs in at 12.3 kg (27.1 lb). This bike is typical of its price range, with gears and brakes comparable to most of its similarly priced cousins.

WHO IS IT FOR?

This bike is for everyone with an occasional or one-off interest in mountain biking. It will fit most people, as it comes in sizes to suit riders from 1.47 m (4 ft 10 in) to around 1.93 m (6 ft 2 in). The *Hahanna* is a bike for anyone starting out in mountain biking, or for experienced cyclists who enjoy a ride whenever they can, but don't have the time to become serious off-road activists. A bike like this is made to last and could be loaded with panniers and trekked hundreds of miles along rough roads. It is suited to cruising rather than high-speed manoeuvring on a tough race course. Bikes at this price are fully working, fully serviceable and can be maintained with quality parts over time.

THE COMPANY

Kona is one of a handful of pedigree manufacturers who have contributed to the design of mountain bikes. The company is based in Vancouver, Canada, and builds in Taiwan. It has nurtured its range, which numbered four steel bikes in 1989, with new aluminium, titanium and suspended models. In 1996, these and the originals numbered 13, priced from the lower end of the scale right to the most expensive mountain bikes. The main *Kona* trademarks are a long, sloping top tube that gives you good crotch clearance with a proper low-torso position, an extended seat tube with reinforcement around the saddle post and own-brand co-ordinated front and rear tyres.

WEIGHT

With mountain bikes one of the chief measures of quality is weight, and when you are straining to make it all the way to the top of a peak, you will know why. For bikes of this standard a respectable weight lies between

The *Kona Hahanna*: good value and a great first mountain bike.

12–14 kg (27–30 lbs). This is achieved mostly by using butted tubing and decent alloy components.

FRAME

The bike's structure is of cromoly steel, the standard alloy with added chromium and molybdenum which is used in the majority of mountain bikes. Virtually all the *Hahanna*'s tubing is double-butted, a weight-saving feature which means that internally it is thinner in the middle and thicker at each end around the joints. The ends are kept bulky to resist the weakening effect of heat on the area when the tubes are joined, and to handle the stresses concentrated at the tube junctions caused by, for example, bungled log-hops.

Kona's own fat, straight *Project II* cromoly forks sit on the front.

GROUPSET, GEARS AND BRAKES

■ Groupset: *Shimano Acera-X*, with a front hub from *Shimano Altus*, a lower quality groupset.

■ Brakes: *Shimano Acera-X* cantilever arms come from a budget groupset that sits in the pecking order above *Shimano Altus* and below *Shimano STX*. The *High Command* levers are of shiny alloy and drilled out, resembling custom levers. This braking set-up provides solid, direct braking and is easy to maintain.

■ Gears: *Shimano Acera-X*
GripShift SRT 300
Chainrings: 42/32/24
Sprockets: 11–28

The main feature of the bike's gearing is that it uses GripShift (revolver) changing rather than separately-mounted thumb-and-finger levers. The first inroad by another company into *Shimano* territory, this type of gear lever now comes fitted on a significant number of new mountain bikes – it is light and simple to maintain, easy to use and has markings to show which gear you are in.

The rear derailleur (gear changer) is longer, to take up the slack in the chain when it is on the smallest 11-tooth sprocket. The chainrings and sprockets are small for reduced weight and better clearance, as is now standard.

PEDALS

Called "LXT" these are simple flat pedals for ordinary footwear. You will have to add toe clips and straps before getting into your stride off-road, or upgrade to pedals with a spring binding.

TYRES

A pair of *Kona*'s light own-brand tyres, the front one is called *Mr Dirt*, a wide tyre with V-shaped blocks that you must make sure to put on the right way round. The rear tyre is called *The Cleaner* which is also "directional", and with its centre block "paddle" pattern, works like a steamer on the Mississippi River.

25

the performance
bike

For the committed mountain biker there are many pedigree bikes that promise great fun and great performance. The average weight of these bikes drops to around 11 kg (25 lb) and aluminium, titanium and carbon fibre frames join bikes with improved steel tubing. With this higher quality, another decision comes into play – whether to ride away from the shop on a bike fitted with a suspension fork, or to buy a rigid bike and fit your own favourite fork to it. A handful of fully suspended bikes muddies the waters of choice further, in this range.

Ah, says the detractor, but the bicycle is simply a tool and the engine is the same – my pounding heart, rasping lungs, and stinging legs. In which case, says the mountain bike lover, you will appreciate the easy handling and lightness of these machines even more. It is an off-road jungle out there and your engine needs all the help it can get.

Buying a performance bike

The *Cannondale F500* is an excellent example of a performance range MTB. It may seem expensive though and there is no obligation to pay this much money – bear in mind that models of this quality are more than functional tools. They are instruments to enhance your riding pleasure, and, of course, if you are competitive, on which you can improve fitness and handling on the cross-country and downhill race courses.

WHO IS IT FOR?

Any committed rider and connoisseur of fine things gets a kick out of performance bikes. They have the reliability of standard models, but, with frames and components specifically designed for light weight and rigidity. They are stronger too, giving you quicker travel and safer manoeuvring – not to mention more years of service. Touring cyclists need to ensure that the frame has eyelets for panniers, and casual riders should see that they are still comfortable with the steeper angles and long, low-slung upper body positions created for racers.

THE COMPANY

The *Cannondale* company turned up soon after the beginning of the mountain bike phenomenon in the mid 1980s, and has been designing and building its own high-quality, fat-tubed aluminium steeds in the USA ever since. The company's research into frame shapes and suspension has won them a unique place among bicycle manufacturers. They are the only builders to have successfully put a front shock absorber in the frame rather than the fork. They have also produced a unique range of radical suspension V-shape "delta" frames that work beautifully.

FRAME

The *F500* (F stands for front suspension) has a standard oversized aluminium frame of the 3.0 series, with added manganese, which cuts down on weight without sacrificing the frame's strength.

The high-quality *Cannondale F500*.

Coming in four sizes – from small to extra-large – *Cannondale* made its reputation with frames such as this one which, on its own, weighs 1.4 kg (3 lbs) including the internal suspension. Another excellent *Cannondale* detail is the "replaceable rear dropout". The dropout is the part of the frame into which the wheel slots. Because it is exposed it often gets bent in crashes; this means unless a dropout is replaceable, the frame is damaged as a whole.

COMPONENTS

Manufacturers usually match the value of a bike's components to its frame, but, as with this *Cannondale*, the bike's price is kept down by fitting components of a lower grade, in terms of quality and weight. This frame is a long-term investment that will outlive its parts, which can be upgraded with lighter versions as time passes. This explains the appearance of some cheaper *Shimano Acera X* pieces around the bike. They are perfectly adequate for riding at this stage, but they are not in the same league as the superb frame.

BRAKES AND GEARS

■ *Acera X* cantilevers and basic Taiwanese brake levers look simple and they are per-fectly adequate and will decelerate and stop on demand. However, as the bike's great suspension means fast descents are irresistible, the owner could fit a more powerful brakeset.

■ Gears: *Shimano Acera-X GripShift SRT 400*
Chainrings: 42/32/22
Sprockets: 11–28
Light, tough GripShift (revolver) changers work the front derailleur from the *Shimano Acera-X* groupset and the rear derailleur from the next groupset up, *Shimano STX*. The particularly easy lowest gear featured on this will be appreciated by an unfit rider. A good, straightforward gearing system.

PEDALS

The pedals are aluminium platform pedals that come without toe clips. It is assumed that the rider will screw his or her own clip-less pedals into what is a superb piece of kit, the *CODA* machined cranks, specified only on *Cannondale*s and designed by a motorbike guru.

TYRES

The cavernously knobbly *Piranha Pro* tyres match the quality of the frame, and have been designed together to grip the trail in muddy conditions.

CODA cranksets are a special feature on some *Cannondale* bikes.

bicycle thrills

Whoever would have thought that the humble push-bike could be invested with so much technology and razzmatazz! On advanced models every tiny piece of the frame and every component reveals the most skilled use of the finest raw materials – with an exciting amount of experimentation proving that although MTB design has come along way, perfection is still over the horizon. A crossover of craftsmen from the realms of motor-cycling and Formula 1 motor racing has elevated the engineering sophistication of the off-road bike with spectacular results.

For superlative quality, full suspension bikes you have to pay a lot of money. There are dozens of these bouncy bikes to choose from, utilizing either elastomer or hydraulic shock units at the front in the forks, with swing-arms at the back that have numerous permutations of angles and pivots.

For the purist wanting simply the best in rigid steel, aluminium or titanium, the choice is far larger, with weights as scintillatingly low as 10 kg (22 lb). This is also the realm of esoteric components, where a race is on for weightlessness. However, when you are faced with a choice between low weight and strength, strength must win every time.

The competition bike

If you are thinking about the thrills of an expensive bike, the professional standard *GT Links Tuned Suspension 1* at 11 kg (24.9 lb) is worth considering.

WHO IS IT FOR?

There is little doubt that, whoever you are, MTBs such as these are the most pleasurable and exciting bikes to ride. If you respect your bike you respect yourself.

THE COMPANY

GT got into mountain bikes early on through building BMX bikes, so a reputation for sportiness is accompanied by the image that *GT*s spend as much of their time in the air as on the ground. The truth is more down to earth. The Californian company, which, like much of the bicycle trade, divides its assembly process between the US and the Far East, now has a range of two dozen bikes for every possible pedaller. One of the biggest players in the racing scene, *GT* has lifted world downhill championship trophies no fewer than seven times since their inauguration in 1990.

However, the company's speciality is a number of full suspension models that come from two basic designs. The first, the *RTS* (Rocker Tuned Suspension), is purely for downhilling; the second, the *LTS* (Links Tuned Suspension) is for cross-country. The philosophy is that the drawbacks of full suspension – extra weight and slower uphilling – are outweighed by its advantages – control and comfort everywhere else. On average, full suspension is now considered to make cross-country, as well as down-hilling, faster and more fun.

FRAME

The *LTS* bike is constructed from basic 6061-T6 oversized aluminium tubing, using a new application of a motorbike link idea in the rear shock, which allows the back wheel to swing.

The wheel is not restricted to moving in a strict arc around the bottom bracket, as are the majority of rear suspension designs, but is double-pivoted. This allows the wheel to follow the line of rough terrain with greater accuracy.

GROUPSET, BRAKES AND GEARS

■ *Shimano XT.* From near the top of the *Shimano* range, this set of parts is influenced by the smooth lines and quality of traditional road groupsets from *Campagnolo*, whereas the one above, *XTR* now copies the trend for squarer edges that has arisen from CNC-machined parts from the US. *XT* is plain, smart and works beautifully.

■ Brakes: V brakes and V brake levers. Styled on US designer cantilevers, the arms are elongated and upright, with an interesting dual pivot on the brake pads to bring them on to the rims horizontally rather than in an arc.

■ Gears: *Shimano XT* 24-speed
Chainrings: 42/32/24
Sprockets: 11–28

Lots of small-ratio gears for reduced weight and clearance with lots of choice, plus *Shimano's Rapidfire* easy-to-use under-bar gear shifters.

FRONT SUSPENSION FORK

Rock Shox Judy XC. This is the beefiest model from *RockShox*, with fat, deeply over-lapping legs and stanchions to overcome the tendency of telescopic forks to twist.

PEDALS

Shimano M-535 – could quick-release pedals be more minimalist?

TYRES

Panaracer Hardcore Dart and *Smoke* with Kevlar for grip and puncture resistance.

The *GT Links tuned suspension* bike.

what to wear

Obsessive cyclists end up with more cycling than civilian wear as they devote their lives to finding the perfect combination for every condition and trend. It is not hard to see the attraction – modern cycle clothing can keep you comfortable, warm, smart, and riding happily whatever the weather.

Pick conservative black for everything, or make a statement with clashing shades that confirm to the unfaithful that colour-blindness is a prerequisite for cycling. In addition to standard polyester or lycra cycle-club clothing, new textiles are everywhere. The jargon is sometimes overstated, but there is no doubt that man-made fibres are great at replicating the warmth and water-proof qualities of feathers and wool, and they easily outclass cotton T-shirts, sweatshirts and shorts, which are chilly when wet and dry slowly. The advantage of the modern textiles is their lightness and their quick-drying and wash-ability – an element that everyone appreciates!

In the heat you can generally wear the clothes you wish, perhaps investing in a high-quality jersey that deals with sweat and dries quickly. In 30°C+ (86°F+) temperatures you will feel much cooler if you wear white.

It is water and wind against which bikers must defend themselves, particularly in cold temperatures, for these are the conditions that carry a high misery-risk. Give up and go home as soon as you, or someone in your party, finds the suffering is greater than the excitement generated by the elements. Getting cold is painful and unpleasant, and, in the worst case, can lead to life-threatening hypothermia, where the core body temperature drops.

HOT/DRY/COOL WEATHER
Short- or long-sleeved jersey
Shorts
Fleece shirt
SPD shoes
Bum bag or backpack
Dark shades
Lightweight showerproof

CHILLING OUT
■ **On a day with temperatures around 10°C (50°F), a 16–32 km/h (10–20 mph) breeze drops the temperature to between 5°C (41°F) and 0°C (32°F). On a day that hovers around freezing, a wind of 16–32 km/h (10–20 mph) drops the temperature to between -10°C (14°F) and -20°C (-4°F) – and that is while you are standing still.**
■ **The temperature drops 1°C (1.8°F) for every 100 m (300 ft) climbed.**

COLD/WET WEATHER
Gore-tex, or other
waterproof jacket
Overtrousers
Winter tights
Fleece jacket
Silk underwear
Boots
Overshoes
Winter gloves
Clear shades
Headband
Gloves

chill-factor, and feet, which are moving faster than the rest of the body and are close to the wet or icy ground, need thick overshoes to stop them going numb.

Short change

An essential clothing item for any cyclist, shorts are cushioned for comfort and to prevent chafing on your inner thigh. Baggy styles are available for the less showy rider.

rate at which it floods from a pumping cyclist. Use waterproofs as much for their windproof qualities as their waterproof ability. Remove them as soon as you have found shelter, to let your body and clothing air.

Keeping warm in winter

Avoid draughts. Plug gaps at the neck with a scarf, use wriststraps and long-wristed gloves. Do not pack layers tightly, otherwise first you will simmer, then chill if they become soaked with sweat and then exposed to cold air. Keep the top of your head warm by wearing a thin headscarf in cool temperatures and a thick fleece headband in very cold weather; use one that covers your ears as well as blocking the gap between your helmet and head. Use an armless body-warmer to keep the chill off your abdomen.

The thrill of the elements is a big draw in cycling, but the chill of wind on wet flesh and clothes needs to be understood if you are to enjoy it safely, especially on remote, exposed rides. Wind speed is chilling enough, a cyclist's speed increases the

Love your Layers

Cycling is hot work and so the correct clothing is a balance between insulation and evaporation. Go for layers that you can remove or add easily. Use thin sports underwear next to the skin for core insulation, then as many mid-layers as you are comfortable with. Add shirts or pullovers of fleece, polyester, lycra, or any of the trade-name equivalents. Finish your layering system with a wind and waterproof shell on the outside. Think of the outer layer as a window, providing a seal from the elements rather than warmth.

Dry – dream on!

Staying completely dry is an impossible dream: nothing, not even the best breathable material, can release perspiration at the

TEXTILES

FLEECE

A textile that miraculously combines cuddliness with sportiness, fleece comes in different densities for warmth and windproofness. In warm and cool conditions go for a lightweight, windproof fleece sweatshirt as a outer layer; in the cold and wet, wear a unfaced fleece beneath your waterproof for insulation without bulk. An option is

ECO-FLEECE

A textile made from recycled non-biodegradable drinks bottles.

POLARTEC

Providing warmth and windproofness, Polartec comes in different thicknesses and is the most popular fleece material.

SILK

Underwear made from silk is not only warm, it feels nice. One long-sleeved high-necked vest on the inside does the job of an extra thick, draughty jumper on the outside.

PERTEX

A great material for wind and shower-proof shells, Pertex is a super lightweight, densely woven polyester that dries incredibly quickly.

GORE-TEX

A super-patent protected material, *Gore-Tex* is the original breathable waterproof fabric invented by Mr WL Gore, now with a dozen labelled competitors.

essential accessories

An essential piece of equipment for any cyclist is a helmet; these are well-ventilated, light and smart enough for all cyclists to wear, wherever and however they ride. For mountain biking, where falling off is part of the fun, helmets have become part of the furniture. Spectacularly broken lids are displayed as trophies by their grateful and healthy owners. The skull is the brain's natural helmet, but it needs help to protect it from cycling knocks because they happen at speed.

Although the skull puts up a good defence against external damage, the majority of sporting head injuries are not caused by skull fractures, but by the crash smacking the soft tissue of the brain hard against the inside of the skull, also twisting and tearing the covering membrane.

Helmets are constructed with a collapsible 10–20 mm (½–¾ in) wall of expanded polystyrene that gives way under impact, absorbing the forward force to slow down the brain's internal momentum and reduce damage. Whichever type you choose, the heavier, cheaper hard-shell helmet with its solid outer casing or the more popular flexibly covered micro-shell helmet, it must conform to one or more of these safety standards; the British Standard BS6863, American ANSI Z90 or the Snell Foundation B84 or B90.

Hard-headed hints

■ Get a helmet that fits. Start with the right basic size, from "extra small" to "extra large" – this does not necessarily conform to your height or girth.

■ Make sure that the helmet rests fully on the top of your head. Use the sticky pads provided to get the fit firm and comfortable.

■ Set the side straps by pulling or pushing them through the clips below your ears to keep the helmet horizontal. Pay attention particularly to the front anchor straps, so that the helmet doesn't get pushed backward while you are riding. Pull or push the chin-strap through the buckle clip for a snug jaw fit. You can tape the chin-strap in place if it slips, as they tend to with wear.

■ Because of their construction, helmets should be ditched after a hard knock and replaced to ensure their integrity. Similar to free coffee refills, *Specialized* and *Giro* have a "new-for-bashed" policy and will send you a replacement for the nominal cost of postage and packaging, which justifies their higher initial cost.

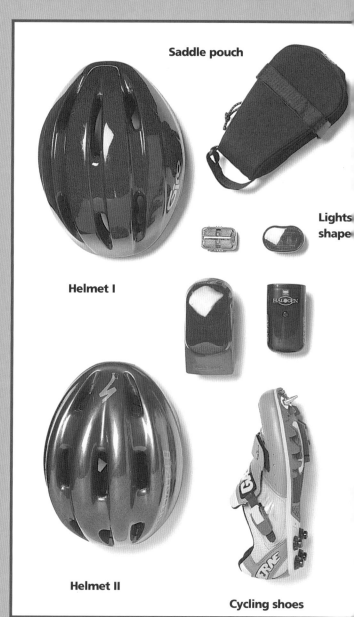

Saddle pouch

Lights shape

Helmet I

Helmet II

Cycling shoes

Thinking on your feet

From pedal-locking sandal to knee-length mountaineering gaiter, cycling footwear covers a spectrum of styles and tough terrain. How much you invest on footwear depends on your saddle-hours and how deeply you want to penetrate the hills.

All cycling shoes have stiff soles, which

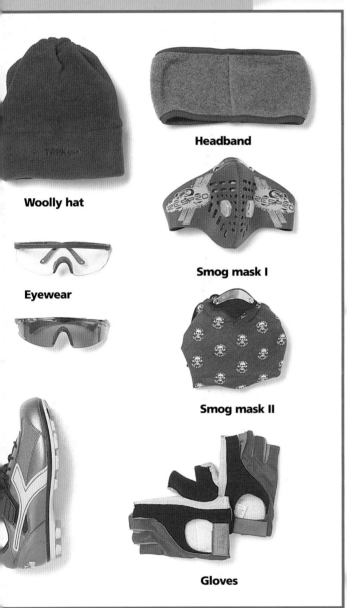

Woolly hat

Headband

Eyewear

Smog mask I

Smog mask II

Gloves

stop your feet forming painful lotus hooks around the pedals. It is impossible to descend properly or to pedal over rough ground without having your pistons somehow tied to the pedal, but what else will you be doing on the trip? If the terrain forces you to do much walking you'll appreciate a pair of MTB boots, or even waterproof walking boots for their ankle support, protection and grip.

The best way to couple foot and bike is with the "clipless" binding, so-called because it uses a spring mechanism in the pedal, instead of toe clips and straps. A quick-release cleat in the sole of the shoe locks the ball of the foot into the pedal at the flick of an ankle, and it releases automatically if necessary. Once connected the pedal bindings work beautifully, allowing even beginners to do impressive bunny-hops. The design has been adapted from road racing, only you can walk and run in off-road shoes with bindings, as the cleat does not protrude from the sole.

The minor drawback of bindings is that the pedal mechanism and cleat get clogged in bad mud and stop working. It can also be a fiddle to feel the connection between cleat and pedal, especially with cold feet, and the cleat's steel surface does not grip wet rock well, should you have to cover a lot of ground on foot. Shoes, boots and now even sandals with bindings are available for riding in different conditions.

Regular toe clips and straps are simple and cheap, not quite as effective, but far more versatile than bindings, and let you ride in ordinary shoes or trainers, or full-blown waterproof hiking boots. The latter are best for off-road touring where you may be wet for days, or cycle travelling where you don't want to carry more footwear than necessary. However, you need patience to control the pedal spin when trying to get your foot into the clips.

Don't forget that wearing thick overshoes will keep your toes warm when it's cold, and when it's wet consider even full-length gaiters to keep off detritus thrown up by the wheels.

Handy Hints

If you do not wear mitts or gloves, your hands will eventually toughen up enough to hold on to the handlebars without blisters or pain from the cold – but frankly, who wants to be that hard? Mitts with towelling on the back are nice for wiping away sweat and a runny nose, while padding and rubber mean comfort and grip.

When it comes to protecting your exposed hands from the cold do not skimp on quality. Every penny spent on a pair of gloves pays itself back in warmth and durability and adds mileage to your riding. The best cold-weather gloves have a kind of mini-layering, with a windproof shell on the outside and a warm lining. A long wrist to tuck up inside your sleeves is useful. If you can find waterproof walking or skiing gloves with fingers that are slim enough to allow you to work the controls, go for them.

the maintenance of a mountain bike

Learn to love the maintenance of your mountain bike.

'You cannot be at ease on your bicycle if you are at its mercy.'

Bridgestone mountain bikes.

Tips and principles for efficient maintenance

■ Look at each component of your mountain bike carefully, to see how it works. All the components are visible – there are few hidden parts.

■ Every time you buy a new component for your moutain bike it should have clear, comprehensive instructions that tell you how the part should be fitted and adjusted; keep these, as you never know when you may need them.

■ New mountain bikes usually come with a whole volume of instruction leaflets, which should be kept as you can use them as step-by-step guides to proper maintainence of your bike.

■ The very least every cyclist should be able to do is fix their own punctures, adjust their gears and know if their brakes are working properly. If, however, you are not mechanically minded – and don't worry as many people who enjoy mountain biking are not – spending many frustrating hours on a task that is too complex for you is just wasted riding time. Also, some of the required tools can cost more than paying someone else to do the repairs.

■ Maintaining your own bike can bring a great sense of satisfaction. By the time you have bought tools and spent time on it there are probably no savings to be made over having your bike fixed professionally, however, the very process of working on it brings you closer to how your machine operates, which, in turn, allows you to ride it better.

■ Regular attention to your own bike means you can pick up and correct faults before they become serious. Ride with niggles and they will inevitably become problems. Being confident enough to tackle small jobs is great, otherwise the problem will irritate you for months and someone else will come along, fix the problem in 30 seconds and leave you thinking, "I could have done that". Small adjustments to your bike make a lot of difference, and it's remarkable how much better a bike can operate after as little as an hour's work.

■ Work in a warm, comfortable and well-lit environment. You can do most adjustments with an emergency toolkit (see pp. 38–41), although you will find that a larger toolkit kept at home will make things easier.

■ For most of the gear and brake adjustments, a stand is essential. Something very simple will do, as long as it holds the back wheel off the ground and the bike vertical.

■ As you take each component apart, lay the pieces face up on newspaper in the order that they come off the bike. This way you will know in which order to put things back together. Clean each part, then wash your hands before reassembling the component or touching clean parts, especially if you are working with bearing surfaces and cables.

■ Take care of tools. Clean them every single time you use them and remember to oil them when necessary.

■ You will need lots of old rags such as old towels and sheets. Old T-shirts are also useful. Cut off the sleeves and cut the body into horizontal strips to make loops to hang on hooks on the wall.

■ Be systematic – always check your work before riding off. Do not half-fit anything, thinking that you will come back to it at the end of the session, It is all too easy to become distracted and forget all about it. Ill-fitting components are potentially dangerous, for you and other riders.

■ Stop work if you get frustrated – in this frame of mind you are more likely to break something than mend it. Take a break for a while, and return to your bike when you feel calm and composed again.

the pre-ride check

Usually, your bike will be in good working order and raring for a ride, but the one time you catch something wrong, you will be glad you took the trouble to perform these 10 pre-ride checks. With a bit of practice, they will take you about 20 seconds, the process will become an enjoyable habit to get you in the mood for a ride, and a ritual to bond you with your bike and your riding companions.

1 PICK UP THE BIKE AND DROP IT

Lift the bike 10 cm (4 in) off the ground using the handlebars and saddle, and let it drop to the ground, catching it before it falls over. Listen carefully to how it sounds, and learn to become familiar with that sound. Anything loose that is about to fall off will sound different from normal; and if something sounds downright weird you know to investigate.

2 CHECK THE BRAKES

The front and rear brakes should be checked independently. Stand beside the bike, and push the bars forward. When you pull the front brake only, the rear wheel should lift up as the front wheel locks; when you pull the rear brake only, the rear wheel should lock and slide across the ground.

3 CHECK THE QUICK-RELEASE LEVERS

Check the quick-release levers at both wheels and at the seat-post. Ensure that

Part of the pre-ride check: checking the rear wheel bearings.

they are holding the component firmly. If you are unsure of how to work quick-releases properly, get someone who does know to show you how.

4 CHECK THE BEARINGS

Bearings are made so that when they are properly adjusted, the item being borne can rotate freely about its own axle, without any

Check for frayed cable.

play (movement) at all across the axle. They should always be adjusted as soon as they become loose, because nothing destroys a bearing surface more quickly. Also check that they are not too tight.

To check the rear wheel (rear hub), bearings, squat on the right-hand side of the bike. Hold the seat tube about halfway down with your right hand. Take the rim of the rear wheel between thumb and first finger of your left hand. Rock the wheel gently toward you and away from you, as in the image opposite. If there is play in the hub bearings, you will feel a slight knocking and probably also hear a little click.

To feel play is to know it, so if you are still ignorant but happen to meet a fellow cyclist with loose bearings ask them to let you feel the wobble before they are properly adjusted.

Next, check the front hub bearings. Take hold of the fork and the wheel rim and rock gently.

5 CHECK THE BOTTOM BRACKET

Hold the seat tube and line the crank up with it. Hold each crank in turn – but not the pedal because play in the pedal bearings might be mistaken for bottom bracket movement – and rock it gently. A loose bottom bracket will click. If you can feel play on one crank, but not the other, the crank may be loose on the bottom bracket axle. If this is the case you must tighten it immediately – riding on a loose crank will eventually destroy it.

6 CHECK THE HEADSET

Stand beside the bike with your hands on the handlebars. Put the front brake on and rock the bike gently forward and backward. If you are using suspension forks it is harder to distinguish a loose headset, as there will always be a fair amount of movement in the area. However, loose bearings make a distinct click and jolt.

7 CHECK THE WHEEL ALIGNMENT

Pick up each wheel in turn and spin it. Watch the rim as it passes between the brake blocks. Check that when you pull on the brakes they hit the rim centrally; too high and they will bite into the tyre, causing a massive blow-out; too low and they will jam in the spokes, bringing you to an abrupt and possibly painful halt. See pages 50–51 for further details about brakes.

8 CHECK THE TYRES

Check that the tyre pressure is reasonable, and not below 35 psi. Check the tread for excessive wear and cuts in the sidewall. Pick out anything that is lodged in the knobbles. Sharp things can take a while to work their way through the tyre casing into the inner tube, which gives you a chance to catch them in time.

9 CABLE CHECK

Check the cables for kinks, fraying or breaks in the outer casing. Cables usually break a strand at a time. They usually break either at sharp turns or where they join the nipple.

10 CHECK THE HANDLEBARS

Stand in front of the bike, hold the front wheel between your knees and twist the bars – not too hard in case you bend the front wheel. The stem should not move. Check the saddle does not twist either.

preparing for breakdowns

Good preparation reduces the chances of trailside breakdown, but everybody's luck runs out sometime. The simplicity of bicycles can turn into a disadvantage, as almost nothing about them is superfluous. You cannot get away with breaking any part of a bike, because every part is in regular use. The priority, if you are in the middle of nowhere, is to be able to get yourself home.

As soon as you realize something is wrong, stop and get off the bike. Have a think. There are few problems that cure themselves. The list of those which could worsen drastically if you were to just "ride over there" is long. Stop immediately, and you will have a shorter walk back to where you heard pieces fall off too.

Every day someone is finding a new way to break a bicycle and, hopefully, a new way to mend it. These are general repairs to cover the majority of breakdowns. They sound obvious, but they work.

Tips and principles

■ Stay calm – panic does not mix with effective, safe repair.

■ After a crash, first check for damage to yourself. A lot of blood, unusual visual effects or nausea may mean that you need looking after more than your bike.

■ You will be able to locate the damage much more efficiently if you are familiar with your bike beforehand. Work out the difference between how it is meant to be, and how it is now.

INVENTIVE TOOLS AND SPARES

■ Zip-ties are very useful, so carry them wherever you go. Use them to help repair pedals, punctures, bags, lights and even to keep long hair out of eyes.

■ Shoelaces and toestraps are also worth taking with you on rides. Anything you are wearing or carrying about your person can be pressed into service.

■ Coil a brake cable up inside the repair kit, as it hardly weighs anything. A rear brake cable will do as a front brake or brake straddle cable and, depending on your gear shifters, may work as a gear cable too.

■ It makes no sense to carry spares for which you have no corresponding tools, or conversely, to carry tools to fit spares that remain back at home.

■ Inner tubes with fat Schraeder valves may fall into this category. Presta valves are narrower, so if your rims are drilled for Presta valves, Schraeder valves will be too wide to fit in the hole.

■ A strip of heavy duty sticky tape wrapped around a spanner may come in handy.

Air-tight inner tube with the correct valve – Presta or Schraeder

Puncture repair kit

Lights

Lights

Fresh batteries

Spare bulb

Mini pump

Tyre levers

A toolkit containing the bare minimum of equipment.

■ Assess the severity of the problem. After your own health, the primary requirement is to get the bicycle rideable, for which the minimum is two brakes and one gear. You may have to be content with imperfect operation, but salvaging a bike so that it stops and starts is enough.

■ Remove as much as possible of the dirt that surrounds any broken part, and get a good look at it. Make sure you have not thrown away any loose pieces.

■ Do not lose tools or parts in mud or grass. Find a clear patch of ground on which to work, or place all the stray parts on your bag or jacket.

■ Be inventive about tools. Rocks, locks and SPD shoes all make good hammers.

■ After completing the obvious repair, survey the bike for related damage before riding off. Did the crash take out anything else?

■ Pick up all your tools, your helmet, gloves and bits and pieces.

■ Is the repaired bike trailworthy? Would it be better to walk home than to risk further damage to it or yourself?

tools for trails

A larger toolkit to anticipate breakdowns on longer trips.

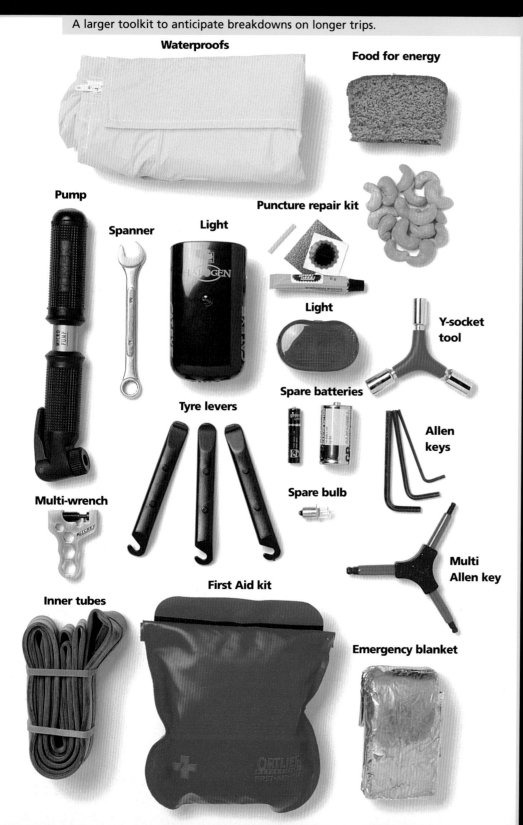

Waterproofs

Food for energy

Pump

Spanner

Light

Puncture repair kit

Light

Y-socket tool

Spare batteries

Tyre levers

Allen keys

Multi-wrench

Spare bulb

Multi Allen key

Inner tubes

First Aid kit

Emergency blanket

Here is a list of the tools most commonly carried by experienced mountain bikers to cover the most common emergencies. Supplement them according to your own experience and learn from what your companions carry. The extent of your trailside toolkit depends on where you are riding. Discovering your puncture kit glue has dried out on a summer afternoon in the country park can be a harmless excuse to retire to the nearest watering hole. The same error in winter twilight up a mountain could have dangerous consequences.

Essentials for fixing punctures

■ Puncture repair kit
■ Pump
■ Tyre levers

Never leave home without a spare inner tube and recently inspected puncture repair kit, which should contain some patches and glue that is still liquid – once opened a tube of glue lasts about six months, even with the lid screwed on tight.

An alternative to the traditional patch kit is one of various glueless versions currently on sale. It is reputed that these were developed by the US army as emergency bullet wound patches, although there has never been any evidence of this application. The two most common makes are the *Park* glueless patch kit, which comes in a re-sealable, waterproof plastic box, and *Leeches*.

Both types of kit are adequate for emergencies, and make puncture repair

A quick-release skewer used as a lever.

easier, but the seal is not as reliable as a traditional patch repair, especially if applied over the seam of the inner tube. It helps a repair patch to stick if you clean the inner tube before application with mini surgical swabs. They come in small individually sealed packets. They are available from chemists and are often found in First Aid kits.

PUMP IT UP

All this is useless however, without a pump to re-inflate the tyre once you have successfully mended the tube. There are many different types of hand pump on the market. If possible, test different makes and models before you buy. The metal ones are more durable, but heavier. Very short pumps are harder to use, but easier to carry around. If possible, get a pump that adapts to both shapes of inner tube valve: Presta (long and thin) and Schraeder (as on car tyres, short and broad), as you never know who you might be riding with. There seems to be a belief among mountain bikers that someone else will have a pump – this isn't always the case.

TYRE LEVERS

Carry at least one tyre lever, preferably two. A stick or a screwdriver may be used as a substitute – but they are drastic measures.

Other alternatives include the 1995 *Shimano LX* and old *Mavic* quick-release skewers. Be careful using them, as it is easy to scar delicate rims and pinch the new inner tube as you are refitting it, which is extremely irritating.

Fixing a broken chain

The next most commonly required item on the trail is the chain tool. It's a good idea to practice with it at home before you need to use it for real. Also, before you leave for a ride, find out if your chain needs special replacement pins. For example, the rivets in *Shimano* chains are not designed to be re-used. Instead, the special black rivet must be located and replaced with a new special black rivet. This is not an easy task in conditions of fading light, deep mud or cold weather, which makes it essential to practice at home first.

Some of the very small, light chain tools available can be tricky to use, although the *Ritchey Chain Tool* and the *Cunningham Chain Pup* are both satisfying pieces of design. Also recommended is the *Park CT-5 Mini Chain Tool*. It is excellent and easy to use even wearing gloves, and comes with comprehensive instructions on the box.

Park chain tool.

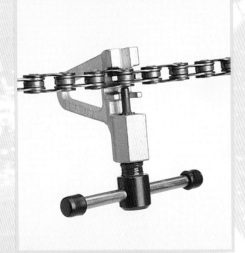

Which spanners?

The spanners you carry depend on your bike. Check which ones you need and take a variety of spanner sizes of between 8 mm and 17 mm. You should also take a small adjustable wrench. Many people manage fine with just one wrench. Make sure it is narrow enough to get in behind your brake unit to adjust the block clamping nut, and that you have no parts that need two spanners simultaneously, such as old-style brake cable straddle clamps.

Which Allen keys?

The Allen keys you carry also depends on your bike, although the bare minimum for most models is shown below. Allen keys are measured in metric sizes.

6 mm – for saddles, stems and some brake systems.

5 mm – for headsets, chainring bolts and some brakes.

4 mm – for some leverless skewers and some brake levers.

3 mm – for some GripShifts, SPD pedals.

2.5 mm – for some GripShifts, some brake-centering bolts.

Loose Allen keys are fine, and those which fold up as a pocket knife are good, as the body of the tools acts as a comfortable handle.

SCREWDRIVERS

Screwdrivers with cross and flat heads are always useful. Some of the multi-Allen key tools come with screwdrivers. They are needed for adjusting gear end stop screws and brake centring bolts.

The packaging

Choose a tool bag from which nothing can escape. You can strap your tools to the bike, in a small saddle bag, which stops you leaving them behind.

fixing trail breakdowns

Creative puncture repair.

Emergency puncture repairs

■ String and zip-ties isolate the punctured area of the tube.

■ A knot tied in the tube works too, but it has to be pulled very tightly to prevent the air escaping. This makes the tube shorter and harder to get back onto the rim and the knot makes a curious lump in the tyre that you can feel as you go along.

■ Anything that will stick to the surface of the tube may keep the air in long enough to enable you to get home. Successful repairs have been done with postage stamps and other bizarre patches.

■ If the hole in the tube is too big to isolate or patch forget the tube and stuff the tyre with something else. Grass is the traditional substitute, although, assuming you can find some, it is hard to get enough of the stuff inside the tyre to protect the rim from knocks, and rims damage quickly if you ride them with a soft tyre. The tyres don't like it much either. If you're forced into this situation ride gently – you lose steering on the front wheel and traction on the back.

■ Any large cuts in the tyre will cause another puncture as soon as the inner tube bulges out of the hole in the carcass – the edges of the hole will simply cut into the tube. Find something to wrap around the tube, to block it from bulging out of the hole in the tyre. Paper is strong enough for the task, so try to improvize with money, sections of map or candy wrappers.

Gear repairs

If either of the derailleur cables snaps then the spring in the derailleur mechanism will pull the chain onto the smallest cog that the end-stop screw will allow.

FRONT DERAILLEUR

Screw in the end-stop screw so that the chain sits in the middle ring. Alternatively, a lump of wood wedged between the seat stay and the derailleur will keep the chain in the middle or largest ring, depending on its thickness. If the front derailleur is broken beyond repair, remove it. Run the chain over whichever ring you want, usually the middle. With practice, you can change gear with your heel as you cycle along!

A block of wood keeps the chain on the middle ring.

One way to fix a broken rear derailleur – with a zip-tie.

a potato chip. Release the brake and remove it. Hold it up and spin it. If the mis-shape is nice and even, with the top and bottom bent one way and the front and back bent the other there is hope that it can be fixed. Remove the quick-release skewer to release the wheel, and lay the wheel on the ground.

Step onto one high point, then ease your weight gently onto the other. Bounce gently up and down. If you are in luck, the wheel will suddenly spring back to its previous shape – which is, hopefully, fairly round. However, take care to jump off the wheel quickly before you go too far.

Finish off the job with a spoke key (see pp. 58–59), if you have one. Refit the quick release, wheel and brakes.

REAR DERAILLEUR

Screw in the end-stop screw so that the chain sits in a comfortable gear. If the rear derailleur itself breaks or falls apart, it is sometimes possible to bodge a repair to it. Zip-ties can be the answer. Shown above, a jockey wheel bolt has been replaced with a zip-tie and the jockey wheel bearing.

If you cannot mend the derailleur, you may have to remove it. Because the rear derailleur tensions the chain as well as moving it across the rear sprockets, if you remove it you also have to shorten the chain to stop it flapping around.

Take out as many links as you need to run the chain in a sensible gear. If you have horizontal dropouts – the slots in the frame into which the wheel slides – try adjusting the wheel to take up all the slack.

Once the chain has been shortened, check that it runs freely and that you can pedal backward. Unless the chainset is perfectly even the chain tension will change as you turn the pedals. Decide how many links to remove to set the tension so that there is still a little slack even when the chain is at its tightest. Do not throw the extra section of chain away. You will need it when you replace the derailleur.

Fixing wheels

It is actually possible to salvage a wheel that has been mangled to resemble

Broken rear derailleur.

cleaning a mucky bike

Cleaning the rims with white spirit.

Cleaning your bike is either considered a boring chore to be carried out as quickly as possible, or as a useful survey and bonding process! Regularly cleaned parts last longer; for example, clean rims will not wear brake blocks out so quickly. Surface dirt needs to be washed off before it works its way into concealed parts, such as inside a cable housing and into bearings. Bike wash time is also a good time to check the condition of your components.

A CLEAN FRAME

Brush off any dry, loose mud. Remove the wheels to make it easier to get in between the stays. If you can, hang up the bike to make it easier to work on. Use warm, soapy water and a sponge, and rinse off afterwards with fresh water. Polish the frame after you have cleaned it. Mud does not stick as well to a smooth, polished surface, so the bike stays cleaner longer. Check for cracks in the frame – they first appear as fine lines into which dirt gets stuck.

CLEAN WHEELS

Keep the braking surface of the rims as clean as possible. Brake block residue accumulates on wheel rims, limiting the effectiveness of braking. If necessary, wipe the rims over with white spirit. Riding down a tarmac road at speed clears most of the mud from the tyres – scrub off the rest with warm soapy water. Check the tyres as they are revealed from beneath the muck for deep cuts or sharp things; remove anything embedded in the tyre.

A CLEAN DRIVETRAIN

The chain, block (sprockets), front chain-rings and jockey wheels are the elements that constitute the drivetrain. The sprockets in particular wear very quickly if not kept clear of muck. Chains last as little as a week in bad conditions if neglected; the dirt they pick up gets carried around the drive-train and forced into the holes between the chain plates. As you put pressure on the pedals, these particles of dirt get further ground up by the chain, wearing the metal surfaces. Ideally, wipe your chain down once for every six hours of riding time; this sounds frequent, but the act takes a few moments for a smoother-running bike. The frequency with which you wipe down the chain also depends on the riding conditions.

BRUSHING YOUR BIKE
Keep a selection of soft brushes, bottle brushes and toothbrushes. Washing up brushes with an angled head are perfect for getting into gaps behind brakes and gears.

CLEANING THE CHAIN

Lean the bike up against a wall, or ask a companion to support it for you. Crouch down on the bike's right-hand side. Wrap a cloth around your left hand. While pedalling backward with your right hand, hold the cloth around the lower section of chain where it comes off the chainring (see below). Gradually increase the pressure with your left hand so that you are cleaning the muck off the chain as it passes through the cloth. As the cloth gets dirty, move a clean part on to the chain. Repeat until the cloth remains clean. Chain cleaning should be done at least once a week in good conditions, and after every ride in bad conditions.

It is better to clean a chain often and gently. Occasionally however, because the chain is constantly exposed, it needs a deeper clean, which involves its removal with a chain tool. Hang the chain on a bent spoke, or hook it over a jar. Starting from the top, work toward the bottom of the chain, driving the muck down the chain into the jar. Use a toothbrush to scrub each link. The visible parts of the chain work best if they are clean. Most of the chain's operation

Cleaning the jockey wheels.

happens on the inside, where the rollers turn around the rivets; therefore, it is important that there is always enough lubricant on the rivets to allow them to run smoothly. Cleaning the chain with harsh solvents will drive the lubrication off the rivets, so re-lube carefully afterward.

Running a clean chain over dirty jockey wheels is a waste of time, so clean these also. Hold a cloth against each jockey wheel while pedalling backward. A stiff brush will be fine for cleaning the block (sprockets) and

chainrings. If you have the tools and time, remove the chainrings from the chainset and clean them separately; this makes it easier to get into the gaps.

CLEANING MATERIALS

Start the cleaning process with warm soapy water and plenty of cleaning cloths. Work gently and gradually get more brutal with the stubborn areas. If soapy water does not work, resort to degreaser, but wear gloves to protect your hands. Try to remove any component you are degreasing. For example, it is better to remove blocks, as it is important that stray degreaser does not seep into the rear hub. Follow the manufacturer's instructions; if they advise washing off the degreaser then do so, otherwise it will react with whatever lubricant you apply. Depending on the degreaser, water also activates emulsifiers, which help lift grease off components. Dry off the degreased part, and lubricate it immediately to prevent the unprotected surface from corroding.

Cleaning the chain.

FLAMMABLE PRODUCTS
Many cleaning and lubricating products ignite if exposed to a naked flame, so handle with care.

45

lubricants and lubrication

Lubrication is easy, isn't it? Buy the cheapest oil you can find in the bike shop, stand in the same room as the bike and spray. If anybody comments on the increasingly disgusting state of your drivetrain, look hurt and say, "but I oiled it three weeks ago, why doesn't it work smoothly?"

Lubrication should be a regular ritual. The rule is to lubricate little and often. It is much better to give your bike a small, regular oiling than a mucky, occasional over-spraying, which just collects dirt.

What does a lubricant do?

A lubricant allows two surfaces to pass over each other with the minimum friction. Ideally, all the energy you put into pushing the pedals around should go into propelling your bicycle and body forward. The more friction the bike has, the less the energy supplied by your legs moves you forward.

A lubricant's second task is to reduce wear on the bike's components. Surfaces that rub together should be as smooth as possible, and lubricated to form a tough protective film between them, preventing their self-grinding action.

Applied on assembly and during your regular maintenance sessions, a thin film of oil or grease on metal surfaces will also prevent corrosion. Bike components should always be greased on assembly.

WHICH LUBRICANTS TO USE

Grease is for bearings. Do not contaminate it – it should always be clean and applied to clean surfaces, so that it stays put. If it is worth opening up bearings to grease them, then it is worth using more expensive specialist bicycle grease so that you will not have to repeat the job in a hurry. Waterproof grease is recommended. Oil, which is thinner, is used in more exposed places on the bike. While grease does not move, oil gets sucked into cracks and crevices by capillary action.

LUBRICATING PLASTICS AND TITANIUM

GripShift gear levers are a plastic-on-plastic friction, and need a special lubricant. Although the plastic will not corrode, it will

wear without lubrication, leading to sloppy shifting. Similarly, titanium parts need an anti-galling compound to prevent them corroding – one make is *Anti-Ti Seize*.

LUBRICATING CHAINS

The principle reason for oiling chains is to get lubricant in between the plates, and

Lubricate little and often.

HOW OFTEN?
The frequency with which you lubricate your bike depends on:
- How often you use your bike
- How often you clean your bike
- The weather and conditions in which you ride your bike
- How heavily you ride your bike

Oiling cable stops.

rear derailleurs are in the firing line of crud thrown up from the back wheel. A drop of oil on all four pivots in the rear mechanism can make an amazing difference to shifting. The back inside pivot is the most awkward to get to, and probably best oiled with the wheel off. Oil the jockey wheel pivots too. Wipe off any excess.

Oiling the pivot points in the rear derailleur.

between the pins and the rollers. Once the chain is clean (see p. 45), drip a small drop of oil onto each link on either side of the top of the roller. Leave it for several minutes to soak in, then wipe off any excess with a cloth.

Using a lubricant

Lubricant is best applied to clean surfaces because it will flow more easily and there is no danger that it will flush dirt into cracks – there is no point grinding muck around. Give the oil a few minutes to soak in, then wipe off the excess – excess oil attracts fresh dirt and defeats the object.

LUBRICATING CABLES

The most common place for the cables to break is at the nipple end, inside the brake and gear levers. The nipple must be kept greased so that it can turn in the seat. If it cannot, the section before it becomes twisted and over-stressed. Be warned – pre-break fraying is difficult to see because it is on the inside of the lever housings.

Good cables are lined with *Teflon*, which is very smooth and does not need supplementing with oil. Without oil, however, the cable itself still corrodes and becomes rougher. Therefore, *Teflon*-lined cables

should still be oiled. Oil them at all cable stops, the places where they attach to the frame, and where the inner cable emerges from the outer casing. Lubricating will help to repel water and stop it collecting inside the cable. *Gore-Tex* cables should never be lubricated at all.

LUBRICATING DERAILLEURS

Derailleur mechanisms work more smoothly when the pivots are oiled. Lubrication should be frequent, as both the front and

Oiling the jockey wheels.

LUBRICATING THE HANDLEBAR FURNITURE

Oil the brake lever pivots. Turn the barrel adjusters so that the slots point upward and you can see the cable. Drop a little bit of oil into the slots. The part nearest the end of the cable needs oiling most – from there the oil will seep into the rest of the cable. Turn the slots back down again, to guard against dirt and rain.

mending a
puncture

Removing the front wheel.

A puncture can occur at any time during a ride; therefore it is essential that every cyclist is aware of how to fix one – here is a step-step-guide to puncture repair.

REMOVING THE ▲ FRONT WHEEL

1 Release the brake straddle cable. There will be a tab on one end, which you pull down and away from the bike while squeezing the brake blocks together with the other hand. This allows the brake blocks

to move far enough away from the rim to remove the wheel easily.

2 Release the quick-release lever.

3 Some front wheels have small tabs at the bottom of the dropouts, because there is a danger that if your front quick-release lever accidentally comes loose, the wheel can drop out – with horrible consequences. The tabs are there to give you time to notice that your front wheel is jolting about and refit it correctly. Release the front quick release then unwind the lever a few turns while holding the nut on the other side. Remove the wheel.

REMOVING THE REAR WHEEL ▼

Rear wheels are just as easy to remove, once you have learnt how.

1 While turning the pedals, lift the back wheel off the ground and change into the small cogs at the front and back for maximum chain slack.

2 Turn the bike upside down and rest it on its bars and saddle.

3 Undo the quick-release lever.

4 Stand behind the bike and put the first finger of your left hand in front of the guide jockey wheel (the one nearest the body of the derailleur) and your thumb behind the tension jockey wheel (the one that normally hangs down, see picture 1, below). With your left hand, push your finger backward and your thumb forward to twist the derailleur out of the way (see picture 2, below). With your right hand, pull the wheel up and forward. Lift away the wheel to the right, so that it comes away from the chain.

STRIPPING THE TYRE ▶

The next step is to remove the tyre. Press the valve to remove any air left in the tube. Now pinch the top of the tyre so that the tyre bead facing you moves away from the edge of the rim toward the centre of the rim. Move around the whole rim repeating the

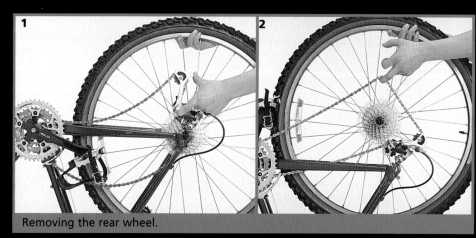

Removing the rear wheel.

Loosening the bead.

Levering off the tyre.

process. The tyre should now be looser on the rim, making it easier to remove. Pop a tyre lever under the bead, flick it down and hook the end around a convenient spoke. Repeat with a second tyre lever until the tyre is loose enough to remove by hand. Remove one side only and then the tube. Leave the tyre on the same place in the rim, so that once you have located the puncture in the tube you can match the position to the tyre and find out what caused it.

LOCATING THE PUNCTURE

Pump up the inner tube to medium pressure. Pass it slowly in front of your lips – they are very sensitive – so you can feel the air rushing out of the tube and you may even hear it. If the puncture hole is very small, you may have to pass the tube across your face several times at different angles to find it.

Once the hole is found, let out the air again and fix the puncture. Remember to let the patch kit glue dry completely before application, which usually takes about five minutes. Alternatively, fit a spare inner tube and take the punctured tube home to fix at your leisure.

IDENTIFYING THE TYPE OF PUNCTURE

Work out what caused the puncture. Two common causes are "snakebite" punctures and sharp-object punctures.

Snakebite punctures occur when you hit a bump or rock with great force, squashing the tyre against the rim and pinching the inner tube. If you get snakebite punctures often, pump your tyres to higher pressures.

Sharp object punctures happen on the outside of the inner tube. To locate and identify this type, run a finger gently around the inside of the tyre, take care, as sharp objects on the inside of the tyre can rip your fingers if you move too fast. Match the position of the puncture to the tyre, using the valve hole as orientation. The object that caused the puncture may be very small, or it may have dropped out already. Check the rim too for sharp-ended spokes or shifted rim tape. Another way in which a puncture can occur is if the brake block is set too high – it can slice open the sidewall of a tyre, causing the tube to bulge out and blow.

REMOVING THE CAUSE OF THE PUNCTURE

Remove whatever caused the puncture. Try not to make the hole bigger. Ensure that there is nothing else poking through the inner tube.

REFITTING THE TYRE

Once the patch glue is dry, pump a little air into the tube. Remember that a patch is not strong until it is trapped between the tube and the inside of the tyre, so you cannot pump a repaired tube up too hard off the wheel in case it blows off the patch. A slightly inflated tube is easier to fit, as it will not get trapped under the tyre bead so easily. Put the valve in place first, then tuck the tube into the tyre. Fold as much as possible of the tyre back into place with your hands, massaging the bead into the centre of the dip as you go. If possible, refit it with your hands, although it may be necessary to use tyre levers.

WHEEL REPLACEMENT

Replacing the front wheel is the reverse of removing it. To replace the rear wheel hold the bike upside down and hold the derailleur out of the way as before with your left hand. Tuck the wheel between the stays, and manoeuvre it until the cassette sits between the upper and lower parts of the chain. Rest the smallest cog on the lower part of the chain, then push the axle into the dropouts. Check with your fingers that the wheel is sitting centrally between the stays. Push the quick-release levers flat along the stays, so that they stand less chance of snagging.

Refit the brakes, pump up the tyres and you're ready to go!

Remove cellophane from the patch.

49

brake replacement
and adjustment

All brakes that use cables work in roughly the same way, so although the images here show a standard *Shimano* style brake, the principles apply to any make or model. If you are in any doubt about the way the brakes are adjusted on a bike, tell the shop about it. It's a good idea to learn how they operate yourself, so that you can determine exactly how you want them adjusted, near or far away from the rim.

Starting from the lever, we work toward the wheel unit, as this is the easiest and most systematic way in which to install or adjust brakes without missing anything.

1 BRAKE LEVERS

Ensure that the levers are as comfortable to use as possible using the reach adjust screw If you have small hands, wind in the screw so that the levers are close enough to the bars to grasp easily The whole lever can be rotated around the handlebar too. Adjust the angle of the brake levers so that you can ride comfortably with one or two fingers on them, ready to use.

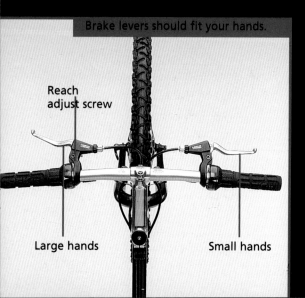

Brake levers should fit your hands.

Reach adjust screw

Large hands   Small hands

2 CABLES

The brake cables work best if they are not kinked or forced around tight bends. However, as excessive cable creates extra friction and is more likely to get snagged on things, find a balance between the two. The correct cable length should make graceful curves.

It is the short sections of cable which seem to cause most problems – try to ensure that the outer casing enters the cable stop aligned as much as possible in the direction of the inner cable. A spot of grease on the nipple before installation in the brake housing on the handlebar will allow it to turn in its seat. If the cable cannot turn as you pull the brake it will soon snap. Fit ferrules to the ends of cables wherever possible; they protect against fraying and catching.

3 STRADDLE CABLES

Straddle cables come in a variety of forms, but all are based on the same principle. Effectively, they translate the pull of the brake cable into the rotation of the brake units around the brake bosses, thus forcing the brake pad onto the rim. This movement should be as effective as possible – this means attaining the most pull on the rim with the least pull of the hands on the lever. Since the end of the brake unit can only move in a circle around the brake boss, it is a waste of energy trying to pull it in any other direction.

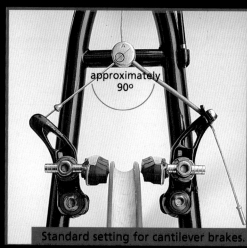

approximately 90°

Standard setting for cantilever brakes.

Set the height of the straddle cable clamp so that the two halves are approximately at right angles to each other – your energy will go into pulling the block on to the rim, not into bending the brake boss. Ensure that there is sufficient clearance between the straddle cable and the tyre for the tyre's knobbles and for any crud you may pick up. Make sure there is room on the front tyre for a reflector bracket - an important safety aid. Reflectors may not be cool, but if the front brake cable snaps, they will prevent the straddle wire jamming over the tyre and stopping the front wheel violently – sending you over the handlebars.

Shown here are *Shimano* "dynamic links", on which the brake wire goes through the straddle clamp and then through a short section of outer casing to the brake unit. Adjusting the brake cable is very simple, since it can be pulled through the straddle without disturbing the brake setting.

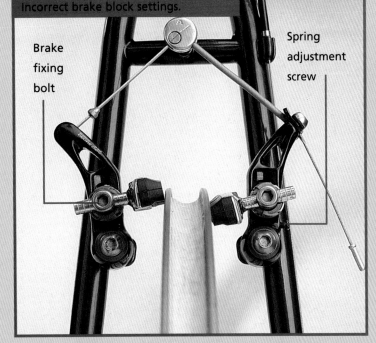

Showing brake-block toe-in.

4 SPRING ADJUSTMENT

This process allows you to match the strength of the spring in the adjustable unit on one side of the wheel to the strength of the spring in the other unit. Screwing in the spring strengthens it, pulling the unit further out from the rim. Since the two units are connected by the straddle cable, moving one unit away from the rim will move the other toward the rim.

5 BRAKE PADS

The brake pads are th brake components that most frequently need maintenance or replacement. Getting the adjustment correct seems to take forever the first few times you attempt it, but the effort is worth it, and you will speed up with practice.

The brake block rod bolts to the unit with a brake fixing bolt. When you loosen the bolt, it can be moved up and down in the slot or rotated against the curved washers that match the curve of the unit. The brake blocks can also be moved toward and away from the rim by sliding the block rods in the brake fixing bolt, this allows you to set up the blocks as follows:

■ Brake blocks should strike the rims centrally. Too high and they cut into the tyre and will cause a blowout within a short space of time. Set too low, the blocks will pull under the rim, and catch dangerously in the spokes. The image below shows that the left block is set too high and the right block too low.

Incorrect brake block settings.

Brake fixing bolt

Spring adjustment screw

■ Brake blocks must be parallel to the rims when viewed from the side, and should strike the rim squarely with the top and bottom touching at the same time.
■ Brake blocks should be toed-in by about 1 mm (0.03 in) (see left). This means that the front edge should touch the rim just before the back edge, stopping the brakes from squeaking.

6 BRAKE BLOCK TRAVEL DISTANCES

Personal preference will dictate brake settings. Some cyclists prefer to set them so that the brakes come into action as soon as you touch the lever. Others set them so that they don't take effect until the lever is about halfway between its original position and the handlebar. Ensure that when the brakes are fully active the levers neither "bottom out" on the handlebars before activating the blocks, nor crush any fingers left gripping the bars – a risk when the blocks get worn rapidly on a wet, gritty ride. Small adjustments can be made with the barrel adjusters at the brake levers. Large adjustments are made by unclamping the brake cable or straddle cable at the wheel units, pulling cable through and reclamping.

51

gear maintenance

Check that the rear derailleur hangs straight below the sprockets

The rear derailleur.

There are three different types of gear lever, but they all work in the same way – one click pulls the cable enough to move the chain exactly one sprocket. The cable can only pull, not push, so both derailleurs are sprung. The cable pulls the chain on to a larger ring, and when the cable tension is released, the spring pulls the chain back on to a smaller ring.

Each manufacturer sets the sprockets different distances apart, so you can only use products by the same manufacturer, or those designed to be compatible. The lever must obviously have the same number of clicks as there are sprockets.

Derailleur differences

The front derailleur moves the chain across the chainrings. The rear derailleur shifts the chain across the sprockets and regulates the amount of chain needed for each gear. Its two jockey wheels do different jobs. The top one is a guide pulley, marked "G". It often has a bit of side-to-side movement to help the gear change. The bottom jockey is marked "T" (tension) and is sprung, so that it always tries to move backward, taking up slack in the chain.

Are the derailleurs bent?

Check that the rear derailleur hangs straight and vertical below the sprockets. Set the chain to the middle ring at the front, and look at the rear derailleur from behind. If it is not straight and vertical, take it to your bike shop, as this is the cause of most persistent gear-changing problems. Do not attempt to straighten it yourself – the hanger should be treated with care.

When viewed from above, the outer plate of the front derailleur should appear parallel to the outer chainring.

SETTING UP AND ADJUSTING THE DERAILLEURS

It helps a lot to have your bicycle up on a stand that will keep the back wheel off the ground and allow you to turn the pedals. If you do not have one, ask a friend to lift the saddle at critical moments.

ADJUSTING THE REAR DERAILLEUR

1 Remove the old cable. Watch where the cable routing goes and where it comes out so that you can refit it later. With *Shimano RapidFire* gears you may need to unscrew a little cover. Don't lose the little screw – it is an odd size.

2 Set the chain to the middle ring at the front, and check that the rear derailleur hangs vertically. If it does not you will not be able to adjust the indexing later.

3 Set the end-stop screws. It is easier to do this now than later after the cable is fitted. Then, if you find, for example, that the chain will not drop into the small ring, you will know that it is because the cable is sticking or the lever is broken, although there is still a small chance that it could also be a wrongly set adjust-screw. Isolate the parts and test each one separately.

4 Screw in the "H" end-stop screw five or six turns (or as far as possible) and turn the pedals. You will find that the chain will not drop down into the smallest ring, because you have deliberately screwed the end-stop in a long way. Continue to pedal, unscrewing the H screw as you do. Gradually, you will see the derailleur moving and dragging the chain toward the smallest sprocket. This is a slow motion version of what happens when you change gear. Whenever the chain is midway between the sprockets, it will clatter noisily, the same sound as your hear riding along with badly adjusted gears. As you unscrew further, the chain will drop into the smallest sprocket. Continue unscrewing until the chain lies exactly below the smallest sprocket, then unscrew a tiny bit further – less than a quarter of a turn.

5 Next, set the "L" end-stop screw, which prevents the chain falling beyond the largest sprocket into the gap and mashing up the spokes. This is a little more tricky. Setting the H screw is easy, because the spring always pulls the cable back toward the smallest sprocket. However, shifting toward the largest sprocket, it is the cable that does the work, but, because you have removed the cable, you have to manually shift the derailleur.

Turn the pedals with your right hand, and hold the derailleur with your left hand, as shown; first finger behind the barrel adjuster, thumb at the front of the derailleur, ahead of the forward pivot points. Curl your other fingers into your palm, to keep them out of the way of the chain and sprockets. Push your thumb away from you, gently and slowly. As you pedal, the chain will lift toward the largest sprocket mimicking the action of the cable. Play with it, find out what happens. Do not push too far, or the chain may fall over the end of the sprocket.

Give the "L" screw five or six turns, then try to push the chain on to the largest ring, while pedalling. If it will not go, unscrew it a little. Keep testing and unscrewing until the chain drops easily on to the largest ring, then unscrew it a little bit – less than a quarter of a turn.

6 Now you are ready to fit and adjust the gear cable. Grease the end of the cable and

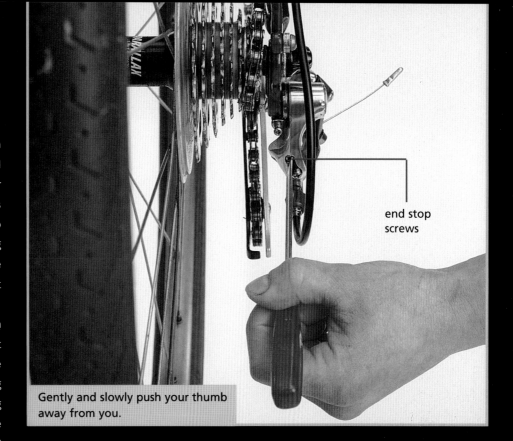

end stop screws

Gently and slowly push your thumb away from you.

Adjusting end-stop screws.

the nipple. The cable must be oiled before being fitted into the casing to keep it smooth. Gear casing should always be Teflon lined. Gore-Tex cables are also really smooth, and do not need any lubrication.

7 Once you have fitted the cable into the lever, put gentle pressure on the end of the cable and test the action of the levers by clicking up and down through the gears. This can save head scratching later, because if the levers do not work properly now, they won't be any better attached to the derailleurs! With moderate tension on the cable, pulling at it directly out of the lever, you should distinctly feel each click. Leave the lever in the highest gear position, ready for fitting.

8 Fit all the sections of outer casing, with a ferrule on each end, and oil as you go. Make sure all the sections of outer casing are a good length – long enough so that the cable is not forced around any tight corners, and so that the bars can turn easily, but without excess. Cut new casing to the same length as old casing, assuming it was the right length. Check the cable as you slide it into each section of casing. If, once the cable is fitted, it does not work, you will have to go back and check each piece of casing anyway. The last section of casing, at the rear derailleur, is the most exposed and needs replacing more often as it soon becomes clogged. Cracking in the old casing where it inserts into the derailleur is a sign that it was not quite long enough.

9 Take up any slack in the cable by fitting it into the cable clamp bolt on the underside of the derailleur, using the little groove usually either in the washer or the derailleur. Clamp the bolt. Turn the pedals and change up to the largest sprocket – or the largest sprocket it will reach – and back down to the smallest sprocket. You have not adjusted

Releasing the cable clamp to fit the cable.

the cable tension, so the indexing will not work properly, but this action settles the cable into place. The alternative is to pull the cable through with pliers, which usually only serves to fray the cable end.

10 You now have to test the operation of the gears. Moving the lever or rotating the barrel one way pulls the cable, moving the other way releases it, folding and unfolding the derailleur, shifting the jockey wheels and thus the chain over the sprockets.

Turning the barrel adjuster to the perfect gear indexing.

ADJUSTING THE INDEXING

To test the gears, move the lever one click;

the chain should move exactly one sprocket, but it probably will not the first time. If it doesn't move far enough, the cable is too slack, so tighten it with the barrel adjuster. Fine tune the derailleur by putting your thumb on the barrel adjuster, then roll the barrel with your thumb moving in the direction you want the chain to go. If the cable shifts more than one sprocket when you move the lever one click, release the cable tension by winding the barrel adjuster back in. If you reach the limit the barrel adjuster will turn, centre the barrel and adjust the cable using the clamp bolt.

THE FRONT DERAILLEUR

1 Check the front derailleur lies parallel to the outer chainring. Check that there is sufficient clearance between it and the chain-rings – a couple of millimetres is perfect.

2 To set the cable tension, set the lever in the smallest ring position. Take up the slack in the cable by unclamping the cable bolt on the derailleur, pulling the cable through, and reclamping the bolt. Change gear up to the largest ring and back down to the smallest to settle the cable in place. If necessary, take up any newly created slack by pulling the cable through the clamp bolt again. At its slackest the cable should be just taut.

3 Check your end-stop adjustment by changing onto the largest and smallest rings. If the chain cannot move as far out as the largest ring, undo the "H" end-stop screw. If the chain falls off the outside of the chainset, then screw must be screwed in. Do the same with the "L" end-stop screw.

4 If the front derailleur is indexed you will have to set that as well. Put the rear gear onto the smallest sprocket, then shift the lever from the smallest ring position to the middle ring. If the chain will not lift, there is not enough tension in the front gear cable.

2–4mm

Shimano LX, sprockets.

Undo the barrel adjuster on the lever to increase tension. Test until the chain lifts easily on to the middle ring. Set the chain on a middle sprocket at the back and the middle ring at the front. Adjust the barrel until the chain runs between the two plates.

NEW CABLES

A new cable often stretches slightly and the cable casing settles into the cable stops, so, after you a while, you may need toadjust it. Repeat the procedure for setting the indexing. Finish off new cables with a cable end to prevent fraying, and road test.

ROAD TESTING

Gears always work differently when you actually ride the bike to the way they work on the stand. It may take several test runs, adjusting the derailleurs to suit you exactly, before they are perfectly adjusted.

Shimano XT rear derailleur.

maintaining bearings

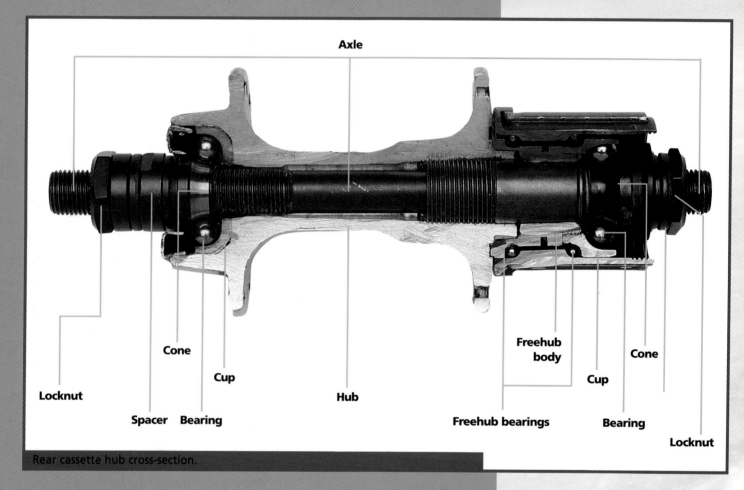

Axle

Cone

Cup

Locknut

Spacer   **Bearing**

Hub

Freehub body

Cone

Cup

Freehub bearings

Bearing

Locknut

Rear cassette hub cross-section.

There are four major sets of bearings on your bike – front wheel, back wheel, headset and bottom bracket. Each allows one part of the bike to rotate freely. The wheels and bottom bracket must be able to spin, but without any side-to-side movement. Headsets must turn easily without rocking backward and forward. All bearing units work on the same principles; the cone is adjusted to hold the ball bearings in place and is prevented from creeping by a locknut.

The cups and cones should provide as friction-less a surface as possible for the balls. If the cones come even slightly loose, they jar against the bearing surfaces every time they are come into play, making little pits. Once a tiny pit has formed, each ball falls into it every time it goes around, and the pits grow bigger. Loose cones wear all the bearing surfaces very quickly.

REAR CASSETTE HUB

The cutaway image of a rear cassette hub (above) shows how cones work. The two sets of larger bearings support the wheel, each sitting in a little cup with visible outward-facing edges. The two cones are screwed onto opposite ends of the axle, so that they come to rest against the balls. The balls are trapped between the cup and the cone, able only to chase round and round in

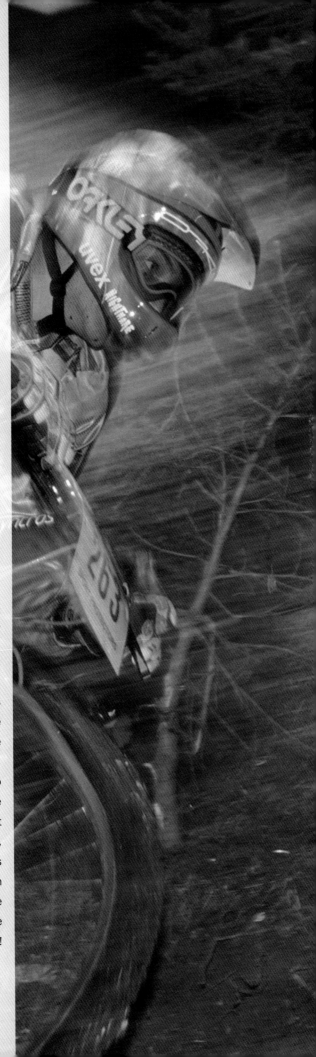

CONE SPANNERS
Take your bike with you to the bike shop when you buy cone spanners to ensure you get the right size. Front cones are usually smaller than back cones.

their allotted space. Once the cone spins freely without play, a locknut is wedged against it to hold it in place.

CLEANING AND REFITTING THE FRONT HUB BEARING

This is the most accessible example of how to clean and refit bearings, and the principles can be applied to the other bearing units.

1 Remove the front wheel, and the quick-release skewer if there is one. The cone and locknut are wedged together, so the first thing to do is release them. The cone is the section nearest the wheel, and will probably have two flat surfaces. It is very thin, so it is necessary to use cone spanners.

2 Fit the cone spanner firmly on to the cone, then, preferably with a ring spanner grip the locknut (the outer-most nut on the axle). Keep the cone spanner still, and unscrew the locknut. Watch out for your knuckles against the spokes.

3 Once the first locknut has been released, transfer the cone spanner to the second cone – this will keep the axle steady. Wind off the loosened first locknut. Remove any washers and lay them beside the locknut. Now transfer the spanner to the opposite locknut and hold the axle steady that way. Use the cone spanner to remove the loose cone. You can now gently withdraw the axle, with one set of cone, washer and locknut still firmly attached.

4 Hold the wheel flat, with a jar under the hub. Knock the bearings into the jar – a small screwdriver is useful for this.

5 Clean the cups and cones thoroughly and inspect them. There should be no pits at all in either cup or cone. The track of the ball bearings should not be more than 2 mm wide. Replace worn or pitted cones. If the cone attached to the axle is not worn, there is no need to remove it from the axle. Grease the cups, making sure you cover the bearing tracks. Fit the same number of new bearings on each side. They should sit up to their middles in grease.

6 Slide the axle back through the hub, taking care not to dislodge the bearings. Screw the loose cone carefully back on to the axle. Start it off by hand, then, holding the loose cone with the cone spanner, wind the axle through using the ring spanner on the fixed locknut. Do not jam on the cone, rest it against the balls. Slide the washers on, and, still holding the axle with the cone spanner on the fixed cone, wind on the loose locknut until it rests against the washers.

7 Adjust the cone carefully, aiming for no play from a freely spinning wheel. Lock the cone in place by wedging the locknut against it. This may take several attempts, as the cone moves as the locknut becomes wedged against it – use trial-and-error. When you think the setting is about right, fit the wheel on the bike. There may be play at the rim that cannot be felt at the axle. Try again!

wheel maintenance

Spin the wheel between the blocks.

3 Dish
A dished wheel sits centrally in the frame, equidistant between the two stays.

TRUEING
Trueing the wheels means balancing the tension of the spokes so that the rim sits in the middle. It is a little like a tug-of-war, with half the spokes pulling to the right and half pulling to the left. When the two teams are evenly matched, the rim will stay still even though both sides are pulling hard.

Trueing is easiest done on a wheel jig. However, most people do not have one kicking around at home, so here is how to do it with the wheel on the bike.

1 Start with the rear wheel. Remove the tyre and tube and replace the wheel on the bike. Suspend the bike so that you can spin the wheel. Sit behind it, so that you have a view similar to the one shown here. Spin the wheel, to get an idea of its condition. Concentrate on the part of the rim that you can see between the brake blocks and use the blocks as reference points. You will see some side-to-side movement and some up-and-down movement. The wheel may not sit centrally, either.

2 Deal with the trueness of the wheel first. Find the section of the rim with the biggest wobble. Draw it toward you, and look at a section of the rim about five spokes long. Look past the rim at the hub. You will see spokes falling away from the rim, toward the hub. Half fall to one side, half to the other.

The best wheels are those you do not even have to think about – and if the attention they get is careful, they should need very little of it. Wheels need slow and gentle work, working in small adjustments. Do not rush the chore – more wheels are destroyed through misplaced enthusiasm than misunderstanding the technique. Catch a wheel as soon as it becomes a bit wobbly, so that you only have to adjust one or two spokes. The longer you ride on an out-of-

shape wheel, the more resistant it becomes to returning to a circle.

TRUEING A WHEEL
There are three steps in trueing wheels:
1 True
A true wheel has no side-to-side wobble as you spin it.
2 Hop
A round wheel has no up-and-down movement as you spin it.

As you look at the wheel from this angle, it is clear that tightening (shortening) the spokes that go to the right-hand side of the hub and loosening those that go to the left will pull that portion of the rim to which the spokes attach to the right, and vice versa.

3 Spin the wheel gently several times to get an indication of how true the wheel is. Just observe at first. Isolate the largest side-to-side wobble. Work in quarter turns of the spoke key and loosen the spoke on the outside of the bulge, then tighten the two on the inside.

4 The spoke is essentially a long screw. It is attached to a funny-shaped nut, the nipple, which has a normal thread that tightens and loosens in the same direction as any other. Choose a spoke key that fits firmly on the nipple. A loose one will round it off, making it harder to turn. Don't be surprised if you get confused at first about which way the nipple should be turned.

5 Always work on the largest wobble first. Then spin the wheel and work on wherever the largest wobble is again. It may be in the same place.

HOPPING

When you have removed the worst side-to-side wobble, work on the hop in the wheel. Spin and watch how the wheel passes the brake blocks. Isolate the areas where the rim bulges outward the most. You will have to spin and watch several times to get an idea of the median position of the rim. Concentrate on the largest lumps and tighten about four adjacent spokes in that area. Spin the wheel again and repeat the process. When you have ironed out the worst of the hops, go to work again on the trueing.

DISHING

Finally, get to work on the dishing. The wheel has to sit centrally in the frame. To test it, remove the wheel and refit it the other way round. A dished wheel will sit in the same place whichever way round it is fitted. If it sits too far to one side, you will have to loosen all the spokes on that side and tighten all the spokes on the other, as if it was one big wobble. You may have to test the wheel several times. It is much better to work in quarter turns of the spoke key, and go round the wheel many times as it puts less strain on the rim.

Once you have dished the wheel you will probably find that you have to work on the trueing and the hop again. You will in the end have to make three or four passes at the wheel. Repeat until you are satisfied and finish with a true.

Long-life for chains, sprockets & chainrings

Like any bicycle components, chains, sprockets and cassettes will greatly appreciate your regular attention. The amount of time you spend looking after them will pay for itself in terms of performance and lifespan.

THE CHAIN DILEMMA

There is a problem with chains. You need oil on them, because it reduces friction, which wears both the bike's surfaces and your legs. The flip side of this is that lubricants attract the abrasive dirt that is thrown up by the wheels, which only makes things worse. However, you can minimize the problem if you follow these three steps.

1 Clean
2 Lubricate
3 Wipe off the excess.

The facts of friction

Look closely at the chain. Sit beside the bike and rotate the pedals backward. Watch a couple of links as they pass over the sprockets. Notice how each chain roller drops into a valley between two teeth and remains in there as the sprocket rotates. The roller can rotate independently around the pin. You can see this if you roll one around with the end of a screwdriver – the chain does not need to slide over the surface of the sprocket. It just drops into the valley at the top of the block, and drops out at the bottom. The roller pushes against the tooth to force the sprocket and the wheel around – it does not slide. No sliding, no friction.

Friction plays a role elsewhere. Watch a section of chain again, but this time watch two adjoining chain plates. As they approach the sprocket, they are in line. As they move around the block, they twist and then return to a straight line.

EXPERIMENTAL FRICTION

Now, place your palms together. Push gently, then twist your hands against each other, as if they were two links of chain. They soon become warm because of the friction that develps between them. However, now try repeating the experiment with soapy hands. The soap acts in a similar way to a lubricant, therefore your hands do not get as warm as they would without it. As well as in the chain plates, friction occurs between the pin and the roller as it turns to accommodate the valley between the sprocket teeth.

The parts of the chain that are really exposed to dirt – where the rollers touch the sprockets – do not slide over each other, so there's no need for the sprockets to be covered in dirt-attracting oil. The places where most friction occurs, in between the plates and inside the rollers, are relatively protected. Large pieces of muck and dirt have difficulty getting into the small gaps between the plates, which are, however, a perfect size for sucking oil to where it is most needed by capillary action.

This explains the instructions on cans of good oil – the ones that everybody ignores – about wiping off the excess. Most of the oil is needed inside the rollers and between the plates. Oil left on the outside attracts dirt, and therefore only increases wear. If you wipe the oil off afterward, the chain is left with a thin layer of oil that is enough to prevent corrosion, but not enough for dirt to stick to. Cleaning the chain first stops too much oil sticking to it, and helps the oil to slide between the plates. Better quality oil is designed to be sucked into small gaps.

CHAIN AND SPROCKET COMPATIBILITY

To work properly, the chain and sprocket have to have a precise, matching shape.

Nevertheless, they wear unavoidably, especially as the chain stretches gradually. Once the chain and sprocket have lost their matching shape, the wear accelerates. The resulting stretched chain wears the sprockets and in turn, the worn sprockets stretch the chain. The chain thus becomes less efficient and eventually will have stretched too much to grip the teeth of the sprocket. Instead it will skip over them. If this happens, a new, unstretched chain will not fit old worn sprockets, and vice versa, so sprockets and chains should always be replaced at the same time.

MEASURING WEAR AND TEAR

There are ways of measuring the wear in a chain, so that you know to change it before it wears the sprockets. Each link is 1 inch (approximately 2.5 cm) long, like many other bicycle components, the links are conventionally measured in inches. So, when it is new, twelve links will measure exactly 12 in (30.5 cm). When a chain has stretched so that it measures 12⅛ in (30.8 cm), both the chain and cassette should be replaced.

Measuring gauges that check chain wear are available from *Park* and *Rohloff* – the latter appears really to be a piece of modern art that can incidentally be used for measuring chain wear!

CARE OF SPROCKETS AND CHAINRINGS

The best thing you can do for sprockets and chainrings is to keep them clean. Remove as much as possible of the dirt in the valleys between the teeth. For a really good clean, take the rings off the chainset. Some sprocket cassettes will separate into individual sprockets, which makes it easier to remove the crud.

the principle of upgrading

A standard mountain bike is inherently sophisticated, however you do have the option to replace individual parts with better ones – infinitely if you so wish. Upgrading can be done as parts wear out; or beforehand if the replacements are more efficient, comfortable, easier to use or even prettier. One beauty of the bicycle is its tinker-ability. With a few tools and a little experience, a bike can be stripped to the frame and rebuilt with different parts in a matter of hours.

Demand for new equipment is partly driven by changes in materials and manufacturing. Once a bike can perform the full quota of off-road tasks to a high standard, the return from upgrading diminishes and you enter the realm of looks and personal experimentation.

Saving weight

Lightweight equipment first became desirable in road racing. Weighing just a few grams less, you achieve a higher speed for the same energy input – a particularly helpful asset when climbing. As the mountain bike suffers considerably more rolling resistance than a road bike – its average speed is around only 16 km/h (10 mph) as opposed to around 25 km/h (16 mph) – a lighter weight counts at all times off-road. You can feel the difference between an 11 kg (25 lb) and a 13.5 kg (30 lb) MTB bike.

The better the bike, the more difficult it is to save significant amounts of weight with individual parts, especially if you take the total weight of the bike and rider into account. Being, on average, two-thirds men's strength and weight, women have marginally more to gain from weight-saving than men.

Never sacrifice strength in the pursuit of less weight. In the UK, the statutory standard for bicycles states that parts must comply with defined performance standards, but independent testing to ensure that they comply is carried out at a manufacturer's request. This means that, regardless of weight, a part's safety testing varies between manufacturers. The best practical advice when buying lightweight equipment is to fit components from established, trusted outfits. Heavier riders in particular are best avoiding the lightest parts, especially handlebars.

Priority upgrades

The lower the quality of the bike you start with, the greater the improvement if you upgrade it. The converse is also true; the higher the quality of the part you start with, the smaller the improvement will be if you upgrade it.

CHEAPER BIKES

Priorities for upgrading a MTB of this value are tyres, brakes and pads and wheel rims – all will contribute to better performance.

PERFORMANCE BIKES

Upgrading a bike of this value will produce a significantly better working machine in many number of ways. Assuming the tyres are knobbly and grippy, try a budget suspension fork. Fit improved cantilever brakes, *Gore-Tex* cable housing and spring-binding pedals. As bearings wear out, replace them with long-life sealed cartridge bearings. If you want an eye-pleaser, replace the hefty seat quick-release lever with a small bolt.

HIGH-PRICE BIKES

How about a good suspension fork with Aheadset steering? Superior lightweight knobbly tyres? Lightweight nuts and bolts, sealed cartridge bearings, slimmer SPD pedals? Wheels with narrow-gauge spokes, slim rims and aluminium hubs? Or anodized cranks, chainrings, seat post, and bar ends? After a couple of years, how about a re-spray and fresh logos? The list goes on...

Customizing and experimentation

Upgrading means customizing, so that what starts out as a model number on an assembly line becomes unique to you. Much MTB part-mania is about opening an identi-

---

UPGRADE YOURSELF!
Your fitness is the single greatest improvement to your riding efficiency; think of it in terms of strength, and weighing less yourself – this is what is known as your power-to-weight ratio.

ty gap between mountain and road bikes. For example, off-road groupsets have previously copied the aerodynamic looks of Campagnolo's traditional road racing components, and are currently less popular than the more rugged look of many individual components. Improving your bike yourself requires a degree of mechanical experience. Do not make mistakes on expensive pieces of equipment. For example, don't round the threads on CNC-cut aluminium cranks. Learn on a basic bike, and get it right with high quality parts.

Much upgrading has to do with experimentation. For every lasting mechanical improvement that comes out of MTB development there are dozens of dead ends. "Trick" equipment is made using new materials and/or new manufacturing methods. It can be practical, decorative or both, but may not be essential. Remember that the trick merchant is making a small contribution to the development process, but is certainly contributing to the gross national product.

When is it time for a new bike?

The price of better quality frames and parts is continually dropping. So, over time it is not worth spending more than a half or two-thirds the original price of a bike on improving it – even to keep up-to-date and on a par with its original quality. If the parts become too good for the frame, it is time for a new bike. You may even decide to build your own bike – several manufacturers sell the frames of their popular models separately. This allows you to fit your own individual choice of components down to the last bolt. However, it is not cheaper than buying a complete bike.

SAMPLE WEIGHT SAVINGS
AVERAGE WEIGHTS

Woman		60 kg	(132 lb)
Average bike	+	12.5 kg	(28 lb)
Woman on bike total	=	72.5 kg	(160 lb)
Man		70 kg	(154 lb)
Average bike	+	12.5 kg	(28 lb)
Man on bike total	=	82.5 kg	(183 lb)

SUSPENSION FORK

Average weight	1.5 kg	(3¼ lb)
Lightest/heaviest	1.1–1.8 kg	(2½–4 lb)

WOMAN

% total bike/rider weight:	2%
% bike weight:	11.3%
Maximum % total rider/bike variation:	+/- 0.5%

MAN

% total bike/rider weight:	1.8%
% bike weight:	11.3%
Maximum % total rider/bike variation:	+/- 0.4%

SINGLE TYRE

Average weight:	625 g	(1 lb 7 oz)
Lightest/heaviest:	450 g–800 g	(1 lb–1 lb 12 oz)

WOMAN

% total bike/rider weight:	0.9%
% bike weight:	4.8%
Maximum % total rider/bike variation:	+/- 0.3%

MAN

% total bike/rider weight:	0.8%
% bike weight:	4.8%
Maximum % total rider/bike variation:	+/- 0.2%

HEADSET

Average weight:	145 g	(4½ oz)
Lightest/heaviest:	100–190 g	(3½–7 oz)

WOMAN

% Total bike/rider weight:	0.2%
% Bike weight:	1.2%
Maximum % total rider/bike variation:	+/- 0.06%

MAN

% total bike/rider weight:	0.18%
% bike weight:	1.2%
Maximum % total rider/bike variation:	+/- 0.06%

upgrading
tyres

Mountain bikers would argue that the creation of the knobbly tyre runs a close second behind the first fish that dragged itself on to dry land in the evolutionary league. The 650C (26-inch) tyre is the signature of the sport. Its deep, mud-beating tread carries you ceaselessly through slime and over rock. The tyres you choose affect the bike's handling and your comfort, as the rubber provides a mountain bike with built-in suspension. Cheap and easy to change, tyres are the number one item for upgrading performance and converting a MTB's personality – especially if it leads a double life as a working vehicle on the road, and a rugged off-road steed.

Mountain biking has witnessed the elevation of the humble tyre from a grubby basic into a big-business fashion accessory. It is great fun poring over catalogues and fingering new rubber in the shops. However, although enough different styles exist to satisfy the most committed rubber fetishist, the basic tyre retains its simple nature underneath. Most knobblies do the off-road job well. For fine-tuning, what counts is the overall tread pattern, tyre compound and the air pressure.

WEAR AND TEAR

The bite of knobbles still sharp-edged and powdery from the mould adds excitement and confidence to the riding. Like the balls in tennis matches, top racers will put on brand-new tyres long before the old ones

Your key to off-road fun: the knobbly mountain bike tyre.

wear out. If you are strapped for cash, choose a tyre for long life with a good, hard compound, designed for muddy conditions, and change to slick tyres when you ride the

bike on tarmac. Do not be deceived by the knobbles, which tend to outlive the trendiness of their pattern and the sidewalls. Although no MOT requires you to renew the

Low air pressure allows a better grip.

tyres, the inner tubes will squeeze through threadbare sidewalls long before the knobs wear out and tear, giving you a nasty shock.

WEIGHT

Tyres weigh 500–800 g (18–28 oz), and, taking into account Newton's laws of mechanics, it is worth paying for lighter ones. Newton's law states that the force (effort) required to accelerate anything is proportional to its mass (F=ma). On a bike it is the wheel that the rider is constantly trying to accelerate to overcome gravity, rolling resistance and air resistance. Since the tyre is on the outside of the wheel it has to be moved further and therefore requires greater acceleration; thus this is the single most important place to consider for lightweight replacements, to reduce the effort required to accelerate, brake and just maintain speed. Equally, the forces in a spinning wheel create an immensely strong and rigid structure, which is what makes high-speed downhilling over rocks and rough ground possible.

Choose a round profile for the front.

ROLLING RESISTANCE

All tyres are designed with the intention of minimizing the area of contact with the ground to keep down the rolling resistance while maintaining grip at all times. This is why tyres vary according to the surface they are tackling. Road tyres are thin and smooth for a small area of contact and low rolling resistance. Off-road tyres must be far more versatile, to dig into soft ground, bridge gaps and cushion the rider against edges. The idea of minimizing rolling resistance still applies, but as the roughness slows down a mountain bike to half the speed of a road bike, it plays a less important role in off-road tyre design than grip.

When conditions are slippery, higher rolling resistance is actually desirable! So we have the "tractor" tyre, which is designed with deep knobbles to dig in to soft mud and to supply enough depth to protect the bike and rider from some of the roughness of the tracks.

AIR PRESSURE

The simplest way to affect handling is to vary the air pressure in the tyres. High performance road tyres beneath a 68 kg (150 lb) rider should be pumped up to 80–100 psi, which means minimal rolling resistance and a sore butt. However, off-road riding needs softer tyres for handling and to isolate the biker from the jolts, especially if the bike has no suspension.

Keep within the recommended pressure limits; you will find these written on the side of the tyre. The lower pressure limit is as soft as a car tyre, at around 35 psi, which is best for slippery conditions. The upper limit should be around 55 psi – this is suitable for hard, dry riding. Tradition says the rear tyre should be harder than the front to take account of the rider's weight: this rule is worth observing.

TYPES OF TYRE

■ For fewer punctures, lighter weight and less twisting choose a tyre with a layer of *Kevlar* beading. This is a carbon-based barrier material that is also used in the construction of bulletproof vests. Kevlar tyres are easier to fit and fold easily, so that they can be strapped to a pannier if you are on a long expedition.

■ Directional tyres have an asymmetric pattern, which is similar in design to a chevron. Tyres such as these are designed to work in one particular direction. The direction may also depend on whether the tyre is placed on the front or rear wheel. Follow the arrow on the sidewall, and expect to think twice to get it right.

■ Some tyres are sold in co-ordinated pairs with different characteristics for the front and rear. The best is the narrower front tyre with a round profile for smooth, controlled cornering, and a chunky square rear tyre for stability and deeper grip.

MUD-CLEARING
Centrifugal force flings mud off the tyres just as the ground plasters it on, which is handy. One optimistic idea says that more widely-spaced knobbles result in better self-cleaning, but it is more likely to be the terrain and speed which decide how much mud gets left behind on your rubber – and no tyre, however gapped its teeth, can perform the impossible. When terrain is drying out, the soil is at its stickiest and the most aggressive tread may become a smooth, skidding slick. When this happens, it is time to stop and get scraping with your fingers.

upgrading brakes

RIM CANTILEVERS ▶

Cantilever brakes that grip the rim are the standard on mountain bikes. Road bike side-pull or calliper brakes with arms that straddle the tyre are lighter, but they are too weak over the double-width of a mountain bike tyre to be feasible. Both hub and disk brakes work better than rim brakes in the wet, but the humble cantilever is the most practical design in combined terms of cost, power, easy maintenance and weight.

Although the commonest and cheapest way to improve your bike's deceleration is to keep the brakes and cables properly serviced, you can increase a cantilever brake's power by paying a little extra for more rigid arms of top quality alloys and better milled fixings, so that there is not a shiver between the brake housing and the boss on which it

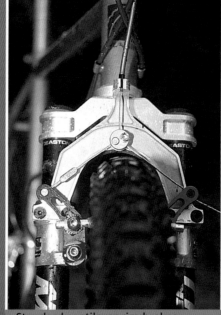
Standard cantilever rim brakes.

fits to the frame. By upgrading to models made of better material, it is also possible to save a couple of grams, which will cheer up the weight-freaks. All manner of different designs exist to accurately position and apply the brake blocks at the rim – cylindrical arms are the current favourites.

Wet-weather braking

Despite industry efforts, no one has yet overcome nature's hindrance to good cantilever/rim braking – wet weather. Braking distances treble in rain – affecting a lot of bikers in the world's temperate climates for a lot of the time. This is dangerous on the road, and means spicy handling off it. A partial improvement in

wet-weather braking can be made by increasing the area of contact with the rim, by using a longer block or softer compound in the blocks; but the play-off is that the block wears down quickly, even in a single day if the conditions are very wet and gritty.

DISC BRAKES ▼

Progress toward the wet-braking solution is being made via the development of mountain bike disc brakes, which have been adapted from motorbiking. A centre-wheel disc, with an enclosed brake pad and mechanism for greater power, is attached via an extra boss at the frame or fork dropouts. Disc brakes are ideal for frames such as carbon fibre monocoques, which do not have standard

The downhiller's choice: the disc brake.

ANTI-SKID IDEAS
When wheels lock up and go into a skid, the rider loses control. Experiments over the years have tried different ways of slowing down the force on the block as it nears maximum clench. This has been done mostly by increasing the leverage both at the lever and the cantilever to enable more gradual braking, but none of the designs have become standard. Outside the design studio, on the trail, it is left to the rider to work the brakes skillfully.

seat stays on which to mount rim brakes. They are also the choice of downhill racers who can afford their weight penalty and appreciate the extreme power. Although the braking force has to pass through the hub, spokes and rim before it reaches the tyres, disc brakes are not affected by wheels that are out of true, nor do they stress the frame or the fork like rim brakes.

BOOSTERS, RIMS AND REINFORCEMENT

Another way to improve back wheel braking is to get a frame reinforced with gussetting or butting at the seat stays. Bolt on a separate booster plate, which bridges the stays to hold them more firmly. On the front wheel add a booster to a rigid fork, while suspension forks come with a booster plate to buttress the independently moving legs.

Another improvement can be achieved at the rims, which are now being coated with materials such as ceramics. This is a costly, but simple upgrade, that will improve whatever cantilever you use – and also makes the wheels look good!

A better brake

The poor braking of a lookalike mountain bike alone is good reason for saving up longer for the real thing. The steel rims and flexing arms of the brakes on cheap bikes weakens the braking to the point where off-road excitement and safety cannot be guaranteed. Above this value, the majority of complete bikes sold have functional, conventional *Shimano* cantilevers. Here, an affordable upgrade is to fit a pair from one of the company's better groupsets; *STX-RC*, *LX*, *XT* or *XTR*. But why stop there, say the anodizing and CNC machining experts, who produce the designer brakes?

DESIGNER BRAKES

Collectors' cantilever brakes of the 1990s have "low-profile" arms of coloured, 6000 or 7000 series aluminium, CNCed – computer numerically controlled, that is cut by a robot according to a computer programme – with a matching straddle cable hanger. The angle of the arm in cantilever brakes has shifted over time and according to fashion, from more horizontal and outspread to more vertical, which is known as "low-profile". That is, from a mode of easy leverage with a big movement, to one of harder leverage and lower movement. Although low-profile cantilevers do not clip the heels of riders on little frames, they probably do not allow the rider quite such delicate application or the same total braking force as the out-spread style. The majority of cantilevers offer a good halfway-house spread, with arms at an angle of approximately 45°. Models to look out for include those by *Shimano* and *Ritchey*.

HYDRAULIC BRAKES

Hydraulic cables and brake pads, available for both rim and disc braking, work by using oil pressure rather than tension in the cable. They are beautifully smooth and do not get "graunchy" in gritty riding. Although they are more complex to set up in the first place, once they are up and running they require little maintenance, with the periodic adjustments caused by cable stretch a thing of the past.

BRAKE TIPS

■ The best brake levers have a short, kinked design for two-, or even one-finger braking and require a smooth-running cable.

■ The rear brake may only be half as efficient as the front brake, because the force from your hand on the lever has three times as much cable to stretch on its journey to the blocks, and twice as much grit and kinking to get through. Make sure the routing is as direct as possible and change to a cable with a low-friction liner, made from *PTFE* or *Gore-Tex*.

Super-smooth hydraulic brakes.

upgrading
gear shifters

The choice of three styles

There are three different styles of mountain bike gear lever. They all use slightly different finger and wrist movements to achieve the same end result. Levers come in pairs, one to activate the front changer and one for the rear changer and it is standard for them to be "indexed". This means that the lever settles into the right position each time you change gear.

Revolvers: They're simple, but they can also be slippery.

All mountain bike gear levers are mounted on the handlebars, rather than on the down tube. This is one reason why mountain bikes are easier to ride – the levers sit within reach of your fingers and thumbs without taking your hand from the grips, so that, in theory, you can hang on, change gear and brake all at once. Apart from a difference in price and availability, the type of gear lever you choose is a matter of taste, as each has strong points. If you have no preference, there is no need to change the version specified on a new bike.

◀ REVOLVERS

Your thumb and forefinger revolve a barrel that fits around the handlebar positioned on the inside of the grips. The leading make is GripShift, a design now fitted on a third of all new MTBs. Revolving barrels have little ergonomic advantage over the other two types of shift, but they are light and simple to maintain as they have few moving parts. Beginners who have not yet mastered the skill of looking between their knees to see what gear they are in will appreciate the at-a-glance indicators on the barrel.

Revolvers have two weaknesses. First, simultaneous braking and changing is more difficult; second, you cannot always get enough grip on the barrel to change gear when conditions are slimy and things are clogging up. To try and solve this, the barrel-grip has been roughened and sharpened, so that it now resembles a knobbly tyre, with

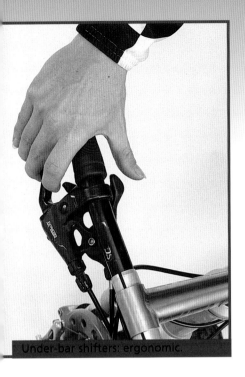

Under-bar shifters: ergonomic.

chunky protrusions to grab and force. As with tyres, you can even colour co-ordinate it.

Upgrading the model will give you stronger, lighter parts, but, just as with wet-weather braking, trouble with severe mud cannot ultimately be overcome.

◀ TOP-MOUNTED ▶ SHIFTERS

The original, but not really the best design top-mounted shifters, the first specialist MTB gear levers, were eclipsed by the appearance of the under-bar shifter. They are still found in small numbers on lower grade groupsets, and on second-hand bikes. The reason for their enduring appeal is slightly mysterious, given that you have to lift your hand from the handlebar to reach them and that you cannot brake at the same time. It is probably due to their simplicity.

With one simple trigger and no ratchet return movement, top-mount "thumbies" take up little space on the bars, cable changing is a doddle and they are light and sturdy. In the beginning it takes practice to work out by looking at them which gear you

are in, but a more useful, if incidental attribute, is that they are the easiest to keep working when the gear changing clogs in muddy conditions. When your fingers are no longer strong enough to shift the lever, you can use the full force of the heel of your hand effectively.

◀ UNDER-BAR SHIFTERS

The most naturally positioned, complex and costly gear lever is also the most common, the under-bar type, known largely by their *Shimano* trade-name *Rapidfire*. There are two levers per changer, one for shifting up with your thumb and one for shifting down with your forefinger. Unfortunately, *Shimano* has complicated the matter by putting them on the same handlebar mounting as the brake levers. It is possible to get under-bar levers separately from the brake levers, but they are rarely specified on new bikes.

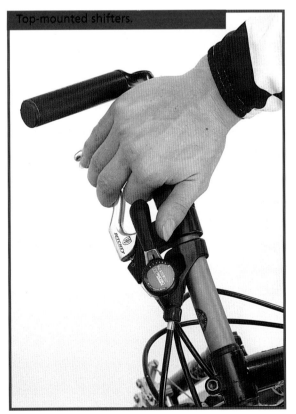

Top-mounted shifters.

Equipment freaks will not fit *Rapidfire*, as it restricts their freedom to fit someone else's brake levers.

Putting the gear and brake lever on the same mounting has a tiny weight and space advantage, but replacement is expensive. Break the gearing and you have to replace the complete unit – including the brake lever. This is particularly unfortunate as under-bar levers are the most susceptible to crash damage and, of the three lever types, have most to break. Their complex internal mechanisms include ratchets and springs, as the lever returns to its position every time. For beginners, under-bar shifters have the clearest indicators, but deciding which lever you need to push is a habit that takes time to acquire.

ONLY NATURAL

So why bother? Although riders have complained of skinning their knees on under-bar shifters, they are the most natural to use. Simultaneously, you can hold the handlebar tightly, press either lever with your cleverly evolved opposing digits and tug the brakes with the middle fingers. It is quite possible, for example, when about to climb up the far side of a trench, to use all the controls at once; to change from a high to a low gear both at the front and back, to brake hard with both wheels and to keep the steering under strict control.

Judged solely by their aid to bike handling, you can see why under-bar levers are the number-one brakes in the MTB charts.

upgrading bearings

The headset.

Bicycles have bearings in five places: the wheel hubs, the freehub or freewheel, the bottom bracket, the steering headset and in the pedals themselves. The latest designs use new materials as part of the complete unit, new working methods and fashion colours. They also tackle the two notorious weaknesses of bearings – coming loose and wearing out because dirt gets inside them.

▲ THE HEADSET: THE STEERING BEARING

The headset allows the front wheel, fork, stem and handlebars to swivel together, although independently from the rest of the bike. This component lives in the front-line position. Sitting on the prow of the frame, the front tyre chucks muck straight into its face, and it is persistently rattled by impacts from the front wheel.

So, while they are fine at providing the steering movement, headsets suffer a tendency to wear out prematurely through grit ingress, and to shake loose with vibration. The best headset upgrade addresses the latter problem. It is a newish adaptation, licensed in the name of Aheadset. It not only improves the locking, but is also 10–20% lighter, depending on the materials used, as it uses a compatible stem with a smaller fastening.

The standard mountain bike headset is similar to the headset found on a road bike. It has a choice of diameters – 1 in, 1.125 in, 1.25 in – to spread the off-road stresses. The principle of headset design is unaffected – there is a race of ball bearings at the top and bottom of the head-tube, to spread the load from impacts to the fork on which the fork turns. The top race screws on to the end of the threaded fork column and is held in place by a washer and locknut, which is what normally works loose. The stem fixes inside the column with an expander wedge and bolt.

THE AHEADSET ▶

The Aheadset stem has no such wedge fixing. Instead, it clamps over an unthreaded steering column and thereby holds the bearing in place, also losing the locknut. It is adjusted by raising and lowering the stem using another bolt in the cap at the top. This is done with a single Allen key, rather than the pair of enormous headset spanners that are needed to adjust a conventional lock-nut – much easier for on-the-go tightenings if the component should, for some strange reason come loose.

PROTECTION

Wobbles solved, how do you protect the bearing, and this really means the lower race, from daily off-road muck? Although grit does not increase the friction in the bearing particularly, it scratches the ball and race surfaces so that they no longer roll perfectly within the casing. Overcome this the same way as with the hubs and bottom bracket, by sealing them inside a permanent cartridge which, unlike conventional versions, need not be regularly stripped down for cleaning and regreasing. They cost a little more, but do extend the part's life for a long-term saving.

HUBS

The hubs, on which the wheels spin, are supposedly a fit-and-forget item. Their task has been fully understood for a long time, so

The aheadset is simpler to adjust.

BEARING NECESSITIES
Ball bearing facts you did not know you were missing!
- Ball bearings have a friction co-efficient of 0.011 – super-smooth! They must be well-lubricated and clean to function this well
- Bigger bearings give less resistance
- The cup and cone design is effective enough to keep working, even when mildly misaligned.
- Bicycles stimulated ball bearing design more than 100 years ago.

(Source: Bicycling Science, MIT Press 1982)

upgrading is a matter of aesthetics and weight-saving and less one of functional advance. However, this is assuming that the bearings are properly isolated from dirt and stay permanently well-adjusted – the recurring weakness in bearings.

Non-cartridge, traditional hubs have adjustable cones, needing slim cone spanners for tightening or loosening the ball movement. An improvement on these, are hubs with cartridge bearing units designed to remain closed; there is a large choice of these available.

SUSPENSION HUBS
Although all hubs are strong enough for the job, a reinforced model on the front is a good choice if you run suspension forks. Called suspension hubs, their axles are up to twice as thick at 20 mm (⅞in) than the standard 10 mm (⅜in), to resist the greater twisting forces in independently moving fork legs. You may even find a version with four rather than two sealed bearings, for smooth turning all along the axle.

THE FREEHUB
What chiefly concerns the rear hub, is how the sprocket unit, which incorporates the bearings for freewheeling and back-pedalling, fits on. The majority are now the improved freehub style, meaning that the spline onto which you slide the easily-interchangeable sprockets is an integral part of the hub. This is as opposed to a freewheel, a cluster of sprockets incorporating the bearings which screws on to a standard hub.

Beyond strengthening, we enter the designer realm of the esoteric. Primary colour anodizing decorates all permutations of hubs made from top quality materials – aluminium, titanium, carbon and even magnesium – in all its sections – the shell, axle, races and flanges. Pick and mix to match your bike.

BOTTOM BRACKET
The bottom bracket, the bearing on which the pedals revolve, suffers the same troubles as the headset and hubs, but in addition it directly receives all the power your legs impart. How do you stop it coming undone,

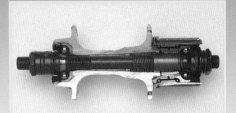

The freehub-style rear nut.

and how do you prevent muck penetration? Judging by the fact that the bottom bracket is the one most frequently found in bits on the kitchen table for greasing, perhaps you simply cannot.

The bracket is closely related to a hub. Both are axles turning at either end on a circle of ball bearings. Just as with the hub, choosing sealed cartridges should cut down on the need to clean and grease and should prevent it working loose and wearing unevenly. The volume of material in the axle is a challenge savoured by the weight-watchers, who favour high-quality titanium and aluminium versions, which can be hollow to save up to a third of the weight over standard cromoly models.

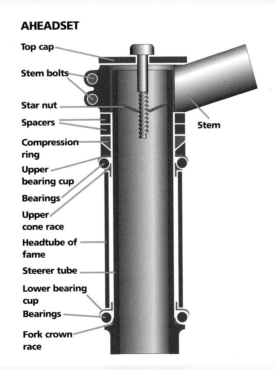

AHEADSET
- Top cap
- Stem bolts
- Star nut
- Spacers
- Compression ring
- Upper bearing cup
- Bearings
- Upper cone race
- Headtube of fame
- Steerer tube
- Lower bearing cup
- Bearings
- Fork crown race
- Stem

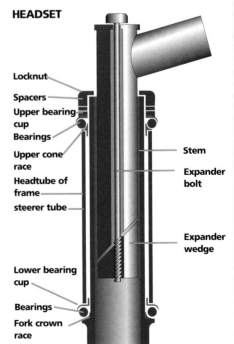

HEADSET
- Locknut
- Spacers
- Upper bearing cup
- Bearings
- Upper cone race
- Headtube of frame
- steerer tube
- Lower bearing cup
- Bearings
- Fork crown race
- Stem
- Expander bolt
- Expander wedge

71

upgrading
pedals

The pedal turns on a spindle which screws into the crank. Other than changing from a platform/cage model to one with spring bindings, upgrading pedals is a simply a matter of saving weight and increasing their chance of long life.

SPRING BINDING
SPD PEDALS ▼

If your new bike comes with ordinary flat models and toe clips, then changing them for a pair of pedals with spring bindings is the simplest way to improve your off-road control. You will also need special shoes with a cleat in the soles. Spring bindings, or "clipless" pedals house a mechanism, into which the shoes clip and unclip. If you have not got a pair of cycle shoes, then upgrading to spring bindings is a good way to combine the two investments. The patent belongs to *Shimano*, and is called SPD, which is to spring binding pedals what Hoover is to vacuum cleaners. Despite the cost and learning period, spring bindings are wonderful. They make acceleration easier, because none of your pedalling is wasted, and handling over tricky ground is more accurate because you and your bike are locked together.

Considering we have split the atom and gone to the Moon, however, we still fail to solve their main drawback. Spring bindings clog up in muddy, wet conditions to the point where they refuse to accept the cleat, which is just as blocked. It makes pedalling impossible, and you find yourself longing for the good old days of platform pedals and

One of the most effective upgrades: spring-binding SPD pedals.

WEIGHT-SAVING PEDALS
Pedals do not break. Their strength limits have not yet been reached in the name of saving grams. Weight freaks therefore should go for pedals with lighter-weight spindles, shaved-down cages or made from 100% titanium.

toe clips. When gears and brakes fail for the same reason, one solution is to seal them inside the hubs, but this is impossible as the spring binding needs to be kept open to take the shoe cleat.

You can either be prepared on occasion to walk, or to find a sturdy twig and clean them out, or you can fit a pair of pedals with a spring binding on one side and a plain platform on the other. As well as being a solution for clogged-up bindings, these pedals save time for competitive bikers. Downhill racers, for example, have to clip in and out a lot – 5 seconds, for them, is the difference between champion and nobody. For the rest of humanity, the platform side allows you to keep your fancy bike permanently mobilized for the dash for last-orders.

New designs reduce clogging and save weight by bringing down the amount of material in the SPD pedal. *OnZa* of the US was the first to bring out an alternative binding to *Shimano*'s wide range of SPDs (available for both road and off-road use), and the choice is growing. *OnZa*s use rubbers rather than springs.

A degree of float is an advantage in SPDs. It lets your foot pivot while remaining securely attached. Grease ports will allow you to squirt fresh grease into the bearings for longer life.

SUPER PLATFORM PEDALS ▶

As pedals for cross-country riding become smaller and neater, trials and downhill riders are fitting the largest, peg-cum-platforms imaginable. Why this should be, is difficult to work out, as they rarely use them, their legs usually swivelling wildly in the air above people's heads.

Measuring up to 10 cm (4 in) across these vicious-looking pedals had all but died out until the full suspension and trials bike renaissance of the early 1990s. Having your feet free is vital for freestyle mountain biking, which is a legacy of BMX and skateboarding. Meanwhile, there is a branch of off-road hedonism growing up around dual slaloms. To make up for having no spring bindings or toe clips, deep serrations on the pedal cages bite into the rubber soles of trainers. Shin gouges are badges of honour among the air-boys and girls.

These platform pedals may be simple, but they are not cheap. The quality depends on the ratio of aluminium alloy in the cage to cheaper resin material around the bearing spindle.

TOE CLIPS AND STRAPS ▶

As well-established as the zip, toe clips and straps are rare examples of a how efficient equipment can cost next-to-nothing. For racing, use shoes with slotted cleats in the sole that, when the straps are tightened, fit into bars in the pedals almost as efficiently

For stunt-riding, the chunkier the better.

as bindings. Toe clips and straps never stop working, and can be expanded and tightened to fit the thickness of your footwear. They are a must when your footwear is incompatible with spring bindings, such as with walking boots or when travelling distant lands where equipment must be simple and repairable. Toe straps also have a myriad of other handy applications around camp. One drawback is the split-second timing it takes to get feet into toe clips – you flick the pedal into a wild spin, and stand on the clip rather than getting inside it. The better the pedal, the less plastic or resin it will contain, also a sign of better bearings and housing.

Everlasting toeclips and straps.

upgrading saddles, cranks and stems

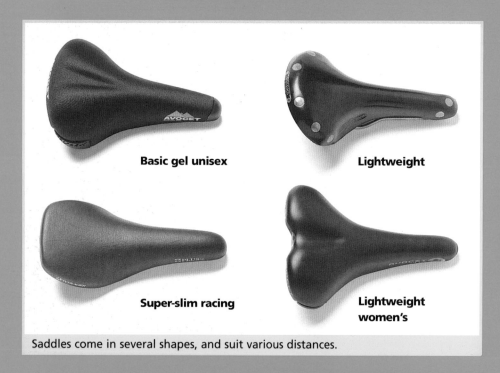

Basic gel unisex

Lightweight

Super-slim racing

Lightweight women's

Saddles come in several shapes, and suit various distances.

SADDLES

Whether riding mountain or road bikes saddles fall into two categories; softer and bigger for beginners and fair-weather riders, and harder and lighter for the tough-bottomed who ride every week. The majority of first-time mountain bikes are fitted with comfortably padded saddles that are just fine for an occasional foray, or for someone who wants to test the mountain biking water. The important thing is to make sure that you are sitting on the bones of your pelvic girdle so that your genitals are not squashed. Women's saddles are broader, men's are slimmer to match the differences in pelvic anatomy, but even so, a beginner of either shape should avoid the extremely wide saddles, which will chafe your inner thigh and push your knees out, affecting pedalling.

However well-fitting, there is no way to avoid a light bruising when you first ride off-road. Your body, which is remarkably adaptable, will toughen to resist this new pressure within a few weeks, and the soreness will go away, permanently if you keep riding.

A BETTER BEHIND

Once you run-in your behind, putting on a better saddle is an affordable bonus for the bike. It may have less bulk, with a slimmer nose and shallower sides, but will probably still be lightly padded. The magic word "gel" can bring solace to the anxious behind, but gel pads deform with age, less so now than when they were introduced, when they would slip inexorably down the sides of the saddle.

The solid leather saddles that parents and grandparents rode need to be worn in like a pair of heavyweight walking boots. Then, without stitching that can come undone nor covering to tear, they last for years, cured and polished by the rub of thousands of miles. Although lightweight solid leather saddles exist, their design has a way to go before they will become the racer's choice.

By minimizing the shape and using titanium, magnesium or aluminium alloys for the saddle rails, the weight of a top-flight racing model has been brought down to as little as 150 g (5 oz). Lighter tends to mean more fragile, and off-road riding, with its run-of-the-mill crashes and abrasion shortens the life of a saddle. The cheaper light models will not last long.

Make sure you get a seat post, to which the saddle attaches, that allows you to adjust the angle of the saddle and slide it forward and backward for comfort. Women like to point the nose down slightly. Remember to keep the seat post greased or it will stick inside the frame and become impossible to adjust or replace.

CRANKS

The crank is a simple creature; a bar of metal, usually solid, with a threaded hole at one end into which the pedal screws, and a

A crank: a simple creature, that also appears in technicolour.

The stem should be rigid under steering force, and not bend after numerous crashes, and that is it as far as upgrading goes – apart from saving weight.

However, there is the matter of the stem's compatibility with the design of the steering bearing or headset. Old-style headsets that screw on to the fork column use stems that wedge inside the column; new-style "Aheadsets" use stems that clamp to the outside of the fork column, saving a significant amount of weight and making them easier to adjust and remove.

Stems featuring suspension are rarities and a little outmoded, having appeared marginally before fork suspension – a development that blew suspended stems away. They are hinged with a spring or an elastomer, and isolate the upper body while the bike gets thrown about as much as ever.

square hole at the other to fit on to the bottom bracket axle. Other than the possibility of lightening cranks further, development has probably peaked, although fashion shows no sign of deceleration. The designer MTB crank of the 1990s is of anodized, sometimes hollow, aluminium, which saves weight and looks smart and strong; it also widens the choice beyond the standard *Shimano*, *Sugino* and *Campagnolo* cranks. Lightening tricks include hollowing out the crank, or carving it down to a minimum. Another lies in the pattern of the "spider", the five, or four arms at the top of the right-hand crank to which the chainrings are bolted. The cranks and chainrings together are called the crankset. MTBs have triple

cranksets, with three chainrings for more gears than the double crankset with two chainrings on most road bikes.

Although the stress placed on an MTB crank, up to around 1,540 kg (700 lb) per stroke, is the same as on a road bike, the MTB chunkiness and colour distinguishes it from road bike components.

STEMS

Connecting the handlebars to the frame, stems are also proof of the different direction that MTBs are taking from road bikes. The road bike's stem resembles a swan's neck. The MTB stem is fatter, and where carved from a billet of material, probably squared-off for rugged good looks.

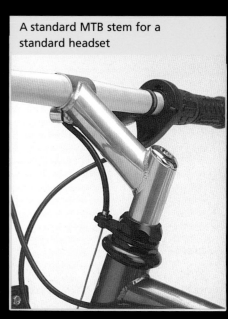

A standard MTB stem for a standard headset

about suspension

Ask a silly question...

Why go suspended? Perhaps because you are stuck for something to talk about with your mates, or because you're seeking a tribal logo to mark your identity as a rough slacker, or maybe you've just got too much money. All these factors may be true to a degree, but the main reasons must be because a suspended bike makes riding easier, faster and more fun.

The idea of suspension systems is to isolate the rider and/or bike from the direct effect of impacts between the tyres and the track. This is achieved by introducing shock absorbers at various points on the bike – most commonly nowadays in the front fork and rear triangle.

With the shock of the trail partially absorbed you can go more quickly with more control. Fundamentally this is because the wheels stay more closely in contact with the ground, as the shock absorption reduces ricochet. The rougher the terrain gets and the higher the speed, the wider the gap between the response of a suspended and rigid bike. High-risk downhillers ride bikes with up to 15 cm (6 in) of shock absorption at the front and rear to get as close as possible to the shortest line.

Benefit boosts

The benefits to a beginner are almost as great. Suspension is forgiving, and allows you to escape the consequences of clumsy handling that a rigid bike could not swallow.

Although suspension was developed particularly for downhilling, it is becoming more appropriate to general riding as the weight penalty decreases with advances in design and materials. The net result – full suspension is now feasible for cross-country riding because a fully suspended bike weighs just a couple of percent more than its rigid cousin. Top quality full suspension bikes can weigh as little as 11 kg (25 lb) or even less – which is light by rigid bike standards. This means that every cyclist should now be able to enjoy the higher speeds, sense of control and lower body stress of suspension.

Stress-relief

Suspension is also a healthy addition where your other equipment is concerned. Back-country hackers who spend all day in the saddle, 5-minute downhill dashers and racing greyhounds will all puncture less and have longer-lasting frames and components because of the reduced stress suspension provides. In theory, to save weight a suspension bike frame can be built less sturdily, although the lateral reinforcement and extra parts it needs usually add the grams back on.

However, suspension should not be seen as a panacea for all off-road ills. It means a loss of sensitivity in the trail, which is in itself one of the highs of mountain biking – and the injury rate among aspiring downhill pros is noteworthy. There is a finely-drawn line between skilled riding and recklessness on a fast, springy bike!

The first MTB with rear suspension: the *Fisher RS-1*.

Early and recent suspension types.

And another thing...

What about loss of speed when you're climbing? And the tendency for fully-suspended bikes to pogo when the extra pressure put through the pedals on a climb sets off an up-and-down oscillation in the hinged rear end? Perhaps that is why some cross-country professionals who grew up in cyclo-cross use suspension for contractual reasons rather than by preference. Whenever our faith falters temporarily in the consumerist belief that new is automatically better, it can seem as exciting to ride a rigid bike again it felt as when you first discovered suspension. Judging by the even split in bike sales the rigid bike is in no danger of extinction. However imaginatively designers experiment with the frame and parts of the push-bike, its performance will always be powered by the lungs and motivated by the nerve of the rider.

Nevertheless, the sophistication and diversity of suspension bikes validates their quest for pushing the capacity of the bike to the limits.

A brief history of suspension

In a cross-over from horse-drawn carriages, the concept of shock absorption has been incorporated on bicycles in one form or another since they were invented in the second half of the 19th century. The roads were much coarser then than now, and any form of springing wasn't just efficient – it was essential just to keep the bike on the ground and in one piece. In what seems like full circle, suspension has become relevant again, as people have taken to riding the rough stuff – now voluntarily.

The low-pressure pneumatic tyre, patented by *Dunlop* in 1888, was a major lurch forward after the solid tyres of the very early years. Until then sprung frames had been considered the answer, although they would become loose too quickly to work for long.

Sprung saddles go some way towards solving discomfort, but they don't make the bike run any better and they do affect the amount your leg has to extend to press on the pedal properly. The Briton Alex Moulton is the man credited with an important development in modern bike suspension. He used metal spring and rubber on his 1960s bike, the small wheels and luggage-carrying capacity of which required some form of shock absorber.

The first major developments in successful MTB suspension are attributed to the American off-road bike pioneer Gary Fisher, and motorcycle engineer Paul Turner. Fisher, in partnership with *Harley Davison* influence Mert Lawwill, brought out an early swing-arm rear end on the 1990 *RS-1* bike, which never made it commercially, but did send a hundred new MTB inventors scuttling to the drawing board. Turner's contribution was the 1989 telescopic, oil-dampened *RockShox* fork, another direct descendant from motorcycle trials-riding, which has become extremely popular and successful in mountain biking, while remaining fundamentally unchanged.

Early full suspension bike developers were *ProFlex*, which used elastomer bumpers as shock absorbers in both a hinged stem – the *FlexStem* – and hinged rear wheel. The design of the rear end has been successfully continued, whereas the stem has been overtaken by suspension forks. *Cannondale* went further with more complex metal spring and oil dampening in a hinged rear triangle. The company followed that up by positioning a shock unit internally in the head-tube, for a properly suspended front wheel, and this style also remains in production.

upgrading suspension

Internal mechanics

The aim of good shock absorption internals is to absorb impact accurately and instantly; indeed a culture has grown up among mechanically-minded bikers ravenous for knowledge about how different materials and combinations achieve this ideal.

Of course, you can enjoy feeling the boing without ever giving a fig about what is going on out of sight; but ignorance is not so blissful when it comes to the extra expense and maintenance which a suspension fork inevitably, demands. At least if a shock absorber breaks on a ride, it is unlikely to stop your wheels turning. You will just rattle all the way home.

How does it work?

If you seek initiation into the equipment fray, this is how gases, fluids and rubber subdue a six-inch edge of granite without damage – be warned: you are now entering the addiction zone.

Shock absorption works by channelling force in a controlled manner through compressible substances. The impact is first taken up by a moving spring, and then drowned by a damper. When choosing an individual piece of suspension equipment, or trying to decide on whether to get a complete bike, it helps if you understand the different combinations of spring and damper around. Why? Because each has advantages and disadvantages in terms of rate of absorption, amount of absorption, reliability and imagination.

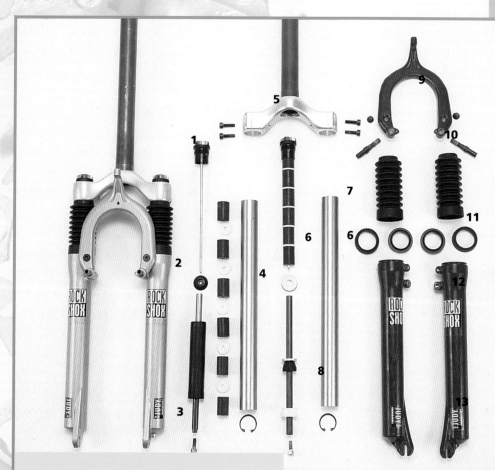

JUDY XC FORK
1 – damper skewer with preload knob; 2 – oil damper cartridge; 3 – 6mm retaining screw; 4 – six microcellular foam elements (one side); 5 – fork crown assembly with cromoly steerer; 6 – *Easton* taper-gauge alloy fork legs; 7 – complete micro-cell stack; 8 – right-side top-out shaft assembly; 9 – magnesium fork brace for the SL and DH model; 10 – brake bosses; 11 – fork boots; 12 – boot air cleaners; 13 – magnesium sliders.

WHICH TYPE OF SHOCK ABSORBER?

METAL COIL

On general bikes the cheap, cheerful spring often has no damper, which means uncontrolled rebounding. On quality off-road bikes, combined with oil dampening, a metal coil spring works well.

HYDRAULIC

This style has more parts and needs high-quality seals to stay air- and oil-tight, but is highly-tuneable and considered the "king" of the big bumps. It takes a larger impact to set off compression in the fluids, so it is not so good for little bumps. Probably because of its motorcycling heritage, hydraulic is considered more authentic than the cruder, yet highly effective elastomer bumper, and is the choice of the big-hit downhiller.

ELASTOMER

This type of shock absorption works better on little bumps and has a mess-free reliability. Advances are being made to refine its adjustability, which is at a disadvantage compared to hydraulic systems, with interchangeable bumpers of different densities for graded shock absorption and a quicker compression on big bumps.

COMBINATION ELASTOMER/OIL

This system of shock absorption may prove to be the best of both worlds. It retains the simplicity of bumpers, which have a fast spring rate for little bumps, and adds an oil damper to swallow the big bumps, which has the fine-tuning of hydraulics.

HYDRAULICS

In a fluid, hydraulic shock, the spring and damper are separated. The spring gives way to the impact, allowing the wheel to move in relation to the ground rather than the rider/frame; the distance it travels depends on the amount of movement in the unit and its degree of stiffness The spring's job is also to transfer the force to the damper where the impact is lost for good. In a hydraulic system, the spring is usually a chamber of air compressed by a piston, lthough it may be an external metal coil.

The damper – the dead end for the shock – is like the foot-pedal operated felt pad that stops a piano string vibrating. It is designed to eat the force instantly, before it can rebound. The damper prevents the impact going into reverse and shooting back out through the spring with the same force that it entered. A hydraulic bike damper is a chamber of viscose oil compressed and extended by the spring; the spring's rate of resistance may be adjusted by opening and closing the aperture of valves through which the oil is forced, or by using thicker or thinner oils. In most telescopic forks the designers have simplified the valve adjustment by putting a dial on each fork leg for the different resistance settings.

The amount of force dissipated by the spring can also be adjusted by manually altering the tension in the metal coil or the pressure in an air chamber.

ELASTOMER "BUMPERS"

Until 1994, elastomer "bumper" shock absorbers used just one material in a single mass to perform the function of both spring and damper. The dual job was tackled by a stack of compressible bumpers. Additional damping in elastomers comes from the resistance to the bumpers' rapid expansion from the internal wall of the fork. The bumpers spring enough for the wheel to move several centimetres, while dampening the force to reduce its rebound. Adjustment in the compression is made by inter-changing bumpers, which have different densities.

ELASTOMER "BUMPERS"

After 1994, an elastomer/oil combination was used. These work as the dampening inherent in the stack of bumpers is supplemented with a hydraulic oil chamber, for better fine-tuning and rebound sensitivity.

which
suspension

For a reasonably priced suspension upgrade suspension forks can be purchased, although a pair may cost as much as the bike itself. Bikes with built-in front suspension are in the medium-to-expensive price bracket, while for a fully suspended bike, you have to consider the top of the range.

What to look for

TRAVEL

Travel is how far a shock absorber will compress, and governs how far the wheel will move on its own separately from the bike. The latest designs have up to 15 cm (6 in) of travel in the rear, an extraordinary amount that compares with motorbike suspension which supports a greater weight. Travel is something that you pay for, and cheap shock absorption will only allow the wheels to move as little as 2.5 cm (1 in). The average quality fork will offer around 5 cm (2 in) of travel. The more travel there is the greater the lateral strengthening must be to resist the frame or fork twisting from side to side, hence, partly, the beefiness of downhill bikes.

PRE-LOAD AND ADJUSTABILITY

The rider's weight and skill, plus the hardness or softness of the terrain are the deciding factors in adjusting the rate of compression. The rule is to set the shock absorber softer as the terrain gets rougher. Heavier riders should always start with harder suspension, to save more of the compression for the trail and not their weight.

A good deal of the adjustment is done in the workshop by changing the oil or bumpers, or the air pressure. However, what has made suspension much more rider-friendly is the pre-set knob now found on a large number of suspension forks models which you use on the trail. With this the shock absorber can be completely turned off, or "locked out", to suit climbing, riding on tarmac or mood.

Despite experiments with handlebar levers, in all but a very few cases, notably *Cannondale*, shock absorbers cannot be adjusted while actually riding along. This means that the ideal, which is to be able to turn the shock absorber on and off at will to suit the gradient, remains a dream.

BRACING AND REINFORCEMENT

The Achilles heel of a telescopic suspension fork is twist, which happens every time one leg compresses further than the other. This is unavoidable in telescopic forks, as each leg contains its own shock. Force from the trail rarely hits a fork squarely from the front, nor does your body weight bear down on it centrally from above when you are rocking from side to side on the bike. The squirm in the wheel, especially standing in the pedals to honk up hills, may be bad enough for the brake pads to rub the rims on each stroke – an unwanted time to brake if ever there was one.

The higher quality the fork, the less the twist. The stiffest versions use strong materials, along the same lines as better frame materials, that is, with higher yield and tensile strengths. There should also be a lot of internal overlap between the legs and the stanchions –as with *RockShox' Judy* fork – and a powerful brace.

HOME ADJUSTMENT

1. Load the shock absorber correctly for your weight so that it never gets to the end of its compressibility – you'll feel a thud every time it does.
2. Use a wheel with a double-thickness so-called "suspension" axle in the hub, as this is all that holds the wheel in place. This contains no shock absorber, it is just stronger than a regular hub.
3. Adapt your riding style. Train to strengthen your legs so that when you stand up on the pedals you are as upright as possible. Rocking from side to side may look good – and is easier in the short-term, but, in reality, it wastes energy and it is a sign that the hill is winning!

Rider-only suspension

Cheap ways of isolating the rider from the trail – but not the bike – include fitting a sprung seat post or sprung stem. The

Telescopic type
suspension fork.

former is not a new idea, and plays the same role as a sprung saddle for a more comfortable butt, with the drawback of slightly affecting the distance your leg extends. The sprung stem largely defends the wrists, and might allow a nominally more aggressive style, but cannot provide more than a couple of centimetres of travel for your upper body. Neither of these pieces of equipment are a replacement for a shock absorber at the wheels, but they are nevertheless popular specialist MTB items that enhance a bike's rugged identity.

Parallelogram type suspension fork.

FRONT SUSPENSION TYPES

The telescopic fork is the most popular style, with sprung legs which overlap the stanchions, each with its own internal shock absorber. The major benefits are simpler aesthetics and few exposed joints. The costs are double shock absorbers with double the faff and a potential to twist, and a linear movement of the wheel in compression – it only moves in and out along the straight line of the fork.

▶ LEADING LINK SUSPENSION FORKS.

This type of fork design uses a single shock absorber and has a double strut the full length of the fork, which is hinged to form a swinging parallelogram. The chief advantage is its better handling. As well as moving in and out as the shock is absorbed, the wheel is allowed to swing slightly forward and back, to follow the surface more realistically. There is also less twist in the fork legs, because they are fixed both at the top and at the bottom. The drawbacks of linked suspension are weight and complexity in the pipework and a potential for weakness in the multiple link-points. These factors are enough to make them a rarity.

◀ PARALLELOGRAM SUSPENSION FORKS

Sharing the same movement as the link fork, also with a single shock absorber, this style uses a small parallelogram at the top of the fork legs to build a swing to the in/out movement of the wheel. The advantages are realistic tracking without doubling up the tubing and joints, less twisting in the legs and

an attendant weight reward, without any compromise in travel. Becoming increasingly popular, but still well in a minority against telescopic forks .

Link type
suspension fork.

HEADTUBE SUSPENSION

Here a single shock absorber is concealed inside the headtube, meaning that the fork legs are rigid and the movement is plain in and out without any swing. The benefits of this type of suspension are that the fork legs do not twist, the internal mechanisms do not get silted up, it has a low weight and the forks are not weakened laterally.

To date. this is the only type of front shock absorber that can be turned on or off while you are actually on the move, such as at the start of a climb. The drawbacks are that this type of suspension cannot be retro-fitted – it is only available on complete bikes that are manufactured by *Cannondale* under the brand name *Headshok* – and it looks to the uninitiated as if you are riding a rigid bike.

widgets–
a bike's bits and pieces

Major league equipment aside – wheels, brakes, bearings and gears – mountain biking is full of trinkets to swap, collect and keep on your bike. Some save weight, others have a functional advantage and some are fashion accessories or toys – it's all part of the game.

BAR ENDS ▶

Bar ends have now become standard equipment. Nearly all new mountain bikes come with bar ends fitted, but if yours does not have them, then get a pair for more comfortable and convenient hand-holds – and racier looks.

The MTB handlebar is perpendicular to your body and rotates your arms about 90° away from neutral. Think about it; if you drop your arms to your side your palms are prone, facing your body. When you grab the wide, flat bars on the bike your arms swivel to bring your hands to position. If they were by your side they would be facing backward. This is not a problem, because the arms are evolved to rotate up to 270°, but it is marginally more comfortable when riding to have your hands facing palms-in rather than backward. Like the drop-handlebars on a road bike a pair of bar ends brings them back to neutral.

A bar end is a short piece of tubing that comes in a variety of lengths and bends, colours, material and knurling. If your bike is on a gram-controlled diet, then forking out for an expensive pair along with other

Bar ends: variations on a theme.

weight-reducing equipment, will help a small percentage loss in overall weight.

CHAIN RETAINER ▶

A cheap frustration-saving device, a chain retainer is a useful aid for when muddy conditions or slack in the chain threaten to derail it. When downhilling on a fully suspended bike, a retainer is virtually obligatory, as a jumping rear wheel continually alters the chain tension. Other risky times are when clogged sprockets and rings

spoil the snug tooth-to-link fit, or when the chain goes slack as you change gear from big to little rings. Momentarily, before the rear changer (derailleur) has time to spring back and take up several centimetres worth of free-flying links, the chain has nil tension, goes floppy and is easily knocked off.

Not with a chain retainer. Positioned halfway between the wheel and the pedals, it provides an extra slot for the chain to run through and thus halves the distance by which it can move off sideways.

FANCY FIXINGS

It is possible to pay an intriguing amount of wedge for nuts, bolts and screws of the latest metals in the latest colours for peppering on the bike. Here is a shopping list of fixings queuing for attention.

- Brake boss bolt
- Crank bolt and cap
- Brake straddle cable hanger,
- Spoke nipples
- Jockey wheel screws
- Wheel and seat-post clamps
- Stem bolts
- Rear derailleur hanger bolt
- Chainring bolts – these items are available in assortments to take the hassle out of individual selection.
- A moment for the mechanics – softer alloys round easily, and titanium-on-titanium surfaces must be properly greased to prevent galling.

Bar ends in uphill action.

QUICK-RELEASE LEVERS

If the knobbly tyre is the symbol of a bike revolution, then the cool quick release (QR) lever or skewer is the symbol of a designer revolution. It is rumoured that engineers have been able to retire young on the proceeds of these wildly popular MTB identity cards, an early focus for colour anodizing and aerospace metals.

The skewer is a simple clamp, with a bolt at one end and a hand-lever that works an internal cam at the other. Each bike has three places where a quick release skewer can be fitted, one at each wheel to clamp it to the frame, and one for the seat post.

A fancy QR will weigh half as much as the regular pair that comes fitted on a standard bike, and it will display some aspect of new materials or machining method, be it aluminium or titanium or having been CNC cut. What was first learned on QRs, which are small, and thus affordable items of equipment, has since been applied to the more critical parts of the bike, such as the cranks, hubs and brakes.

Avoid QRs which do not clamp smoothly or which have skinny levers. They can be difficult to open and close with numb fingers in cold weather. Unfortunately QRs make it easy to steal bits of your bike. If you often have to leave the bike unattended, for security's sake switch to nut and bolt skewers and save the QRs for the MTB festivals.

Make dropping your chain a thing of the past with an extra retainer.

mud glorious mud

You can't beat it, so why not learn to love it.

The ministry of mud defence

Tips to help you deal with the mountain bike and biker's favourite foe – mud!

■ Go for the chunkiest tyres your frame will take while keeping 1 cm (½ in) clearance. Wider knobbles shed mud more quickly from the tyre, but at a rate which depends on its stickiness. Directional tyres, such as those with chevrons, are good, with an alternative choice in "semi-slicks", smoother tyres which cut through the surface slime to the firm surface beneath. Also there is mileage in the idea of going for slimmer 4 cm (1½ in) tyres.

■ In mildly muddy conditions spraying your frame with lube will slow down mud build up.

■ Use thick lubes – thinner lubes like WD40 or GT85 are not intended for the chain. They are water-displacers and will wash off quickly in mud and rain, leaving the links grating and scratching. Always use a thicker oil – the extra pennies are worth it – and apply liberally if you are expecting hell.

■ Tyres pressures should be low at around 35–40 psi, to mould around every available contour for grip.

■ Before starting out on a ride that will be very wet and gritty, either renew the brake blocks, or pack a spare pair so you can change them mid-ride. Brake blocks can wear down to the pegs or housing after a few long descents in very wet and gritty weather – the wetter it is, the more like sandpaper is the combined action of the mud and rims. If the metal is exposed it can split a rim which is worn – which is incurable out on the trail. Use the barrel adjusters at the levers every hour or so to take up the wear this action causes. Don't forget the 10 mm spanner or allen keys necessary to adjust the blocks.

■ If out in boggy hills, wear walking gaiters, preferably breathable ones. These will protect your leggings and keep the mud away from your skin.

■ Gradually exchange all non-sealed bearings (bottom bracket, steering headset and wheel hubs) to models with sealed cartridges. Until that day, clean and regrease them frequently after grotty, gritty rides.

■ Remove the seat post of a steel bike and hang the bike upside down to dry after a wet, muddy ride, to make sure water doesn't rust the tubes, especially around the bottom bracket.

■ Fit top-quality brake and gear cables, preferably PTFE or Gore-tex, for extra slide-ability for when the mud gets serious.

■ Grease is the bike's protective layer. It protects it from the elements and ensures long life. Squirt the stuff into the little breathing holes in the chain stays, smear it around the headset races...

■ Are you bunged-up? What about in the end of the handlebars, the end of the bar ends, underneath the fork crown going up into the fork column? The top of the fork legs, the gaps around shoe cleats, crank bolt caps, the spout of your water bottle, your ears, mouth and nose? Only kidding!

Muddy fixtures and fittings:

■ Mud guards for the down-tube and front wheel – for maintaining a clean front.

■ A mud guard for the rear wheel – for a shiny rear end as well.

■ A sprocket scraper – fixes at the rear hub and combs away the crud from between the sprockets.

■ An anti-chainsuck plate – fixes beneath the chain stays at the chainrings and stops the damage that is caused when a derailled chain gets pulled up between the stays and the rings.

■ A chain retention device, as otherwise clogged rings easily derail the chain.

■ Make sure suspension fork legs are pro-

tected by gaiters. Lube the fork legs frequently. Service them to check that the seals are doing their job.

■ Don't round bolts. Clean out muddy allen bolts before undoing them, in case the allen key does not insert properly and the bolt gets rounded.

■ Spray the spring bindings of SPD-style pedals with lubricant – they are one of the first things to seize up. Or go back to straps and cleats for huge amounts of mud.

■ Keep on brake covers. Do not remove the rubber covers on the brake lever pivots. Do cover up the lower headset race with either a commercial neoprene and velcro coat, or make your own from a piece of inner tube fixed with zip ties.

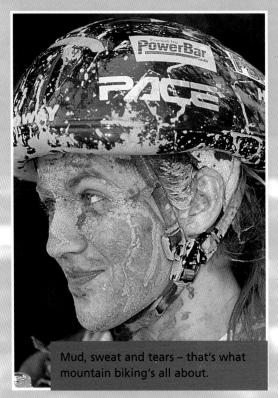

Mud, sweat and tears – that's what mountain biking's all about.

Mud and the Mountain biker

■ Eye protection – wear it. It is not just mud that flies up into the eyes from Farmer Giles' pastures – and it can cause infection.

■ Shiny rider – at home in the post-ride bath, do not forget to clean inside your ears! Get used to having lightly hennaed skin for a couple of days after getting muddy in areas with reddish soil!

■ Gear grip – keep a grip on revolver gears by getting covers with the sharpest profile you can find.

■ Clearance – in the bike shop satisfy yourself that the clearance between the chain stays and seat stays is big enough on the bike you fancy.

■ Second saving – racers with serious ambition can carry a second full water-bottle to flush the mud off the sprockets, and should consider on-the-move chain lubing devices. They could make the difference between

becoming a champion and staying a nobody with jumping gears and recurring chainsuck.

■ In the car – buy or make water and mud resistant seat covers to keep the car upholstery clean. Remember several plastic bags to stuff revolting muddy gear into. Carry around another couple of bin liners for sitting on to placate respectable publicans and café mistresses.

■ Sock sense – put aside a couple of pairs of socks solely for muddy riding – you will have to give up on their original colour. Ditto, a few old and worn bath towels.

■ Recycle the mud you collect on your travels – wash the bike on a flowerbed.

■ Cleaning tips – thick mud is much more easily removed when wet and scratches the paintwork less. A thin layer will come off more easily with a dry cloth when dry, but can take the shine off new paint.

■ Stop-gap lubing – if you have no time to clean and dry the bike properly after a ride, then at least spray some lube on the chain to stop it going rusty overnight.

Every biker will have to confront mud at some point on the trails.

this chapter is concerned with building the mountain bike's engine – your body – and acquiring the knowledge to drive so that you can get the most out of mountain biking. Don't be fooled by the number of hints on skills and fitness into thinking that there is anything difficult about the sport. Anyone with a minimum of mobility can have a go and will improve with practice. After a short search, everyone should be able to find some easy-to-reach track within a few kilometres of home – whether it be a state park, or an urban canal towpath.

The nutrition and stretching sections are here to remind you that mountain biking is an easy way to a healthy lifestyle and to show you, in easy steps, how you can get there. According to the British Medical Association, a regular cyclist has the body of someone 10 years younger. Regular exercise is also an excellent guard against heart disease. We explain how to build fitness in a year from scratch, then how to train for racing. All the wider sports health issues are covered, such as how to cross-train indoors and outdoors, how to prevent colds and to eat for energy.

Anyone who is seeking a way to fit the sport into their busy lives, or who is unfamiliar with life beyond the city limits, will probably find their first effort bruising – but persevere! Try to think of every pedal-stroke as an investment that will pay you back with improved health, stronger legs and higher self-esteem.

Although you can ride a mountain bike from the second you swing your leg over the saddle, you may soon want to go faster, over harder terrain and cover longer distances. That's the way to get the most from your valuable bike and to get a feel for the landscape. Each time you are out on the trail you are intuitively using your balance in harmony with the pedals and brakes to guide the bike forward or to resist the pull of gravity. The technique and terrain pages identify the handling skills needed to ride long and hard off-road. They also give detailed explanations of how to survive most of the surfaces and gradients you will face.

Few mountain bikes are street virgins for long. Between trips your bike will probably double up as a daily transporter, so survival in traffic is an important and vital skill. Learn to recognize the danger spots, and how to shine in the dark. As urban bike theft is such big business use these tips to build up your defences against thieves, and to limit the damage if you are unlucky.

And when the call of the wild becomes irresistible, it's time to load the bike with panniers, get out the maps and respond. In this chapter you will discover the information and equipment recommended to survive a long-distance trip

William Morgan, a sports psychologist, claims that running is a wonder drug. Mountain biking is the same, but with better views and tales. What are you waiting for? Get out and ride!

the fit mountain biker

Riding a bike is exhilarating yet hard work – but don't panic. Assuming general health, inside everyone is a fit body trying to get out, and how better to release it than from the saddle of a mountain bike.

A beginner's first aim is to enjoy an afternoon's ride on their shiny new bike. However, even this needs a level of fitness, especially if you choose a hilly or muddy route. Sporty types, who regularly do aerobics, run or swim will have little problem adapting to mountain biking, although the cycle-specific muscles in the calves and thighs take 6 to 12 months to develop. However, for the couch potato drawn to mountain biking by the call of the wild, the waistline and trick componentry, that first afternoon will be a righteous challenge.

How fitness works

Whether you mountain bike regularly, or you consider walking to the burger bar an act of heroism, your natural body fitness is set at the following level:

Weekly demand + energy for emergencies = (un) fitness level

Take little exercise and your body will "relax". Exercise steadily and your body will at first feel as if it is resisting, before growing to a stronger and heartier setting. Unfortunately, there are no short-cuts.

When will I be fit?

Broadly speaking, it takes a year for an adult's body to adapt from meeting the mellow demands of inactivity to those of a hard, hilly day in the saddle. Young women and men, teenagers and children have abundant energy and fewer bad fitness habits, although their endurance may need work.

Regarding individual sessions, it takes 2–3 days to recover your energy after a session and a week or so for soreness to go away. It takes 3–6 weeks for your body to grow stronger in response to a session. It takes 3 years of committed training for endurance athletes, like cyclists, to attain their full potential.

Fitness tips

■ Avoid overdoing it – sometimes in their enthusiasm, unfit people can overdo their riding, and suffer a consequent long-term loss of energy. Do not let your mind push your body faster than it can grow.

■ Quality not quantity – riding for a short time regularly is as effective and more sustainable than once-monthly blowouts that will make you want to sell the bike.

■ Commute by bike – ride to school, college or work. These "invisible" kilometres are of benefit to the environment as well as your heart and head.

■ Do hills get easier? Yes, but it doesn't feel like it. As your fitness improves, rather than settling back to enjoy it, you will find yourself with a new-found ability to climb bigger hills faster and more frequently. The reward lies in more mountain biking fun, rather than being able to laze on the bike.

How to ride to fitness in a year

1 GOAL-SETTING
Set yourself low or realistic goals, attainable within the amount of time you have to ride, otherwise you will quit at the first hurdle.

For example:

- In a month's time I want to be able to ride for 20–30 minutes, 3 times a week.
- In 3 months time I want to be able to ride off-road for 1 hour without resting.
- In 6 month's time, I want to be able to ride every day for short distances – commute to school, college or work, or do my first one-hour race.
- At the end of a year I want to be able to ride all the way up "Grief Hill".

2 THE PLAN

Your aim in your fitness programme is to concentrate on steadily increasing the amount of time spent riding.

Months 1 to 3

Start with the three 30-minute sessions a week of exercise. Try riding, running, swimming or aerobics – any form of exercise that gets you out of breath.

Months 3 to 6

Increase one of the regular weekly sessions to an hour's ride, keeping up the other 30-minute sessions. By the end of this period you may be able to spend a whole afternoon every weekend riding on rough terrain. Try to ride all the way up small hills, and practise the handling as your speed increases.

Months 6 to 12

Try your first fun race, to last less than a hour. Keep up the shorter sessions and make every other weekend ride an all-day one. Ride all the way up difficult hills that require balance as well as strength. How about marking the anniversary of buying your new bike with a 2-day camping trip carrying all your own gear...

When the going gets tough

- The first 20 to 30 minutes of riding feel awful. It is a transitional phase when, as with any engine, your body's systems are adapting to work more efficiently. After that, things get easier.
- The burning pain in your legs when climbing a steep hill is as a result of lactic acid – a by-product of the energy conversion process – which cannot be removed as fast as your body produces it. The burning stops when you rest, and over time, its onset is delayed.
- If your enthusiasm wanes in the face of pain or rain, that is not failure. Take a break from the bike for a couple of days. Revise your plan and goals and review your equipment, but don't give up. Perhaps your clothing isn't up to the conditions? Why not treat yourself to a inspiring piece of equipment for the bike.
- However difficult or lonely the riding, however weak your body feels, the workout is doing your legs and heart good. Be patient, and go for the goals you've set yourself not those of your friends.

Build up your fitness with regular stretch and strength exercises.

sports
fitness

Having reached the point where they can happily ride off-road non-stop for 1 or 2 hours, many bikers push on with their fitness. They are enjoying themselves and plan adventures such as doing 80 km (50 miles) in a day, having a holiday in the mountains or even racing. Unlike simple fitness, sports fitness does not slot easily into a casual lifestyle. It needs performance goals, a seasonal training plan and usually some dietary amendment! Some old pleasures will go, but they usually amount to little more than hours wasted on the sofa.

The training plan

Here, intensity is added to time in the saddle. The quality of the workout matters as well as the quantity. The amount of energy you put into a ride is divided into three percentages of maximum effort: the easier the effort, the longer the ride. The table below shows these, using approximate heart rate values, with an average rate of 185 beats

A good training plan will help build your race fitness,

Effort level	% max effort	BPM	Builds	An/Aerobic	How it feels
Level 1	Below 40%	sub–74 bpm	Nothing	Aerobic	Easy to chat
Level 2	50%–70%	92–130 bpm	Endurance/ strength	Aerobic	Hard but sustainable
Level 3	80%–100%	148–185 bpm	Strength/speed	Anaerobic	Unsustainable

...per minute (bpm). This is measured with a heart rate monitor (HRM), preferably with a chest strap detector and a wrist-strap or handlebar monitor. A HRM tells racers how hard they are working, and whether to give more or to ease off.

Off-season racers do long low-intensity level rides to build endurance, say an all-day 112-km (70-mile) ride with several stops. As the competitive season approaches, the rides are shortened and the intensity increased to high level 2 and level 3 efforts, to build strength and speed, say, a 1-hour stint or a set of 1-minute repetitions (intervals) at maximum. Refinements are built into the plan to prevent over-training and to a peak for the big events. Some plans use 4 levels, further sub-divided.

Motivation

When the novelty of training has worn off a lot of riders drop their training plans out of boredom or demotivation. Perhaps you cannot find the time to stick to an over-optimistic plan, or you are beaten in a race by someone you have had no trouble pulverizing in the past. Also, mountain biking is one of the sports which is great fun in practice, but a lot of training work is done on the road, in the gym or on rollers.

Find ways to put fun into training. Build rewards into your diet, seek training partners for companionship and comparison. Do not neglect other pleasures – the cinema, family and non-biking friends – but do not quit! As with any long-term project, you will suffer low points. Build as much as a 25% lost-time factor into your programme to allow for illness, relationships, family or loss of motivation.

■ Cross-country mountain bike racers train 75% on the road, 25% on the trail because tarmac provides the predictable environment needed for controlled-intensity training sessions. Off-road work is essential to develop faster handling. Improvement comes from exposure and testing your nerve and control on harder and harder obstacles and slopes.

■ Downhillers are purer trail devotees, as in their split-second discipline what counts is high-speed bike control as well as fitness.

■ Train your weaknesses – whatever you work hard at you will be good at. For example, if you ride for 160 km (100 miles) steadily, that is the area in which you will shine, but your speed will not improve. If you are poor at downhilling, sign up for a downhill competition! If you cannot mount the bike from the right-hand side, get practising. If you fall behind on hills, write more climbing into your training plan.

■ Eat a balanced diet with approximately 55% carbohydrate, 30% fat and 15% protein. Eat fresh fruit or vegetables at every sitting, replace desserts with fruit, and cream with yoghurt.

■ Keep a diary (possibly even in the form of a computer spreadsheet) in which you keep a daily record of what cycling and exercise you have, or haven't done.

■ Over-training causes a long-term drop in performance. You have done too much too soon and your body, rather than adapting to the extra effort and becoming stronger, cannot catch up and is defeated. An unfit or semi-fit rider is at just as much risk from over-training as the sports rider. It can occur at quite low levels and such people are usually less aware of the problem.

■ Always rest properly between sessions, remembering that the harder the session, the longer the recovery period, be patient – do not rush back into the saddle.

■ Trust your body. Do not expect to feel great for a few days or even a week after a big ride. It takes 3–6 weeks to feel the benefits of a training session. Controlled rest is the prescribed cure, in the absence of a full understanding of over-training.

■ Good weather and exciting terrain.

■ A heart rate monitor.

■ Indoor static trainers – indoor rollers or turbo trainers provide the most controlled cycling conditions and are highly effective if used to their full potential.

■ Handlebar computer – to monitor time and distance, as well as speed, and perhaps cadence.

■ Try a training partner – not only is this more fun, it will also help with your pacing.

A handlebar computer.   Measure your pedalstrokes.

eating and drinking
for mountain biking

Start with a healthy diet

The average Westerner eats double the amount of fat and half the amount of carbohydrate recommended for a healthy body. So the priority for active bikers is to get the daily balance right first, then to tackle the detail.

Experts recommend that the daily diet contains the following proportions of the essential food groups.

- 55% complex carbohydrates – for energy. Carbohydrate is found in starchy staples such as bread, potatoes, pasta and polenta.
- 10–15% protein – for growth. Protein is found in eggs, dairy products, beans, lentils, soya, fish, chicken and red meat.
- 30% fat – an essential dietary aid. Good sources of fat are oily fish, dairy products, vegetable oils and margarine.
- Eat fruit and vegetables at every meal

and you will also be getting the other essential nutrients – fibre, vitamins and minerals.

What should I eat before a ride?

After 1–2 hours of solid exertion, glycogen, the body's fuel derived largely from complex carbohydrates and stored in the muscles, runs out. Suddenly, you tremble and lose power. This is called "hitting the wall", or "getting the bonk". At best it is uncomfortable, for competitors the event is over.

What happens is that your fuel system is switching over from short-term glycogen to long-term body-fat, in effect, your reserve tank. However, during this time, which lasts an hour or so, the rider is not worth much. Eat, instead, for short-term energy. Munch carbohydrates in the form of sugary or mixed sugary starchy foods – for example, a banana or an energy bar – and you should be able to get back on your bike and pedal within 30 minutes.

To avoid hitting the wall in the first place you need to carbo-load. Serious athletes carbo-load properly; that is, they exhaust their glycogen supplies a week before the big event by working out desperately hard, then pack their plates with little other than rice, potatoes, pasta or bread for the 3 or 4 days before the ride to give the body time to gather the maximum glycogen in the muscles. Carbo-loading for fun riders just means paying careful attention to your intake and eating

Fresh fruit – a vital ingredient in the recipe for healthy eating.

On every ride, drink plenty of fluids.

more than your usual amount of carbohydrate-based food in the days running up to a big ride.

When and what should I eat?

For any ride over about an hour, on the day eat a hearty breakfast of cereals, toast or muesli, but nothing heavy, such as sausages, which take time to digest. Allow 2 to 3 hours between your last meal and the ride, because when you start riding the blood is drawn away from your digestive organs to the muscles, and anything undigested will stay that way until you stop. Worse, there is a risk of being sick.

DURING

On the ride eat little and often, before you get hungry. Pack your backpack with convenient forms of moist starchy sugary foods that you can swallow on the move. Try dried fruit, sultanas or raisins, energy bars, bananas, moist biscuits. If your legs and spirits need a boost, resort to an energy bar or a sports drink, but by preparing properly you should be able to avoid having to fall back on these cheering but non-essential eats.

AFTER

Eat carbohydrate-filled calories within 2 hours of stopping your ride, while your body is still efficiently converting that energy. Studies have shown that eating in this phase will aid your long-term recovery.

Liquid-fuelled

Two litres (3½ pints) of water is the recommended daily quantity that all adults should drink. Cyclists can hardly get too much of the stuff, using and losing it at a surprising rate. Always drink a glass of water before you start a ride – whether you feel like it or not. Your freshly filled water bottle is an essential piece of equipment on any ride so use it. Start sipping from your water bottle after just quarter of an hour. Drink little and often all the way to the end of the ride, and a larger quantity afterward.

The human body can process about a litre (2 pints) of water an hour, so it is easy to leave it too late to catch up with the amount you've sweated into your clothes – and that gives little indication of how much has vaporized. Post-race headaches are caused by dehydration, just like alcoholic hangovers. If a headache develops, even if you don't feel thirsty, try steadily drinking a half a litre (1 pint) of water, and another, if you feel like it. Some racers in hot climates have been known to hydrate themselves before an event, to the point where their urine starts to run clear.

ENERGY BARS

The advantage of commercial energy bars and drinks is first, their portability, and second, the ease with which the energy giving ingredients can be digested. If riding in wilderness areas such bars are survival aids, and another advantage is, just as with a chocolate, they make great comfort foods when the going gets tough! A typical bar will contain a thorough compote of complex and simple carbohydrate for immediate and delayed energy, plus minerals. So well-prepared are they, that, like vitamin tablets, you are unlikely to need or use them all unless you really have hit rock bottom. Remember that a big banana, home-made oat and sultana flapjack or moist cake, or water with added fruit juice may be just as refreshing and restorative.

> **HINT**
> **Out on a ride, eat before you are hungry, drink before you are thirsty.**

Cool water feels great on a hot, tired mountain biker's body!

stretching
for cyclists

Why bother?

Stretching is excellent for cyclists because it helps to prevent injury, increase flexibility and ease soreness. Everyone, can feel better with this kind of gentle movement. However as with any exercise program you should consult a doctor before attempting anything new.

Stretching is not enough, unfortunately, to get you fit, but what other healthy task can be so easy to fulfil, and such a pleasure to perform? Whether you work a single throbbing muscle for a few seconds in the sandwich queue, or get down to a half-hour head-to-toe routine stretching can feel great. It has characteristics in common with yoga and other relaxation techniques, with a potential to stimulate deep concentration and a sense of well-being. When training feels all work and no play treat yourself to an extra dose!

For racers stretching is not a luxury. It is an important piece of maintenance for muscles stressed by riding hard or training. When a muscle activates it contracts. At rest, after working hard, the muscles shorten and become tight. Stretching opens out the muscles, tendons and ligaments again, by pulling them gently in the opposite direction to the contraction. The movement flushes whatever is being stretched with oxygen- and nutrient- carrying blood, which is necessary for operation and healing. It also feels nice. This pulling and flushing guards against side effects of heavy exercise on muscles and joints while they are strengthening for future exertion.

Soothing, preventative, stretching

In the short-term, a stressed muscle shortens while it recovers. This feels somewhere between stiffness and soreness, and is, in fact, the body's warning not to use the area. The area loses normal flexibility and can be damaged by day-to-day movements, which you normally would not notice, let alone expect to cause damage. During this phase sudden exertions, such bending to pick something off the floor or running late to an appointment, could actually tear a muscle, ligament or tendon. Stretching prepares the body gently for day-to-day movement until the muscles have finished recovering and/or growing and return to their normal elongation.

> Gentle stretches regularly performed are of benefit to all of us, whether we cycle or not. Practised regularly they will increase your flexibility.

THE KNEECAP AND ANKLE

In both the short-term and long-term, a shortened muscle can pull and harm the joints adjacent to it. If a joint becomes sore after training, think about what is connected to it. The muscles around the joint may feel fine, but by stretching them gently you may find that the soreness in the joint starts to ease immediately.

The ankle joint is connected to the calf muscles via the Achilles tendon, which runs from the heel bone to halfway up the calf. If the calf muscles shorten they pull on the Achilles tendon. This may limit the movement in the ankle, to the point where it affects your gait. In this state a short sprint may be enough to tear the tendon, a serious injury that takes time to heal and can recur. Stretch your calves to ease the ankle.

Stretching the quadriceps can help avoid misalignment in the cyclist's most crucial and vulnerable joint, the knee, which should be taken care of to prevent damage. Just like

CAUTION!

- Stretch gently – do not bounce, it is risky, ineffective and hard work.
- Over-enthusiastic stretching done too quickly or taken too far does damage. Do not hold a stretch beyond the point where the muscles or joints are not able to relax into it. Ease off the moment you feel pain, or if you start to tremble.
- Play safe and stop if in any doubt about whether a stretch has become a pull. Take care and don't overdo it.

1 Achilles tendon (lower calf)

Stand astride the bike with one foot on the floor, the other on the pedal set at the bottom of the stroke. Straighten the pedal leg, so that the ankle drops below the pedal. Repeat on the other leg.

an unevenly tensioned wheel, the patella (kneecap) can be pulled out of true as the thigh muscle group adapts to training. This affects rock hard cyclists who ride enough to alter the proportion of their muscles.

The quadriceps are the powerful four-muscle group that provides most of the pedalling force, and can alter the alignment of the kneecap. Three of the group attach to the outer edge of the kneecap. The inner edge of the kneecap is held only by the single vastus medialis muscle. As the thigh grows stronger, the outer muscles begin to overwhelm the force of the single inner mus-

cle, and to exert an uneven pull on the knee. This can result in painful misalignment, as the kneecap gets pulled out of the groove along which it should travel smoothly with each leg flexion and extension.

DIAGNOSIS

Try stretching as a home cure for minor aches, but consult a doctor if the pain persists after more than 3 days. Be careful not to work a joint or muscle that you even suspect is damaged rather than strained. With experience, you will be able to tell whether a twinge requires medical attention.

2 Quadriceps (thighs)

With your back to a wall, place the lower leg flat against the wall, the knee on the floor touching the wall. Place the other foot flat on the ground, comfortably forward from the wall, with your hands aligned either side of the front foot for balance. Get comfortable, without stressing the knee. This stretches both thighs simultaneously, but after a minimum of 10 seconds, it should be repeated on the other side.

3 Head

Tilt your head to the left, then to the right and forward. You may tilt it back as long as it is done gently. Turn it to the left and right, but do not rotate.

Warm-up and cool-down stretching

Stretching before you get on the bike can supplement a warm-up routine, although it shouldn't be used to sidestep a controlled 20–30-minute build-up on the bike!

Warm-up stretches prepare the muscle responses. Concentrate on the legs and back. Do a few gentle knee-bends of not further than 90° flexion, and calf and quadriceps stretches, as shown here (there are variants). Rotate your ankles and swing your hips. Lean your head from side-to-side.

After a hearty bash, muscles are relaxed and stiffness and soreness can be eased with more gentle leg and back stretching. This also helps to flush stinging lactic acid out from the muscles, the by-product of energy production. Again, however, stretching should not replace a low-effort 10-minute cooling-down ride. This allows your body temperature and heart rate to fall gradually, and will also contribute to removal of lactic acid.

The developmental, "big" stretch

Deep stretching makes you extra flexible, and is good for everyone, not just sports people. Men, being less flexible than women, are particularly advised to follow some sort of developmental stretching regime from puberty, to stand them in better stead in old age. Mountain bikers, who squat to fix punctures, jump on and off the bike, crash, recover and carry 14 kg (30 lb) of rubber and metal about on their shoulders, will benefit from the flexibility stretching provides. Watch the champions – every one of them will be able to bend over and squat with ease, as well as perform twisting, heavy motions, such as pulling the bike out of ditches, without a problem.

Developmental stretching is easy. It requires only the patience to hold the positions for longer than the recommended minimum of 10 seconds and, over a period of weeks or months of regular application, to

4 Hamstrings, upper calf, lower back and shoulders
Face the bike. Place one hand on the handlebar, lift the same leg and place it on the top tube, taking your weight on the standing leg. Keeping the raised leg slightly bent, put your other palm on the raised knee and lean over gently. Repeat on the other side.

5 Upper back
Stand astride the bike, both feet flat on the floor. Take hold of the top tube behind you with both hands. Lean gently back – not far – and hold for a short while.

take the stretch further. It is during these sessions that the joy and pride of having achieved a fit, lithe body can flood the soul with happiness.

Stretch technique
■ Warm the muscle up for the stretch by flexing it gently and relaxing it once. This is the initial trigger for the blood supply to get moving.
■ Go to the point of solid resistance then relax back. Settle at two-thirds full stretch.
■ Feel and hold the stretch, for between 10 seconds and as long as you like. Relax into it. Think of opening up, rather than pushing or forcing. The move is an extension, not a contraction and should not speed up your heart rate. Think about the specific muscles

and joints you want to work, and shift the pressure about to get the stretch as accurate as possible.
■ The muscle will gradually relax into the stretch. Be patient and enjoy it.
■ At the end of that stretch, either return to neutral, or gently go further to two-thirds the next degree of complete resistance and repeat until time or patience runs out.
■ Shake out gently after the stretch.

When to stretch
Regular riders and racers should do maintenance stretching daily, and developmental stretching once or twice a week to increase flexibility; in addition they should also perform warm-up and cool-down stretches

before and after riding. New riders, feeling the effects, should stretch before riding, but are unlikely to do so, but particularly after riding for recovery, plus regularly for health and mobility. Everyone should stretch just a little when they first get out of bed; with knee-bends – not further than 90° flexion – neck and back.

Illustrated stretches
This is a sample of five stretches out of two dozen or so suitable for cyclists. Several of these can be performed in different positions. Three use the bike as an anchor for example, although any convenient floor or wall will do. Hold each stretch for a minimum of 10 seconds.

Cross-training

Aerobics provides a solid level 2 winter-time workout.

Although compared to different sports cycling uses very few specific muscles, all that heavy breathing – the cardiovascular effort – is a feature it shares with most of them. If you cannot or you do not feel like riding, perhaps your time is too limited, the weather is inclement or your bike is broken, there are other workouts that help mountain bike fitness. This is what is known as cross-training.

Circuit training

This is an indoor workout that road racers traditionally endure off-season. It involves an hour or so of repeated circuits of a series of simple power exercises, called stations. These consist of such exercises as crunches, push-ups and bench-lifts. The effort is in short, hard bursts that last a minute or two. Improvement can be dramatic.

DRUGS AND MOUNTAIN BIKING

The international cycling federation (UCI) and the national cycling federations each have lists of substances whose limits must not exceeded. Mountain bike racing has, so far, kept clean, despite its close relative road racing, where drug-use is never long out of the headlines. Drugs are controlled for two reasons; first, to provide a level playing field for competitors; and, second, to protect them from harmful and even fatal side-effects. The amateur racer should be aware that some proscribed substances feature in over-the-counter cold relievers and energy drinks. Nevertheless, the limits are reasonable. For example, on an empty stomach the UCI caffeine limit may be exceeded only after a few cups of strong coffee. It is hard to break the rules innocently.

Aerobics

Well-named, an hour of this upper level-2 workout is tougher than it looks, and you do not have to wear a leotard to get in. The teacher warms up the group, then takes it into a pulse-raising non-stop level-2 workout. Resistance is increased by using a step – good for cyclists' calves and thighs – and using hand and wrist weights. An aerobics session is not to be under-estimated.

Snow sports and skating

Cross-country Nordic skiing is both low-impact and leg-based, and thus one mountain biking's closest relatives. Snowboarding is beloved of the downhill fraternity for its speed and need for quick responses, and snow-shoeing is excellent high-resistance work. Rollerblading has similarities with mountain biking, because it aids balance and coordination.

Running and swimming

These are good cross-training activities that can be done at varying levels of effort. Running is high-impact, and it is easy to jar cyclists' highly tuned but inflexible limbs, while swimming stresses on the arms more than changing gear.

Weight loss by cycling

Mountain biking is renowned for transforming unsuspecting overweight guys and gals into slimline figures without a minute's rationing. Losing weight by building fitness rather than by dieting has numerous advantages. First, it is fun, which makes it easier. Second, you burn up calories on the ride and while recovering – including while asleep – as the body strengthens in preparation for the next trip. Third, you don't need to cut down much quantity, but to keep your intake balanced and below the amount you burn up on rides. In principle, one afternoon's hard ride could burn up more than whole day's food. Within as few as 6 months, more riding and an informed diet can mean significant weight loss. Within 1 to 2 years, it can transform a fat person's life and outlook.

A healthy, balanced diet itself usually brings an automatic cut in calories, because it reduces fat to the recommended level of 30%. Cut portions of dairy products, processed food and red meat by a third. Cut out and replace chips, cakes and biscuits with bulky or low-fat variants like carbohydrate (pasta, potatoes, bread) and fruit. Eat fruit and vegetables at every sitting.

A healthy level of body-fat is about 25% for women, 15% for men. An athletic level of body-fat is around 15% and 10% respectively. Long steady outings burn fat rather than glycogen (carbohydrate), but these are for the very fit who cannot get a lot better. For the majority, getting out on the bike regularly will do the job.

Looking at intake, a healthy daily calorific intake, which keeps the body functioning and supplies energy for effort, for adult women is about 1,800 calories, and for men is around 2,500. Munch regularly throughout the day to aid digestion and to avoid the risk of hunger-bingeing.

Looking at output, one hour's steady riding uses up about 350 calories, and an hour at maximum, such as in a race, uses up about 600 calories. Bearing these figures in mind losing weight becomes as easy as falling off a bike.

Stick to the recommended calorie amount and by riding twice during the week for an hour, then doing a day ride or race at the weekend, you will boast a slimmer figure within a few months. Of course, equipping your bike with light and expensive componentry is one way to lose a kilogram overall, but reducing your waistline costs only time spent having fun on the trails and in the kitchen.

Roller blade for balance.

Ease yourself gently into running.

young and old

Mountain biking is a new sport that has benefitted enormously from modern attitudes toward women's and older people's participation. As long as you have basic health – a check-up at the doctor will establish if any condition advises against it – and a bike you can stand astride, off-road cycling can be celebrated by people from six to sixty. An active lifestyle is the greatest natural defence against ill-health and lively people are attractive whatever their age.

Health tips for men

Men are naturally less flexible than women, therefore are advised to stretch a few times a week (see pp 94–97).

Health tips for women

■ Osteoporosis is a devastating and common condition in post-menopausal women that involves crumbling bones caused by calcium deficiency. It can be avoided by lots of physical activity in youth. This, and the shortage of women involved in mountain biking, is good reason to get teenage girls and young women out on rides.

■ Fitness and health are more desirable than being thin, and, should you wish to lose weight, concentrate on riding on a balanced, rather than meagre, diet.

■ Women may wish to take iron supplements to guard against mineral loss during menstruation.

Britain's pioneering veteran female mountain biker, Beth Mottart.

Mature riders

The older you are, the more difficulty you may have in learning trail handling; also, the longer it may take to recover from a long ride or a regular crash. However, as long as your health is generally good – have a check-up – there is no reason whatsoever to miss out on the fun. Lifelong cyclists indeed often just will not slow down. It is something to do with the cardiovascular and endurance systems – road racing men and women in their fifties are renowned for showing whipper-snappers how it is done. As mountain biking enters its second decade, the veteran, master and super-master race categories continue to swell, with old road bikers as well as mountain bikers, showing that biking enthusiasm dwindles at an even slower rate than performance.

Junior bikers

■ Children love to ride bikes, and mountain biking carries the kudos in current cycling fashion. The traffic-free trails engender a familiarity and respect for the land and a sense of self-sufficiency. You can start children off from 10 upward on their own bike, but ensure that it is not too big and has gears. It goes without saying that a child must wear a helmet. With younger ones, put them on a trailerbike, a one-wheeled trailer with a proper saddle and pedals that fixes easily to the parent's bike. This way, they get to ride, but you decide where, and don't have to do all the work.

Children love to cycle off-road.

■ Many parks have graded mountain bike trails suitable for children and family groups. If yours does not, how about organizing one with the authorities.

Leading mixed rides

■ Successful group rides should go at the pace of the slowest rider. Send faster riders off ahead, asking them to wait at junctions, and do not drop anybody.

■ Ride leaders may notice that women tend to progress to harder terrain with strict self-control, whereas men are more likely to take risks and assume they can ride something tricky, even if they cannot. Be ready for both learning processes and carry encouraging words and a first aid kit.

■ Be prepared for mechanical breakdowns and a wide range of mechanical ability in any cycling group, but let riders learn the repairs themselves.

■ Childrens' energy often outdoes their stamina, so ensure that a ride is not too long for them. Their bike can weigh more than they do.

■ Novices tend to tear off ahead, or to the top of a climb without warming up properly, and burn out quickly. Pace the ride properly, and do not destroy their enthusiasm.

staying healthy and injury free

Cold Free

The cold virus is always with us, ready to activate if we get chilled, which is a bind, as this is an occupational hazard of mountain biking. Research has shown that the immune system is at its weakest after riding, training or racing. But you can minimize the risk of catching a cold.

■ Don't stand around chatting in sweaty clothes. Sweat cools rapidly, chilling the sur-face of the skin and bringing you down from an overheated power station to a shivering jelly within a few minutes. Change into dry clothes as soon as possible, and take a spare under-layer on day rides.

■ Wind on wet clothes or skin is bad news. Every molecule of vaporizing moisture carries off with it some of your body warmth. Look for shelter behind walls, tree-trunks or in ditches.

■ Do you ride through streams at the start of a ride on a cold day, ignoring the plank bridge that would keep your feet dry? Well don't. Keep your feet dry if at all possible and wear good quality overshoes once the temperature drops below 5°C (41°F) or if it is wet.

Cold cures

It is ill-advised to keep going through an infection or a cold, however minor. Be patient with your immune system, and allow it time to contain the virus – about 3 days. If you are impatient there is a risk that illness will take a firmer hold that may take up to 6 months or longer to loosen. Many young endurance athletes have suffered the long-term effects of a premature return to riding, a great personal and even national loss. Guarding health is an important part of the top racer's lifestyle. Casual riders are also at risk, usually because of inexperience.

Many cyclists believe in taking high doses of vitamin C during a cold, although a balanced diet provides the recommended daily amount and excess is flushed out of the body harmlessly as waste.

Hypothermia

Hypothermia, a condition in which the core body temperature drops, will kill unless the patient is warmed up quickly. A loss of just one or two degrees is enough to stop the major organs working properly. One particular sign to watch out for is impaired judge-ment – a patient may deny that there is anything wrong with them. Warm the person up with blankets, bodies and warm, but not hot drinks. Try to carry an emergency blanket on any long rides.

A lot of mountain biking is done in exposed areas and in low temperatures. Before venturing out when the temperature is freezing, especially if it is wet or slushy, check that every member of your party is wearing enough warm, windproof clothing from head to toe. Always make sure that you know the weather forecast and plan rides with intermittent exits so that you can get people home in case the full distance of the ride proves too much for them or the weather deteriorates suddenly.

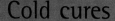
Most cyclists can expect at least a few scratches.

Sticks and stones break collarbones

As in horse riding, the most common fracture in mountain biking is the collarbone, caused often by pitching over the handlebars at speed and landing upside down forward of the shoulder, or on a desperate outstretched arm. It is not a serious break, for the collarbone is a static strut, but it is painful and needs strapping. Riders are frequently back in the saddle after 3 weeks, a little longer if the fracture is multiple, although full movement returns after another month or so. What is usually more debilitating in the long-term is the loss of confidence in your riding, which needs re-building.

Reality bites – wear a helmet at all times off-road.

Nurse your knees

Unlike metal components knees cannot be replaced if you wreck them. It is hard to care about the dull old kneecap when you are out enjoying a ride with friends, but maintaining healthy knees, just like avoiding colds, is a

Clean cuts and use sterile dressings.

hidden skill of cycling. Take advantage of the fact that the sport is low impact. In high impact sports that pound the body, particularly running, the knees can crumble away.

Take seriously every ache, soreness or pain in knees. Is it caused by pushing gears which are too high, or staying out too long? If in doubt, stop riding and consult a doctor. The damage may be temporary and curable with time and rest, or permanent if the patella is dislodged by an uneven pull from developed thigh muscles.

TIPS FOR HEALTHY KNEES

■ Equipment – get your saddle height right (see pp 22-23). Your knee should almost straighten with every stroke. Set it at the correct position along the rails, so that the angle of bend in your knee is comfortable. Make sure that SPD (spring clip) shoes are set at the right angle for your foot, and that you are pedalling with the ball of your foot. Wear over-the-knee shorts during chilly weather, to keep the joint insulated.

■ Pedalling – warm up the knees before setting off, with a few gentle bends, and quadriceps stretches. Start and stay pedalling lightly until the stiffness has gone. Do not hurry this phase. If in doubt, do not continue.

■ Home treatment – stretch the thighs, so that it is not temporary contraction in recovering quadriceps muscles that is affecting the patella. Second, stay off the bike for a while. Finally, if the pain recurs or makes it impossible to ride, go and see a doctor.

Staying healthy is a hidden skill of mountain biking.

handling the bike

Impress others with a running mount.

Good technique begins before you even get on your bike. The ability to "handle" your bike, that is to manage it when you are not actually pedalling, is a useful asset on any ride. As with all techniques, those included here require practice and perseverance.

TURNING IT UPSIDE DOWN

Stand with your legs apart beside and facing the bike, lean over it and place your hands as far down the seat tube and fork as possible. Turn it over, with the saddle toward you. The further down your hands are, the easier it will be to manoeuvre.

LIFTING A BIKE

Stand with your legs apart, facing the bike- and bending your knees not your back, place your hands as far down the fork and seat tube as possible so that the majority of the bike's weight is above your hands and under control. If you are hanging the bike up, warm your arms up first to avoid straining them.

Getting on your bike

MOUNTING FOR ABSOLUTE BEGINNERS

Get the bike into an easy gear and straddle it. Use your toe to position the right pedal at 2 O'clock (10 O'clock if it is the left pedal). Place your foot on the pedal and give it enough of a push to allow enough time to hoist yourself into the saddle and to get the other foot on the pedal and moving.

STATIONARY MOUNT

Place the bike in an easy gear while you are learning. Stand beside it, lift your right (left) leg over the saddle, place it on the right (left) pedal and push down. Slide on to the saddle and get pedalling.

MOVING MOUNT

This mounting technique takes a little practice, so put the bike in an easy gear as you learn. Lift your right (left) leg over the saddle. Push off with the leg that is still on the ground as you slide onto the saddle. For a short moment both feet will flail in midair before they find the pedals while the bike has momentum.

RUNNING MOUNT

This is simply a faster version of the moving mount. It requires predictable ground, and can save several seconds in competition, although, it does use up precious energy. Properly executed, the running mount is an impressive technique. Do it wrong and you will injure yourself as well as look stupid. Work up to it with the moving mount.

Have the bike in an easy gear and with your hands in position on the handlebars, run along beside the bike, pushing it. In a version of the moving mount, push off with

FOR THE LEFT-LEGGED
Instructions for left-legged cyclists are in brackets.

Yet another mounting technique.

SHOULDERING THE BIKE

Stand beside the bike, steadying it with your left (right) hand on the handlebar. Bend your knees and crouch to put your right (left) arm through the frame. Now stand up, with the top tube resting on your right (left) shoulder. Steady the bike by holding either the stem, or the right or the left handlebar with your right (left) arm. Use the other arm as a counterweight to balance while you are walking or running along. Racers use no shoulder padding, but beginners may appreciate a piece of pipe lagging, or shaped frame pad to prevent bruising.

USING THE MOUNTAIN BIKE AS A PROP

To cross streams, gullies, or bogs, use the bike as a staff to leap from safe point to safe point. You may even be able to climb up on to high walls, and down the other side using the saddle like a ladder.

THE SHORT, QUICK LIFT

If you are running alongside the bike, the fastest way to get it over a small obstacle, is to take the weight off the front end, using the handlebars and the back end using the empty bottle cage.

the left (right) leg, with the right (left) leg lifted to land on the right (left) perch bone.

UPHILL MOUNTING

Put the bike in a very easy gear. Set the right (left) pedal in the 2 (10) O'clock position. Hold the bike steady with the brakes on. Swing your right (left) leg over the saddle and slip on to it. Importantly, for maximum momentum, get the right (left) pedalling foot properly inserted before you push off with the left (right) leg and let go of the brakes.

Push or carry?

Covering very rough ground on foot with a firmly shouldered bike is surprisingly effective. You don't have to find a line for the wheels as well as your feet, or push the bike against uneven ground. However, there is the extra 14 kg (30 lb) in weight involved in carrying – especially if it is muddy, which will add to the weight of your load. The act of lifting the bike on to your shoulder is also strength-sapping.

Getting off your bike

STATIONARY DISMOUNT

Unclip your left (right) foot from the pedal and slow down, with the leg ready for landing. Stop the bike, transfer your weight to stand on that leg, and swing the other leg over.

RUNNING DISMOUNT

Riding along, unclip the right (left) leg, stand up on the opposite leg in the pedal. Swing the right (left) leg over the back of the saddle, pass it between the left (right) leg and the bike, and step ahead on to the ground. Rapidly disengage the left (right) leg as you are doing so to hit the ground at a run.

The first rider in this picture is shouldering his bike correctly.

mastering pedalling and gearing

Good pedalling

Although theories extol the idea of pushing the pedals in a circle – spinning – rather than pumping them up and down like pistons, the style of pedalling you employ most of the time – assuming you are even thinking about it – depends on the terrain. The method that feels natural to you is probably right. However, spinning is an efficient road riding technique that works at medium to high speeds off-road. On predictable, although not necessarily straight track you can pedal in smooth circles at a high cadence, between 80–100 rpm (revolutions per minute). This is a great way of picking up speed quickly after a corner, but you need to be fit to sustain it. Concentrate on keeping your upper body motionless – no swaying – and all your weight on your backside, not your legs. It may help if you go into a slight crouch. Your legs are then free to rotate hard and fast, so pick up your feet as well as putting them down. Once you are up to full speed, spinning takes on a momentum of its own – feel that wind!

GET YOUR SADDLE HEIGHT RIGHT
Efficient pedalling is difficult unless your saddle is at the right height. See pp. 22–3 for information.

For slow work in low gears, when each stroke feels like your last, pumping the pedals is unavoidable. Visualize pushing down on each stroke. Pull on your arms, rock as much as you like and pray you make it!

Changing gear

The terrain alters so often in mountain biking that the ability to time a perfect gear shift is an essential part of riding. As with all mountain biking technique this comes with practice and exposure to tracks of different speeds. Gear components are now excellent, with pre-set gears and ramps on the sprockets and rings to help the chain slip easily from one to the other. All you have to do is shift the correct lever the correct way at the correct moment!

HOW GEARS WORK

■ Mechanically speaking, gearing adjusts the pedalling load so that you can adapt to the fluctuating resistance of the track. This alters your speed accordingly.

■ A gear is most commonly described by the number of teeth on the rings you are using. A 36–18T gear means the chain is on the 36-tooth chainring and the 18-tooth sprocket. A gear is also described in inches, proportional to how far the rear wheel travels for one pedal stroke. To obtain your gear in inches use this equation:

front ring teeth ÷ rear sprocket teeth x wheel diameter.

Typical MTB gears are 22–109 in. The easiest gear is 24–28T, the hardest gear is 46–11T, a range that means you can pedal at any speed from walking pace, approximately 3 km/h (1.8 mph), to the speed of a cruising car at around 50 km/h (31 mph). This is gentler than a typical road gearing, which spreads from 41 in to 117 in – or 42–28T to 52–12T.

For speed, change "up" to a 100 in plus gear, described as big, hard or high. Change "down" to a small, low or easy gear, below 40 in, for slow work or singletrack where you persistently recover lost momentum.

GEAR RATIO

This is the relationship between the front chainring and rear sprocket in use.

If they have the same number of teeth, for example 32, the rear wheel turns once for every pedal stroke, and the gear ratio is 1:1. If the chainring has 34 teeth and the rear sprocket 17 teeth (a common gear) the rear wheel revolves twice for every pedal-stroke, making the gear ratio 2:1. On slow ground, when the sprocket has more teeth than the littlest chainring, the wheel turns more slowly than the pedal stroke, with a minus ratio, for example, 24T:18T, which is a ratio of 1:0.75.

Get into the correct gear before you need it.

UNDERSTANDING RATIOS

The greater the chainring and smaller the sprocket, the greater the gear ratio. The greater the gear ratio, the greater the pedalling load and the higher the speed. The idea behind gear ratios, is the fact that different combinations of chainring and sprocket, supply the same amount of resistance. For example, the 48:12 gear is the same as the 52:13 (a road bike ratio) – a ratio of 4:1. Understanding gear ratios is the key to realizing that having more gear combinations does not mean higher and lower speed limits, but rather a finer distinction between gears and a larger choice of combinations.

KEEPING A STRAIGHT CHAIN-LINE

The chainring and sprocket combinations

you can use are restricted to those which keep the chain-line relatively straight. You cannot use the big-to-big nor small-to-small combinations for two reasons. First, with these combinations the chain is askew, which damages the chain plates; second, the ideal chain length is not long enough to go all the way around the big chainring and the big sprocket. If you get your chain into that combination, you may find it will not come off again! If the chain becomes too loose, as it would if you used the smallest chainring and smallest sprocket, there is a risk of it bouncing off. The same ratio is given safely by the middle chainring with a mid-range sprocket.

The desirable gear combinations are to use the largest chainring with the smaller sprockets, and smallest chainring with the

bigger sprockets. Simply, the gearing is toward the bike for easy gearing and away from the bike for harder gearing. The middle chainring is the most ubiquitous, and you can safely use it with both the biggest and the smallest sprocket.

INDEXING AND OVERCHANGING

All modern MTB gears are indexed, which means that they are pre-set, and will click into place. Changing into a bigger ring or sprocket is a push because the movement is against the spring tension in the derailleur. So that the chain can make it up and on the new teeth, push the lever a little further than the resting position before releasing it. On under-bar or top-bar mounted levers this is done with your thumb, because it is stronger. With revolving gear changers, for example, GripShift, you turn the barrel away from you.

Changing to a smaller ring or sprocket is a lighter action, because the lever is releasing the spring tension, allowing the derailleur to be pulled into position. On under-bar or top-bar mounted levers this is done with the index finger. With revolving gear changers, such as GripShift, you turn the barrel toward you.

You can change several gears at once, either with one movement or several quick clicks, depending on your gear levers. If the chain falls right off the chainrings or sprocket block, it needs adjusting (see pp. 52–53).

Beginners tips for good gearing

■ You cannot change gear without turning the pedals. Therefore, to change gear when you are not on the bike, stand on the bike's left-hand side. Pick up and keep holding up the rear of the bike with your right hand at the back end of the top tube. Change the gears while turning the left pedal with your other hand.

■ Sprockets are used for small changes in speed, such as when you are creeping up a long, steady climb. To make small changes with the right-hand gear lever, start with the chain on the middle chainring (front) and the middle sprocket (back). Pedal off and work the right-hand lever until you can set the pedalling harder or easier without even thinking about it.

■ Chainrings are for bigger changes in speed, such as going over the summit of a hill into a descent. Using the left-hand gear lever, start with the chain in a middle sprocket, pedal off and work the lever up and down to change the chainrings. Note

that there is a greater difference in resistance between each chainring than between the sprockets

■ The ideal gear to begin cycling with is usually somewhere in the middle of the sprockets and the middle chainring.

■ Beginners tend to concentrate so hard on steering and pedalling that they forget that the gears are there to help them – remember to change gear.

Gear changing hints

CHANGING DOWN IN ADVANCE

Get into the correct gear before you need it. All the time you are out on the trail there are sneaky obstacles and rises waiting to try and steal your energy and speed. Safeguard that speed by dropping your gear well before the trail overcomes your pedalling power.

MISCALCULATING THE GEARS

There is little more frustrating than climbing up a hill, holding the line and your seat by a whisker, knowing you have got a gear left, only to find you have actually run out of them. Keep tabs on which gear you are in, either by reading the indicators on the gear levers, or by looking down at the rings and sprockets. Getting the hang of this will take some practice, but is well worthwhile as it should help you avoid miscalculating and accidentally jamming or dropping the chain.

TRICKY GEAR CHANGING

A drastic drop in your gear and speed needs a smooth gear change that neither jams the chain nor throws it off. The best place to practice high speed large-ratio gear changes

is on a stretch of rollercoaster-like track where you can roll speedily down one side and then crawl back up the other side. As you approach the bottom of the dip, which will probably be at immense speed, decide well in advance the gear that you need for the ensuing climb. Pick as smooth a line as possible through the dip so that you are able to concentrate on braking and changing gear, rather than keeping the front wheel under control.

When you actually hit the bottom, change down to the lowest gear – smallest chainring – at the front, and down to the third or fourth sprocket at the back – this saves a couple of sprockets for the worst of the climb. Shift both gears simultaneously. Then wait for just an instant to give the chain, which will suddenly have lost all tension, a chance to catch the new teeth and for the derailleur to take up the slack, so that it is not thrown off.

Be prepared to spin the pedals like fury as the bike slows down to its new speed, from a ratio of 4:1 say, to 1:0.75. For a few seconds, before the bike gets into gear, you will probably find yourself spinning against thin air.

On bumpy, fast tracks and downhills keep the chain in a large sprocket and middle or large chainring to prevent it being bounced off.

SINGLE-SPEED MOUNTAIN BIKES

Single-speed bikes, as their name quite rightly suggests, have just one gear. That means that the bike has just one chainring, one sprocket and no gear levers. An element of the attraction of single-speed mountain bikes is that they are utterly simple in a mountain bike world of ever-increasing complexity.

good climbing technique

Put your weight forward as the climb steep

Climbing is the great challenge of cycling. Living up to its name, the mountain bike is the best bike in the cycle shed for taking on the challenge. The broad, gripping tyres, the position of the rider over the back wheel and the 3 km/ph (2 mph) gearing endow the MTB with a surprising caterpillar-like ability.

Mountain bikers have a love-hate relationship with climbing. It is hard work, but it makes life clearer. In comparison with the complications of money, friendship and the future, the goal – reaching the top – is simple. Beginner or expert, little matches the pride at achieving the peak of a rise, after either a patient slog or a maximum strain. The descent is that much sweeter for it.

Technique summarized

In the hands of a good rider, a mountain bike will mount inclines on badly broken ground close to 45°. This is done by a combination of two factors that can be learned by everyone; balance and power. Balance is acquired through awareness and practice. Power is acquired through repeated effort, an investment in muscular and cardiovascular fitness.

CLIMBING AIDS

1 Lower total weight of bike+rider = less work.
2 Use wide, knobbly tyres to aid gripping ability.
3 Bar ends offer a variety of hand-holds to open out the chest slightly and provide a distraction when the going gets tough.
4 A frame with short chain stays, under 42 cm (16.5 in) will keep the rider's weight at the back of the bike for balance, power and grip. Radical frame designs that tuck the rear wheel further under the saddle may have elevated stays or kinked seat-tubes.
5 Suspension has positives and negatives for climbing. It wastes rider energy yet increases grip by a degree, so set adjustable shock absorption harder for a compromise. It is also important that suspended bikes, which have extra joints and pivots, are laterally strong.
6 Setting the saddle with the nose slightly downward will relieve pressure on delicate areas if you have to crouch-climb.
7 SPD-style spring binding pedals and shoes make climbing easier – once you've got used to them!

CENTRE OF GRAVITY

The centre of gravity of a bike and rider is the abdomen. To hold the line and to avoid tipping off backward while climbing, an imaginary line drawn from where the rear wheel touches the ground to the abdomen must not become greater than 90° from horizontal, in front of you. Draw your body weight further forward as the climb steepens, otherwise the front wheel will gradually become unweighted. Then it will lose grip or lift up, and eventually you will either lose the line or slide unceremoniously off the back. Watch out! If your abdomen is too far forward, the rear wheel becomes unloaded and will spin and momentum will be lost, eventually you will lose too much to stay in the saddle.

STANDING UP

In a middle gear the most effective and – until you are strong enough – painful way to climb, is to stand up on the pedals. It adds your weight to the muscular force of your legs pushing on the pedals, but takes effort for the same reason. Rocking the bike from side-to-side, called honking, maximizes the weight on each pedal, but be careful that you are not wasting energy.

SITTING IN THE SADDLE

When things are getting very steep in order to keep your weight as far forward as possible without tipping up assume the following position. Slide forward on the saddle and get into a crouch by bending your arms, and dropping your wrists and back – concentrate on your position.

This sitting position is a technique unique to mountain biking, thus takes practice and a build-up of strength. The back and abdominal muscles have to resist the invisible force of gravity, rather than the pedal or handlebar.

GEARING

The gradient will tell you which gear to be in. Getting it right comes with practice and familiarity with your gear levers!

■ Get into the right gear a fraction of a second in advance.

■ On a long drag try changing up for a few seconds to a harder gear, so you can stand up and pump the pedals for momentary muscle relief.

■ Try to save a last gear for emergencies.

PICKING A LINE

Grip is number one priority in choosing where to steer, and improvement comes with practice on many different hills.

■ Look ahead.

■ Follow other tyre tracks.

■ Choose a line which is clear of loose stuff; leaves, pebbles or dust bowls.

Beginners' tips

■ Every time you press the pedals you become a stronger cyclist, which is a key to better climbing. Any increase in the amount of riding you do will help with the hills!

■ Try not to get demoralized. There are no shortcuts to good climbing, so every time you expose yourself to a horrible new

The 3,874m (12,705-ft) high Pearl Pass between Crested Butte and Aspen in Colorado, USA was first ridden by mountain bike en-masse in 1976. The ride is now a focal point of the Annual Crested Butte Fat Tyre Festival.

ascent, or get something wrong, you are doing yourself good!

■ Don't compare yourself to other riders; measure yourself against yourself. For example, try to ride further up a difficult hill each session.

■ Climbing gets more rewarding, but not necessarily easier!

Advanced training

■ On or off-road specific hill repetitions are the most effective – and painful – way to improve your climbing. Ride up a hill several times as hard as you can in a half- to one-hour period, with a brief rest just spinning the pedals easily in between.

■ Rest sore legs for a couple of days after a training session, or just ride gently. If performed regularly, you will feel the benefit, or hard riding, but do not overdo it.

PSYCHOLOGY NOTES AND TIPS

■ Do not anticipate falling off. If you do, you will. Let the bike lose its grip before you do.

■ Feeling sick on a climb is a laudable sign of high effort. It occurs because the blood is rapidly called away from your organs, including your stomach, to supply the muscles with oxygen.

■ Racers approach a hill thinking about going over it rather than up it.

■ Much climbing is a test of patience. When you begin to wonder if you can stand the strain, try mental distractions, such as your reward; the descent, the café menu, what you are going to eat tonight. Say the alphabet backward, recall formulas or vocabulary, or recipes, or people's birthdays, dates from history, *Shimano* part numbers, the shipping forecast, the States of America, capitals of the world, poetry, Shakespearean quotes.

■ In your mind break up the climb into sections, and take them one by one.

"London, Paris, New York, Moscow...".

descending
techniques

Descending is a joy of mountain biking that is open to everyone, regardless of fitness or talent. But, however easy it may seem there are techniques that can help you get the most out of a downhill run.

Centre of gravity

The centre of gravity of a bike and rider is the abdomen. To stay on the bike down a steep descent an imaginary line drawn from where the front wheel touches the ground to the abdomen must not be greater than 90° from the horizontal behind you – the reverse of when climbing.

As a descent steepens, if your centre of gravity falls ahead of the line, you will go over the handlebars, or at least have to dismount before things get that serious. Keep the centre of gravity behind the vertical, and the angle of slope that a skilled rider can descend can be steeper than 45°.

CONFIDENCE TIPS

**The mountain bike is capable of staying upright down surprisingly angular slopes, so on very steep, slow slopes, as with climbing, trust the bike and let it give up before you do.
A skid feels as if you are out of control, when, with practice, you are not.**

DOWNHILL TECHNIQUE

Descending is a combination of balance, will and controlling the brakes well. Competitive downhilling requires nerves of steel with the addition of explosive power for acceleration out of the corners.

There is little mystery about descending, but there is a variation between each cyclist's natural ability. As with all mountain bike technique, becoming competent and safe is a matter of practice, but with downhilling particularly, each rider has a personal speed limit that is hard – and usually painful – to exceed. Never allow yourself to be pressured into riding beyond your ability. Crashing does more damage than being forced to buy the refreshments as a penalty for being last to the bottom!

Beginners' descending

1 Sitting down to descend is only possible on gentle, smooth slopes. As soon as the ride gets bumpy, you need to stand up to let your legs absorb some shock. This frees the bike from your mass and allows you to easily distribute your weight. A descent technique popular with beginners is to grip the saddle with the inside of the thighs.

The steeper a hill the further you have to get your weight

2 Ensure that the pedals are level – a common MTB technique used whenever riding uneven ground.

3 Keep your legs slightly bent, and use them as shock absorbers.

4 Straighten your arms and bend your legs the steeper the hill gets, to keep your weight as far back as possible. On extreme slopes, stability and traction are supplied by slipping your rear over the back of the saddle.

5 The front brake has more strategic value than the rear, when descending. Use the front brake to control speed and steering.

Apply with care – it is quicker to react. Slam
it on too fast and the combined moving
mass of the back of the bike and your body
will try to overtake the front wheel. The rear
brake is slower to react, and is better used
as a supplement to the front brake, for controlled skidding and emergencies.

6 Over very fast, bumpy ground, to prevent
your hands being bumped off the

TIPS AND
SPECIALIST EQUIPMENT

■ **It should go without saying,
but always wear a helmet. Body
armour is also available, such as
elbow and knee pads.**

■ **Keep your brakes serviced and
done up. The world's most successful MTB racer, Juli Furtado,
with world titles in both downhill and cross-country, had to
drop out of the 1992 world championship cross-country, for which
she was the favourite, when her
front brake cable pulled through
at the brake block and landed her
in a bush.**

■ **Suspension bikes are made for
downhilling. The shock absorbers
work to the limit to keep you on
line for better control.**

■ **Flat pedals are great for specialist downhillers, who use their
legs as outriggers on the corners.
The rest of humanity finds SPD-
style spring binding pedals the
best way of stopping feet being
shaken off the bike. The clever
compromise is double-sided pedals, with an SPD fitting on one
side and nothing but a plain platform on the other.**

handlebars, lock your thumb and forefinger
around it, keeping the middle and fourth
fingers free for braking.

7 Look at where you want to steer, a few
metres ahead of the bike.

8 The best way to improve is to repeatedly
practice a steep downhill or drop-off that you
find a uncomfortable. Once conquered,
proceed to the next most difficult descent.
Racing is good for downhill technique, as
you repeat descents on each lap.

Speed descending

■ Descending is about allowing gravity to
do the work, while you operate the brakes
and distribute your weight. Anticipate rough
terrain and corners by decelerating enough
to flow over or around them. Try not to over-
brake so that you lose momentum.

■ Speed is itself an aid to staying on the
bike. A spinning wheel is a highly rigid
structure that helps you hold a straighter
line, and which will carry you over small
patches of roughness that might catch you
out at slower speed.

■ Take the shortest line, cutting corners
closely, and going for the smoothest piece
of track you can see.

■ Keep your wheels on the ground. Low
jumps, taken in a crouch with bent arms and
legs, help keep a clean line, and the wheels
level. Travelling through the air further than
a couple of centimetres will slow you down.

Safe descents

At all times, stay aware of other trail users
– you may be the fastest thing on the track
but you do not have right of way. Hikers and
horses always have priority over your enjoyment of a descent. Slow down for humans
and stop completely in advance of horses.
Know your terrain – never let fly if you do not
know what is around the corner.

cornering

A controlled skid is a joy to execute and behold, but is not for beginners.

As with other mountain bike techniques, improved cornering comes with exposure and repetition, which, happily, is the same as saying you learn more the more you ride. On any one ride you will turn dozens of corners, over grass, on loose gravel and in ruts, either steeply downhill or sharply upward. On some pieces of track you will not travel in a straight line at all. This emphasizes the differences between off-road and much faster on-the-road biking, which runs along far straighter lines. It also explains why mountain bike design favours strength and manoeuvrability over aerodynamics.

Technique

As you take a corner you will feel a force, known as centrifugal force, pushing you outward away from the inner curve of the bend. This force is derived from three factors, each of which, in theory, you can influence with good riding technique. These factors are: the sharpness of the bend, your speed and your combined bike and rider mass.

1 SOFTEN THE ANGLE

The tighter the corner, the more powerful the force, so the aim is to soften the angle of the bend, keep the speed higher and

make a quicker exit. This is done by completing most of the turn in the first half of the corner. As you approach the bend, swing outward away from the sharpest point or apex, then turn inward and aim for it. By the time you are alongside the apex, you should be facing more or less the right way. Use the full width of the track if necessary. Sweeping around a corner this way saves speed and feels great.

2 CONTROL YOUR SPEED

Centrifugal force is squared as speed increases, so your aim is to enter the corner

For successful cornering
watch out for:
- Balance
- Braking
- Progressive position of the bike around the corner.

slowly and to exit quickly. If you maintain your maximum speed, as if you are still going along in a straight line, you will be shot into the middle of next week!

To take a corner any faster than at cruising pace, use the brakes on the way into the bend and the pedals on the way out again. Get into the right gear for the exit and brake in advance of the bend, to allow for the outward swing. Keep your fingers over the levers ready for trouble on the way round, applying them equally. Don't panic and jam on the front brake, which could stop suddenly and twist the front wheel.

Start pedalling at the point at which you have subdued the corner, which may possibly be well before its apex. Assuming you got the gear right, stand up on the pedals to sprint away.

3 USE YOUR BODY TO BALANCE

Lean your weight to the inside to neutralize the centrifugal force; the sharper the corner, the sharper your lean. Standing up is tricky, but useful, when you are experienced, for bumpy corners, allowing you to use your legs as shock absorbers as well as to get immediate control over where you throw your centre of gravity.

Sitting down is good for smooth, fast corners. It allows you to bend your inside knee and to press down on the straight outside leg, to push against the force. Resist the temptation to lean backward, because

this unloads the front wheel and may endanger the grip and steering. Do this by consciously bending the inside elbow to pull your weight forward and inward.

BEGINNERS' CORNERING TECHNIQUE

Slow cornering off-road is simpler in reality than it appears on paper because MTBs are so well designed. Just as with climbing, if you want to take a sharp bend easily, the wide, knobbly tyres will help you all the way round – just as long as you keep up the momentum. If you are just getting the hang of how the bike feels there isn't even a need to swing it out before the corner, nor to stick out a knobbly knee. Those techniques come into play at higher speeds. Just roll around that corner at your own pace, and think about the next obstacle.

Most people find left-hand bends easier than right-hand ones, so practise the right-handed ones!

EXPERIENCED CORNERING

The more familiar you are with off-road biking the more you use your body's weight rather than the brakes to get around corners losing as little momentum as possible. Put your body to one side then the other off the saddle, stand up and sit down, hammer for the pole position.

What you are riding over is critical. Try to plan the move so that you get as clean a surface as possible. Ruts are dangerous so keep clear and avoid wet roots at all costs! Sand is like a sponge, gravel is risky. Mud is in fact a better bet than most of these, and a puddle usually has better grip still, although be aware of the powerful braking effect of water more than a couple of centimetres deep, and its ability, in extreme cases, to send you soaring over the handlebars.

Lean into the bend.

SKIDDING

Expert riders use skids to get around corners quickly, braking hard with the back brake once they are well into the bend. This locks the rear wheel and allows it to skim across the terrain's surface with rapid deceleration. A well-executed skid is a thrill to behold, and is also a useful skill to accomplish. However, skids are more tricky to control than rolling wheels, and the unpredictable off-road surface increases the risk of falling and injuring yourself.

BANKING AND BERMS

Exploit gravity's natural pull by using man-made berms and verges, or taking advantage of natural banking whenever possible. This tecnique will help you to slow down your speed as you enter a corner and assist your speedy exit from a bend. In additon to the technical benefits, this technique is also extremely good fun.

115

airborne
techniques

Getting air is one of the joys of mountain biking.

Getting the bike off the ground

Unexpected obstacles litter the route of the off-road rider, lying in wait around that sharp bend to bring you down. So the most useful handling skill to have is the art of making air, that is, to be able to lift the wheels off the ground, either one or both at a time. The technique can be applied to anything between a simple log-roll to a full-blown jump, with bunny hops somewhere in between the two. Add this string to your bow, and you will ride faster and more confidently – and well impress your friends.

Log hops for beginners

To hop or roll over a log you lift first the front wheel in a little wheelie, and then the back wheel, but don't leave the ground altogether.

Find a 15 cm (6 in) log or construct a log-like object on flattish ground with a nice approach in front of it and a run-off behind.

Pick up enough speed, to get you over the obstacle with perhaps just a little extra press on the pedals. A metre or so in advance, stop pedalling, set the pedals horizontal, and, still sitting down, shift your weight backward to unweight the front wheel. Just before you hit the log, give another half-pedal, finishing with the pedals horizontal and pull up on the front wheel – have all your weight at the back of the bike

When log hopping, bend your knees to keep the bike flat.

little logs, or painted lines on the ground.

Approach the obstacle at a medium pace. A metre or so in advance, stand up, crouch and bend your elbows and knees and shift your weight forward to take the weight away from the back wheel. Spring upward, bending your knees and pulling up on the pedals to bring the bike with you in unison, all the while keeping the bike as flat as possible. Your arms do a lot of the work. Beginners have a tendency to let the bike rear up, as the back wheel stays fixed near Mother Earth.

so that you are not just pulling up against yourself. The wheel should rise into a wheelie to skim over the top of the obstacle.

The instant the front wheel hits the ground again, stand up in the pedals, push your weight forward and bend your knees to unweight the back wheel. This minimizes the impact and lets the back wheel bump freely over the log a moment later.

In between, if the chainring teeth catches on the log, give the pedals a push to keep the bike rolling – it's uncool to get stuck see-sawing like this.

Bunny hops

A bunny hop is, as the name suggests, where the bike lifts completely off the ground so that light shows under both wheels at the same time. It is a useful trick for getting out of all sorts of scrapes and to avoid disaster in unexpected potholes on the road! At first

you will probably enjoy the feeling of clearing heights of 5 cm (2 in), but, with practice, you may even break the bunny hop records with a run-up of only a few feet!

The most difficult part of a bunny hop is unweighting the back wheel enough to lift it. Here, pedals and SPD shoes are a great aid, adding to the mystery of how stunt riders perform enormous jumps using just plain pedals and trainers.

For the less able, a bunny hop can be created just by getting the approach speed right. If you are travelling fast then it is easier to get the bike airborne, along the same lines as long jump in athletics. However, a true bunny hop moves more vertically than horizontally, and you should aim to perform it with virtually no momentum. This depends mostly on timing the moment when you jump with your body to bring the bike up and along with it smoothly. Practise first over

Jumps with launch pads and lips

Using ramps and edges it is easy to make air, but here the skill lies in landing safely. Off a launch pad even a medium pace is enough to fling the bike and rider quite far off the ground, following which the main danger is a front-wheel touchdown. The bike rises through the air, levels out and then tips downward, hitting the ground vertically. You end up either going over the handlebars or having the front wheel twist beyond control and falling to the side.

Prevent this happening as soon as you have lifted off, by consciously preparing the bike for a horizontal landing, with both wheels touching down at the same time. Place yourself in a crouched position, straighten your arms and bend your legs and push the whole bike forward beneath you.

riding
single-track

Most mountain bikers rate single track as second only to a good downhill. It is fast, yet not stressful and pulls flatteringly quick reactions from the recesses of the brain. Single-track is the creme-de-la-creme of the dozens of natural varieties of trail, because no two sections in the world are the same. Flicking your bodyweight from one side of the bike to the other and timing the acceleration through the pedals is one of the more intellectually stimulating types of riding. Along a single-track's twist and turns, a bike and its rider come closest to that mystical feeling of union.

So what is single-track?

The name comes from the USA, and is distinguished from wide double-track, which is named after the tyre-marks vehicles leave. Unlike so many so-called off-road tracks with which bikers are supposed to content themselves, the single-track trail is utterly inaccessible to vehicles. It is, at best, rough under-tyre and no wider than the bike. Preferably it is too narrow for horses – with which bikers are usually lumped together in the eyes of the map makers – and so often populated by walkers, who do not know what fun they are missing. A bike's footprint is only 5 cm (2 in) wide, so given just a few more centimetres each side for shoulders and hips, the mountain bike can slip through any subtle wrinkle in the countryside about

0.6 m (2 ft) wide. At full speed that is glorious, absorbing fun. Just watch out for the foot soldiers, especially as vision is usually little further than to the next tree.

Riding single-track is fundamentally simple and can be appreciated by a beginner. It is as close as you will get to a complete crash course in mountain bike control, for pure single-track is 100% balance, steering, braking and pedalling. There is no time for cruising and looking about at the wildlife. The speed at which it is tackled is left entirely up to the rider – there is no painful gradient to pedal or to brake against or to humiliate the novice.

The aim is to maintain as high an even pace as possible throughout the full length of the section. Practice raises the speed which needs tighter and tighter timing and takes great concentration. The skill lies in how fast you dare take it. Anticipation and cornering, plus knowing when to put in a burst of forward power, are the keys. As with most mountain bike technique, improvement comes mostly with exposure and to a lesser extent with fitness. Eventually you reach a stage where with a little feathering of the brakes and a few pushes on the pedals creates a momentum a little like floating at speed in the tightest terrain.

The best single-track occurs through natural woodland – as opposed to gridded forestry plantations – where it twists and turns around irregular tree trunks over crackling twigs, leaf pools and slimy roots.

SINGLE TRACK TIPS

■ Cut the corners tightly, as your speed is unlikely to be high enough to throw you off the banking, and get pedalling as soon as you are pointing the right way.

■ Chopping the handlebar as close as possible to the tree trunks is one of the thrills of single-track, and a way to gain a nanno-second of an advantage over timid companions. The consequences are nasty if you mis-time it.

■ Learn to pedal from any position so as to sail over rough patches, roots or bumps and to pull and push the bike.

■ Some single-track can close right down to little more than a tyre's width – and this is where you get trouble with overhanging branches whipping the arms and face. Expect to steer one-handed occasionally if brambles or holly-bushes close in on one side. Wear mitts and a helmet.

■ Brake and change down gear ahead of sharp corners or bumpy patches.

■ Dry conditions are best. In the wet be ready to bunny-hop damp roots, which can take away the back wheel.

■ Crested Butte in Colorado, USA, is renowned for its narrow, fast woodland single-track trails.

Surviving
the street

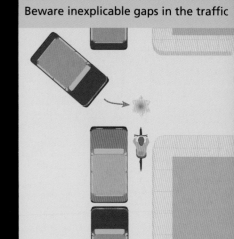

Opening doors

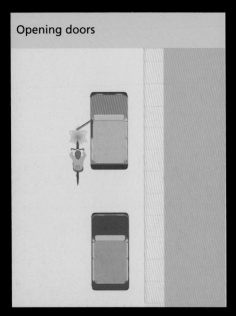

Sudden turns without time to react

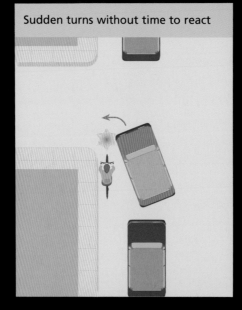

Drafting

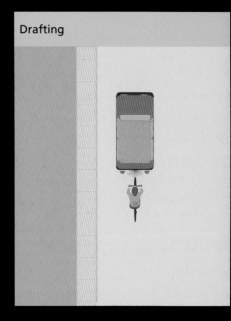

No mountain bike is ridden exclusively on the trails, so a mountain biker has to adapt to riding the roads, and to avoiding cars as well as trees. On the street, a biker has all-round vision, but a driver's is severely restricted. A cyclist can hear and feel the effects of speed, but a car driver is undergoing a form of sensory deprivation.

Safe practice

■ A little visual dialogue goes a long way. Do no be too shy or too cool to direct the traffic with hand signals. Make eye contact and reward a helpful manouevre with a thumbs-up.

■ Know everything that is going on 360° around you. If you cannot comprehend the traffic's behaviour then approach with caution with your hands over the brakes.

■ Flowing with the traffic disrupts drivers less, and makes it easier for them to accom-

modate you. It is also highly enjoyable, but needs a degree of fitness and speed.

■ Use cycle lanes where they are provided. Campaign with your local authority to cut down motor-dependency and to improve the cycle network.

Danger spots

■ Opening doors – give parked vehicles at least a metre (3 ft) of clearance, which is a door's-width, to avoid being hit if one is unexpectedly swung open into you.

■ Car escape routes – when undertaking in a traffic queue watch for the side streets and be ready for drivers to turn in front suddenly in an escape bid.

■ Beware inexplicable gaps between vehicles ahead. When these coincide with side streets they are often being left open to allow across an oncoming vehicle.

Beware lorries turning

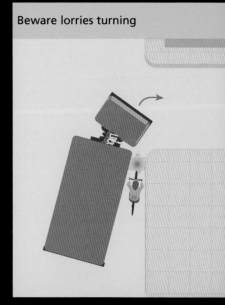

■ Beware lorries at all times – the drivers cannot see you alongside and nor hear warning shouts, nor feel warning thumps. Never, ever be halfway along the inside of a turning truck, as the what starts out as a yawning gap is slashed to nothing. A high number of the annual cycling fatalities are due to cyclists being crushed either against railings or by the wheels of turning trucks. The seconds you save are not worth the high risk.

■ Roundabouts – indicate clearly the entire way round as you change lanes. Also be aware that fast-joining traffic may scan behind you for potential collision vehicles and overlook you entirely.

■ Riding fast – both vehicles and pedestrians underestimate how fast you can move on a bike. They often mis-time when they turn or step out because they consider bikes to be virtually stationary.

■ Drafting or slipstreaming vehicles is fast, furious fun, so naturally, it is dangerous. Vehicles brake more quickly than bikes, especially in the wet.

Bicycle thieves

Beware the bicycle thief. A shiny bike is a ready-made escape vehicle, that is easily converted into cash and difficult for the law to recover. Security cannot be guaranteed, but it can be tightened with diligent locking-up and a sound insurance policy that will limit the loss.

Lock up your mountain bikes!

Urban riding – a test of skill for the most experienced cyclist.

Insurance

A bicycling budget should include an approximate extra ten per cent of the cost of the bike for the annual cost of insurance. Although it is the easiest thing to forget, should the bike be stolen, then insurance is worth every cent. Advice on the best policies is given by the national cycling clubs and federations. Otherwise quality bikes should be covered as named items on the household contents policy, for which you will probably have to pay a supplement and observe the small print, which may have restrictions on certain situations.

The right lock

The steel-bar U-shaped or shackle lock is the undisputed ruler of the world of bike immobilization, although none of them is 100% impregnable.The flexible, covered heavy-duty motorbike cable or chain has gained popularity, but again, this is still fallible.

Locking up

■ Find an immovable object.

■ Remove the front wheel. Slip it between the rear wheel and the fixing. Mount the lock through the rear wheel, frame and front wheel, placing the mechanism on the far side of the railing, away from any heavy prising tools.

■ Remove everything loose – lights, pump, sad-

dle bag and front wheel – even the front wheel quick-release if you are in a high-crime area.

Where's the risk?

■ Your bike is at risk inside the garden shed and garage, so secure it to a wall fixing or even bring it indoors. Beware the hallways of shared accommodation.

■ On the car rack. Either U-lock the bikes to a rack which in turn can be locked to the car roof, or never let them out of your sight.

■ Parked loose outside a shop – the "I only left it for a second" scenario. The opportunistic theft is the most common one – don't risk it.

■ In the open guards' wagon on a train. A friendly guard may promise "to keep an eye on it" but he may be to busy and the authorities will accept no liability.

Precautions

■ Cut down on the time the bike is parked and vulnerable. One answer is to use a secondary hack bike as your local transport.

■ Note the number of the key, so you can get another one cut in case the bike is locked up when you lose it.

■ Record and register the bike – keep a description of the bike, including distinguishing features and the frame numbe. Get the bike registered and tagged.

unmissable – night-time visibility

During the daytime, declare your presence in *Day-Glo* yellow. In darkness, use reflective strips and bands for fun and fashion, and powerful lights to illuminate the night-time road and off-road worlds.

High-visibility clothing

One contradiction of cycling is that cyclists tend to side with environmental issues, yet have to cloak themselves in fluorescent yellow that is too ugly to occur in nature. However, a bit of *Day-Glo* never does any harm, and anything that reduces the feeling of vulnerability, which puts so many people off cycling on the roads, is a good thing.

A neon-yellow or reflective, strip-coated breathable rain-jacket is essential on wet days when drivers' vision is worse than normal. On drier, warmer days, neon jerseys are useful and abundantly available, and a thin *Pertex* windproof shell is a good compromise between the two.

Reflectives

When illuminated in the dark, reflectives are as effective as lights, and demonstrate an assertiveness in the rider that draws respect from drivers. For daytime riding the grey *Scotchlite*-type coatings are easier on

Light up the night with *Day-Glo* strips and clothing.

the eye. At night they are transformed by headlights into dazzling silver.

The Sam Browne belt, named after the nineteenth century army officer's belt and strap, is the most common and effective strip, as long as it is untwisted and not obscured by a backpack. Next for effectiveness are velcro-fastening ankle straps, which are less restrictive and arouse curiosity at a distance as they flicker up and down. Wrist straps are helpful for indicating in the dark, while helmet 'halos" work wonderfully from all sides.

A little silver piping can go a long way. For the times when a backpack obscures the piping on a jacket, or renders a strip belt useless, then use patches of reflective material on it, which can be bought pre-cut or by the metre. Stick them over everything that is visible from the rear; the seat stays and mud-guard, the back of the helmet, and, if they will stay on, shoes and overshoes. Buy models with reflective material in the design.

Reflective tyres with a bead of *Scotchlite* around the wall are compulsory in the Netherlands, and very effective from the side. They are recommended for commuters and anyone else travelling much after nightfall.

Unfortunately, no mountain biker seeking the ultimate in cool will be caught dead with the reflectors sold compulsorily with the bike on the front and back wheels. A pity, as the front bracket not only provides emergency illumination if you end up light-less, but catches a rare snapped front brake cable before it snags the front wheel and throws you over the handlebars.

Lights

A lamp's first job is to mark you out to traffic. This where the largest choice of models is found, most of which are both good at the job and instantly removable for parking. The majority use standard replaceable alkaline batteries, while rechargeable batteries save

Shedding light on the matter – be seen in the dark.

money and are more environmentally responsible, although they are slightly dimmer and fade faster and faster as they age. Do not forget to charge them after each ride.

When it comes to the bulb, halogens use up the batteries quicker, but it hurts even to look at them. LED (light emitting diode) lights are light, cheap and long-lasting – with double-life on a flashing setting – but are officially supposed only to supplement standard bulb lamps. In the UK, despite their enormous popularity with cyclists, LEDs are controversial. The establishment also disapproves of the flashing setting, believing it is a distraction to drivers. This is somewhat peculiar, because anything that attracts a driver's attention increases the cyclist's safety; and any driver who genuinely mistakes them for indicators should not be on the road.

The best place to mount lights is, as ever, on the bike frame, but there's extra visibility to be gained by dotting others around the body and on accessories; on the

helmet, attached to a waistband, on the arms or wrists and even in the pannier pockets. Many models come with special clips for just such creative mounting. Light such as these should only be used on their own in emergencies.

At a higher price are the brighter lighting "systems" by which to see, as well as be seen, the same as car headlamps. Working on bulbs between regular 6 watt (W), strong 10W and a dazzling 50W these are excellent for urban visibility, country roads and the nocturnal off-road forays, when they can be supplemented by a helmet-mounted light.

The majority of super-systems are front light only, some with two lamps for an option of dipped/full, narrow or wide beam and more or less wattage to conserve the battery. Powerful remote battery packs may mount on the bike, either in the bottle cage or beneath the top tube, and supply the extra power needed to light up the night, but they weigh quite a bit and are clumsy to remove and carry around when parked.

Use 1:25,000 or 1:50,000 maps.

planning
trails

Day tripping

The essence of mountain biking is the afternoon, day or weekend ride, beloved by most bikers for the exercise, the sense of discovery and as an easy way to make friends. With little more than a marked-up map and a banana you have the keys to a new world at the end of the road.

The pleasure principle

■ Build in refreshment stops where muddy bikers are welcome.

■ Include beauty spots, viewpoints or historical features. Use your imagination. It is sometimes possible to follow international road races by taking off-road short-cuts.

■ Flat routes along the bottom of valleys or waterways are pleasant for beginners and children.

■ The optimum air temperature for a ride, is around 15° C (59° F) with a gentle breeze, which means no overheating or chill.

■ Close to home, discover the undiscovered land that lies between the local roads.

■ Head out for enjoyable, thrilling descents and challenging, satisfying climbs.

The challenge

■ Break personal bests for distance covered, altitude climbed and time taken.

■ Explore the splendour of high mountains using steeper trails. The thrill is heightened by bad or exhilarating weather conditions.

■ Seek out the difficulties of nature to counterbalance the tedium of urban living.

Where to ride

There is joy in spontaneously exploring a new area without having a clue where you are or where you are going – but this keeps you close to base and needs good weather. It does not take more than a couple of rides for such charming off-road innocence to fade and for the biker to become hungry for bigger riding opportunities and a closer

intimacy with the land. Experience also thirsts for longer distances ridden at speed, and for these you need a map.

To plan a route from the beginning first find the land, preferably hilly, by reading the bike and outdoor magazines or asking others for their recommendations. Obtain the right map in the right scale (see pp. 126–7) from outdoor shops or map specialists found in every country. Then, using a fluorescent highlighter pen, either mark just the route you want to take, or all the legal trails in the area.

How far to go

Decide how long to make your trail, according to the daylight hours available, how many refreshment stops are desirable and

Take time on a day trip to enjoy your surroundings.

Take two wheels and face a world of adventure.

calculate the distance according to the average off-road speed. A realistic guide is the fact that even top racers travel at about 16 km/h (10 mph), rarely any faster. Reasons for getting home late include:

Excuses such as:

- ■ "Time flew at the café"
- ■ "I'm fat and unfit"
- ■ "I got a punctures and the bike broke."
- ■ '"I got lost."
- ■ "I crashed."
- ■ '"The group went slowly."
- ■ "We had to keep stopping to read the map"

Conditions such as:

- ■ A sudden strong headwind, rain or snow.
- ■ Darkness.

Blaming the trail conditions:

- ■ Too much climbing.
- ■ Rough under-tyre conditions, including rocks and mud.
- ■ Having to carry the bike.

Be realistic

A realistic distance to cover in an afternoon is 16–24 km (10–15 miles), although it may be a lot less. A day's ride with relaxing stops for lunch and tea can be set comfortably at 32–40 km (20–25 miles). Fit riders in dry conditions without much risk of getting lost, can tackle 80 km (50 miles) off-road in a day. This is achieved by spinning out one's limited energy with short rests and a sub-maximal pace.

The bike

Having a properly working bike is more of a priority than having a very expensive, high-quality performance mountain bike. For day rides a basic, well maintained mountain bike is ideal, although the more stimulating the gradients and exploration the more a performance bike will be appreciated for its lightness and handling.

Every cyclist knows that their bike should be trailworthy. However, faced with a smiling sun and friends, it is a rare beast who will not head out, putting their faith in the spirits of the trail and denying the rattles. Ignoring repairs will only lead to a disappointing ride so remember the pre-ride check (pp. 36–7).

125

equipment
for the trail

Bicycling bags

Travelling without baggage is a skill that takes practice and is usually learnt by making miscalculations that leave you cold, ravenously hungry or with a long walk back. Accept that this is a rite of passage towards full off-road indefatigability.

Travelling lightly is achieved by exploiting the back-pockets of cycling jerseys and jackets and stuffing saddle pouches with the minimum of tools, a spare inner tube and levers. Mount the pump and water bottle on the frame. Gossamer-weight windproof shells scrunch down to a manageable size and sit imperceptibly in a backpocket.

BUMBAGS

The bumbbag is the first choice for carrying kit on a simple day ride, as it is capacious but leaves your shoulders and back free and dry. The best models are waterproof and padded on the body-side for comfort, with a strong snap-clip. Unless you are travelling in climates that are so hot that two water bottles on the bike aren't enough, avoid the bumbags with bottle containers as they are intended for runners. The disadvantage is that they tend to crumple maps and when the large models are overloaded, they turn into a wagging spare tyre around your middle. In this case, the only way is up, to...

LUMBAR PACKS

In between a bumbag and a rucksack sits the hybrid lumbar pack. It's a high-framed waistbag with the capacity of a small rucksack that climbs halfway up the vertebrae. First developed for runners, its particularly neat feature is minimal bounce straps, so that it stays glued to your back however bumpy the descents – and stops maps getting chewed up. Recommended are the editions by *MacPac*.

BACKPACKS

The maximum baggage for carrying on your back without affecting your balance is the amount you can contain in a regular backpack used by hikers and climbers. Any load bulkier and heavier than this should be placed in panniers, rather than a larger rucksack. You may feel a slight pull on the shoulders with a rucksack, but otherwise, as long as they have a waist-strap, they have few disadvantages and a clever packer can get enough for a month-long (non-camping) trip inside. In addition to holding the usual snacks, tools and light clothing, the extra depth gives room for more foul weather gear if the weather forecast is not good, also a full-length pump if it will not mount on the bike. A waterproof external map pocket is a good idea, as it is frustrating to keep stopping, removing the pack and getting it out.

A couple of specially designed cycling rucksacks are available, with good padded frames for protection from objects such as big tools. They also have compression straps, mesh pockets, key and pump clips.

The sturdy hiker's backpacks are the closest you will get to waterproof, as they are intended as travelling and mountain-wear. Choose models with a wide waist-strap to help minimize bounce and to distribute the weight over the hips, even better models offer a chest-strap to keep it in place when full to bursting, and hacking down a menacing trail.

Day trip kit list

■ Pack the right tools. Wrap and pad them so that they do not bounce around nor dig in to your back. Favour lightweight multi-tools. See emergency repairs, pp. 38–4.

■ Think about foul-weather clothing. Use the calculation that the temperature drops approximately 1°C (1.8° F) for every 100 m (300 ft) climbed, and never, ever forget the drastic cold brought on by wind. The temperature difference between the sheltered trailhead car park and the mountain-tops could be as much as 20°C (68°F). Ask yourself if the weather could worsen; whether you are climbing high; Is it windy? Are you likely to be late back? Have you a change of clean clothes for the train, car or café? A plastic bag is handy for muddy clothing or to protect upholstered chairs.

■ Check that everyone in your group has a

helmet and is fully equipped.

■ Remember to take a map.

■ Money – either pack notes in waterproof wrappings or take coins.

■ Trail snacks. Energy bars come into their own on a long day ride, with convenient packaging and concentrated starch/sugar and nutrients. Nature's equivalents are bananas and dried fruit, with flapjacks and moist cake as the halfway house. These all take more thoughtful packing. An uneaten loose banana at the end of a bumpy ride has to be seen to believed. Take excess food for comfort and emergencies, should plans go awry.

■ First aid – even an afternoon's ride can turn nasty if one of your party has an messy crash. Antiseptic cream and plasters used initially on cuts will ease shock, although they must be properly scrubbed out later. An emergency blanket could be vital. Take repellant in insect-ridden areas and anti-histamine tablets in case a party member reacts, also sun lotion to guard against skin cancer in later life.

Keep your map handy.

MAPS

What scale map for mountain biking? The larger the second number the smaller the area and greater the detail. The best scales are 1:25,000 – 20 km x 10 km (12 x 6 miles) per oblong sheet, showing walls, naming farms and tree types, or 1: 50,000 – 40 km x 40 km (25 x 25 miles). The standard hikers' maps show enough ridable trails to plan several all-day circuits.

■ **Use contour lines, which are set at 5 m or 10 m (15 or 30 ft) vertical intervals, to anticipate climbs and descents. The closer they are, the steeper the gradient – a solid block means a sheer cliff. You can, for example, work out a route to climb steadily for a couple of kilometres to the top of a demonically steep 500 m (1,640 ft) descent.**
■ **Weatherproofing. One wet ride can be enough to turn your crucial green line into soggy, illegible pap – costly as well as awkward. Various methods for protecting maps exist, running from buying ready-laminated editions, which fold badly, to DIY spray-laminating, or covering it with sticky-back plastic.**

trail protocol

THE OFF-ROAD CYCLING CODE

1 Stay on the trail
Only ride bridleways and byways. Avoid footpaths. Plan your route in advance, using proper maps.

2 Give way to horses and walkers
Make sure they hear you approach. Ride carefully when you pass.

3 Bunching is harrassing
Ride in twos or threes.

4 Be kind to birds, animals and plants
And keep your dog under control.

5 Prevent erosion
Skids show poor skills.

6 Close gates behind you
Do not climb walls or force hedges.

7 Stay mobile
Wearing a helmet will reduce the risk of head injury.
Take a first aid kit.
Carry enough food and drink.
Pack waterproofs and warm clothes.

8 Take pride in your bike
Maintain before you leave.
Take essential spares & tools.

9 Be tidy.
Take your litter home.
Guard against fire.

10 Keep smiling

Never ride the trails alone. Because of the risk of crashing or breaking a limb, it is better not to ride solo in exposed areas, especially in bad weather. Two is ideal and three is fine. A group should travel at the speed of the slowest rider, but more realistically what happens is the front will dash off and wait for the back to catch up at junctions or on the brow of hills.

As the off-road code says, mountain bikers in bunches are unwelcome by walkers, horse-riders and farmers, so keep it to not more than ten, and resist indulging in the power of the mob mentality.

Holy slopes

While mountain biking is now well-established as a wilderness sport, hostile authorities can inflict legal damage on it if they so wish, so bikers share a responsibility to respect the land, and to give way and be courteous to walkers and horse-riders. With horses you should come to a complete halt well in advance, as the beasts misunderstand bikes and can take fright. Unfortunately, even sacred downhills must be forsaken if there are hikers are anywhere on the holy slopes – for obvious reasons these folk do not cherish a last-second, close-quarter 40 km/h (25 mph) shriek.

"The Mountain Bike Terror"

"Mountain bike craze sparks ban call". This is the sort of publicity that needs to be avoided and it is the responsibility of every rider to ensure this. Ride on land that will not mark permanently, or contain the bike's impact by sticking to the middle of thread-

Unlike these cyclists – always stop for horses.

Take care not to worry the wildlife.

bare trails, so that the wear does not creep. Rather than being caused by the tyres themselves, erosion is caused by water washing away marked soil and stones that have been dislodged, which is common in upland areas. In delicate habitats, such as the desert of Moab (see pp. 162–3) or on tundra such as in Iceland or Canada, vegetation can take a half-century or more to grow over a mark, so if in doubt, don't ride over it.

Wear on the majority of legal bikable trails is a reality that designated land can handle. The mountain bike lobby wants the establishment to accept this as reasonable and containable, without distinguishing between boots, hooves or tyres. Tyre-marks tend to cause more emotional offence than the other two sports, although studies have shown that the area and depth of tyre imprints are not significantly greater. The onus will remain on mountain bikers to prove themselves worthy of the trails for many years to come.

The law

Where you can and where you cannot ride varies from land to land, but is settling down into a worldwide network of hundreds of thousands of kilometres of tracks to satisify the hungriest soil sampler.

In the heavily populated, formerly horse-bound UK there are two main types of trail; footpaths which are out of bounds and bridleways, which are ridable, but few other countries are as strictly regulated. Generally, the fewer talking heads in an area, the freer the riding controls. Each popular destination, such as the US National and State Parks, the European Alps and Pyrenees, has its own legislation which is usually clearly stated on widely available maps and trail signs. As a rule of thumb, be satisfied with worn, marked tracks.

In much of the undeveloped world, designated highways are dirt tracks that challenge a mountain bike and extra off-road is often surplus to requirements.

equipment for long-distance travels

For any long-distance travelling the best mountain bike to take is a regular model, which has bosses for pannier racks. The worst bet is, deceptively, the old, reliable and usually much-loved model. The fact that your faithful *Trakker Tuffbum* hasn't given you any problems for 3 years on your local trails is a warning – it is about time something major came critically loose or broke, such as the bottom bracket, a crank, a pedal, the headset or a wheel.

The best bet is a newish ridden-in bike, or one that has been well-maintained throughout its life with good parts, and the wear and tear on each of the critical components is understood fully. A major breakage in a remote location could mean disappointment and the end of the road.

Componentry

■ Keep the componentry simple. Use toe-clip/strap pedals. Favour items that need minimal tools to maintain. Do not experiment and avoid performance lightweight componentry which may not survive a round-the-world trek.

■ At best, avoid anything like suspension, which will not work smoothly if it breaks, although if you are a suspension addict, pick elastomer types over hydraulics, and take spare bumpers.

■ Know your saddle. Wear it in, so that you know you can survive sitting on it for hours and days, although some initial touring soreness will be unavoidable.

■ The cables should have settled, but carry spares of the right versions too.

■ Take chainlinks, or a complete chain, the right version for your bike.

Good-sized saddle bag

Bar bag – for maps, snacks and cash

Put 65% of the load at the back

35% of the load at the front

TOOLS
Carry tools based on the trail-side toolkit see pp. 38–39.

■ The wheels must be young. Rims get worn thin by the brake blocks and when they split can lead to a collapsed wheel within a few minutes.

■ Mudguards make a difference to comfort in wet conditions, but bend easily and rarely survive major trips.

■ The headset should be worn-in, and should never come undone. Such a headset is, unfortunately, a rarity.

■ The bottom bracket should also be worn-in and never come undone, this is the norm.

■ Start with new, quality tyres. They have an approximate life-span of 1,000–2,000 km (620–1,240 miles), so take spares for longer journeys in remote areas. Slicks and knobblies can be switched around according to the terrain to reduce wear and weight.

Travelling equipment

PANNIERS

The quality of good panniers is outstanding, with great capacity and waterproofing, secure rack couplings (traditionally their Achilles heel) and quick pockets.

Some travellers prefer front-loaders, which are no hindrance to steering, but the majority use back-loaders with a supplementary bag on the handlebars that holds the map and valuables, but should be kept light for climbing out of the saddle. For a full load use panniers both front (35% load) and back (65% load), although still keeping the weight as low as possible.

Remember to leave inessential luxuries at home and yet to allow enough space for the local purchases, which accumulate on every long trip.

THE PANNIER RACK

Break a pannier rack and the adventure is under threat, so it is vital that you buy a quality model, such as one from *Blackburn*, or as recommended by the pannier manufacturer. Cheap steel versions bend and snap. Check the bolts frequently to make sure they don't shake loose. Try glue if they do.

FIRST AID, POTIONS AND LOTIONS

The best outdoor sportsperson's first aid kit availabable in the UK is the *Gregson Pack*, which, although it is bulky, houses all the equipment and instructions to deal immediately with accidents and emergencies inside a waterproof pack. Travellers in remote places should consult further on what they should carry.

Use the strongest brand of insect repellant available if travelling through wet areas during the biting season. For sunny climates high factor or total block sun lotion is essential to avoid burning, which can cause peeling and blistering in the short-term and skin cancer up to 25 years later. Use a lip salve, with a high Sun Protection Factor (SPF), especially in sunny or snowy conditions.

SLEEPING BAG

Lightness, compactability and the right degree of warmth are the desirable factors in the bike traveller's sleeping bag. Pick a two-, three- or four-season grade to suit the night-time temperatures you will be encountering. The better the bag, the smaller it will go using a compression sack. If you feel you need a bedding mat, use a portable, inflatable *Therm-a-rest* or good copy.

TENT

For weather-resistance, low weight and easy construction traveller's tents nowadays are superb, but they are a compromise on living space – so anticipate cramp and enforced tidiness.

COOKING

Stability, easy fuel supply, low weight and compactness are the qualities in a camping stove. Several models have this combination of advantages.

Survival aids for every trip

On any trip, whether short or long the ability to navigate with a map and compass is essential for proper enjoyment of the wild country. With a compass you can decide the right trail, re-find yourself after getting lost and work out escape routes in bad weather or in the event of accident. Landmarks cease to exist in cloud or fog.

Another essential is water- and windproof clothing. This keeps bodywarmth and morale at the right levels. It is particularly important to understand the value of sealed, windproof jackets and trousers, so that even if wet, you stay relatively warm on the inside.

FIT TO TRAVEL?
Are you healthy and strong enough to enjoy the journey? If you do not cycle regularly, then start three months before departure. Also have a medical and dental check-up to avoid becoming the thousandth hapless victim of emergency tooth extraction in a remote area.

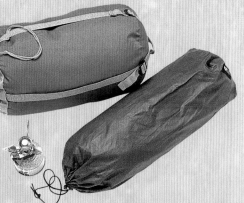

frost
biking

Ice and snow are the elements in which the mountain bikes comes into its own, both as a plaything and as a working vehicle. In cities, when public transport grinds to a halt, when people cannot walk to the corner stores without hitting the deck and cars are entrapped by snow-plough mounds, the mountain bike finds a unique urban niche. The bike always gets through – so long as the rider can stand the conditions – and the fat-tyre townie can silence the smart-ass who is contstantly pointing out the rest of the time that there aren't any mountains in Toronto, Boston, Berlin or Manchester.

Leaving the city grot behind, out on the land or in mountains in soft snow there is little that the bike cannot cope with, which is great for beginners. In the muffled silence that descends on a wintry landscape often all that can be heard is the soft, continual "crump" of snow being compacted under the knobblies, as the steam rises from the backs of trailmates after a big climb.

In the right conditions, a little below freezing, you may even be able to relax the handling a little. The grip of the tyres is enhanced by the forgivingness of a few centimetres of white powder that can be harmlessly scuffed and skidded. At last there is the freedom to dibble the temporary surface as much as you wish and to fall off on to a soft wet mattress. Mark a piece of white virgin trail with your presence, or try a trivial pursuit identify-the-tyre quiz and guess the tyre-make that has beaten you to it.

Who needs skis and snowboards?

Watch for the ice build-up on the tyres, and clear it away before tricky descents, which will be less snowy if they occur in woodland. On exposed tops, such as moorland, be prepared to be hacking along and lose the front wheel into a drift or depression. Watch for concealed boulders on rocky single-track where the snow can fill up the spaces in between.

Perhaps the trickiest sub-freezing surface to predict is the icy patch. Where streams cross paths or stone slabs, an ice rink several centimetres thick can form. If you take your chances and pedal onto the slippery slab just try to stay upright – the tyres have absolutely no lateral grip. Any lean to the side greater than a few degrees and you will go down – hard. Rough ice is sharp, as well as being like concrete, so wear a tough shell if you can to protect quality clothing from getting ripped.

One word of warning – do not venture

out far in winter if a blizzard threatens. Swirling snow and cloud can obscure even a well-known landscape almost immediately. After riding on slushy, salted highways, rinse off the bike. The salt can do more corrosive damage than a winter's worth of muddy rides.

Snowy events

The best-known winter-time extreme event is the Iditibike race in Alaska, which takes 2 days to complete along sled-trails and frozen rivers and has a small, expert entry. The Alpine countries turn almost exclusively to ski-ing in the winter, but fun events are held occasionally, such as coursing down the Olympic Cresta Run at St Moritz in Switzerland or doing time trials around the high Alpine frozen lakes in France.

Frostbike equipment

STUDDED TYRES

Just as hikers attach crampons to their boots when it is icy, ordinary MTB tyres can be brilliantly enhanced with screws and a little patience. Take four hundred ordinary 10 mm versions, and screw them through the tyre lining from the inside so that they protrude a couple of millimetres beyond the knobbles. Space them regularly at the sides and on top so that about four are in contact with the ground at any one time.

EFFECTIVE GLOVES

Warmth and waterproofness is a requirement of the gloves needed on snowy rides. If the temperature hovers around freezing, then the wind-chill on soaking wet fingertips is the first step towards frostbite and can be horribly painful. Growling macho men have been reduced to whimpers by the agony of thawing fingertips.

One recommendation is lobster mitts, where fingers are arranged into double pincers to keep each other warm and while still being able to feel and work the control levers. Ski gloves tend to be too bulky but are extremely warm.

OVERSHOES

They may look silly, but like good gloves, overshoes are an investment that makes the difference between a great day playing polar explorer, and a day spent in misery which ends with the bike being flogged in the January sales. Buy a pair a little on the large size, as most of them are made for road shoes, and will otherwise be tight, and possibly restrictive. If you anticipate heavy going all day through deep snow the best things to wear on your feet are solid hiking or mountain bike boots with gaiters. This might mean exchanging pedals with SPD bindings for platforms and wide open toe-clips and straps; but this is not such a bad idea in very cold conditions when the spring in SPDs freezes up anyway.

SHADES

Dazzling snowy days are made for wearing cool, dark shades to block out the glare from the snowfields. Choose models that wrap tightly around your face, to cut out reflections on the inside of the lenses.

Covered in layers of the white stuff, trails take on a new dimension.

coping with rock, sand and grass

Better handling comes with exposure to many different surfaces.

Sand

It is a safe to say that the majority of riders will never tackle sand on a Saharan scale, but it occurs frequently enough, and is troublesome enough to merit some tips. A sprinkling of the stuff deposited in a watercourse is quite harmless, but as soon as fine sand is more than a couple of centimetres deep riding it becomes like riding on sluggish marbles, or in thick treacle, or like having a loose steering bearing. Even when bone dry, the stuff can somehow be slippery. There is little more frustrating than flopping about like an idiot on an formerly muddy, but ridable bridleway that has been sanded to provide "grip".

Sand patches like to catch bikers out. If it is a sandy corner enter a little more slowly and in a lower gear than normal in case you suddenly lose traction. The front wheel can slew off at an angle and bring you to a

halt. If the back wheel spins out, this is less of a problem – as long as you are in that low gear. Just sit in to keep the wheel weighted and pedal for all you're worth. As long as you have about 50 per cent grip you should haul yourself through and back on to a pure surface, gasping. Beware hitting sand patches at speed, which can be like someone else slamming on your brakes without asking and, in the worst case scenario, could throw you over the handlebars.

Equipment-wise, sand and water wear down brake blocks rapidly. Anyone living in a sandy, wet area is advised to keep their bearings tight – a grain of sand in the races does not turn into a pearl, it ruins them.

On beaches, below the tide mark is about the only place where sand is firm enough to hold you, but, as with winter roads, the salty air and water will corrode the bike and should be rinsed off as soon

as possible. The sand dunes above beaches are usually fragile protected habitats and out of bounds.

Rocks and stones

Rocks and bikers just about mix. Boulders are the props of the trials competitions, inspiring bike acrobats to mount, pirouette and jump. They are the thrill in single-track descending, and they are the curse of the medics.

There are three explosive-free ways of beating a big mid-trail rock. One extreme is to get off and carry, the other is to jump it and the third is to ride it. Although textbook tips follow, better rock riding comes only with exposure. The more differently shaped lumps you tackle, the better you get at coping with them.

Learn to wheelie – unweight the front wheel and pull up on the handlebars, balancing on the rear – to lift the wheel to the obstacle. This keeps up the bike's momentum and minimizes the risk of slamming into it and sending the rider flying forward to remodel their tender parts on the stem.

Balance rather than strength is the key to rock riding. Stand up in the pedals on approach, and keep the weight back, especially if riding downhill. With enough speed, the back end will follow the front end over the top. Resist the temptation to bail out prematurely. Trust the bike to finish the manoeuvre without sending you forward or backward. Visualize yourself cruising over the outcrop, and let the bike give up before you do.

Whereas dry rock presents no surface problems, damp and moss changes the nature of the beast entirely, making them harder to control. Rubble patches and individual stones present all sorts of dilemmas. As well as destroying traction on corners they lie around looking innocent until the front wheel hits one at the wrong angle and

speed and sends the rider into a neat trajectory. Never become complacent about the trail. It is full of tricks and surprises – which is why we go mountain biking.

Grass

The most abundant plant on the Earth's surface, grass moves in mysterious ways. Usually it presents no problems but when long and tough, or tussocky, riding across it becomes desperately hard work. Possibly the most laborious surface in the mountain bike world is a high moorland crossing without a marked trail over such stuff.

Take care on a cambered piece of green hairy trail, especially if it is wet, when you may lose traction and slip downward. If you are about to go into a slide or a spin (whatever the surface) stand up in the pedals for quick weight distribution and take control of your speed. In muddy conditions grass loses significance, but it can bind mud to the bike, and make clogging worse.

Riding thick grass means pushing in a lower gear.

Learn to skim over loose surfaces.

the water margin
–mud, puddles, rivers and streams

Mud

Mud, a variable-strength solution of water and planet, is a surface familiar to most mountain bikers most of the time, but there are few textbook tips to solve the messy difficulties the stuff throws up. As with most mountain biking, with mud you play it by ear. The more you ride, the more used you become to the way that terrain alters beyond recognition according to the season and amount of rainfall. What resembles tortoiseshell during the dry season turns to swamp during the wet one. Your handling shifts in response. One of the marks of a true mountain biker is an ability to keep a steady pace whatever the terrain.

Much of the time surface crud gives better grip the more dilute it is. Rain does not make trails unridable, the sunshine after the rain does, so do not cancel the ride in the middle of a cloudburst, thinking that mud will block your way. Apart from the slipperiness, mud's main effect is to slow you down – climbing, descending and along the flat. Utterly sodden ground on bridleways can be more of a problem, as the bike sinks with every pedal-stroke into the soft surface already deeply churned by horses hooves. If possible, avoid these types of track, they turn an enjoyable ride into a bore.

Traction is usually less reliable in areas with very fine clay soils or chalk, where the loam becomes slippery. Watch it on the corners, especially if there are exposed tree roots which are hazardous. Approach more slowly than in the dry and be ready to stand up if either of the wheels suddenly spins. The wetter it is, again, usually the better the grip, not vice versa.

Along double-track, the line to choose varies from the puddly tyre tracks at the sides to the grassy central reservation. You get better with experience at making the right instant decision. As a rule of thumb go for surface that you can see, and when conditions are truly dire, even tiny pieces of vegetation can hold the tyre momentarily. You will also see with experience that wet conditions are the ones when most damage is done to the trail, so for the future's sake, judge when it is better to sacrifice traction and less resistance and go for the harder, ready-churned track, which is already beyond hope, than to mark the virgin edges. You will get a nice eyeful of mud as the tyres begin to clear at speed.

Watch out for water

On ski slopes and exposed moorland, keep an eye open riding along for the dreaded water-bars, either raised or dug. These little jokers are a good opportunity for experienced riders to show off their ability to bunny-hop at will and for beginners to bump across clumsily. The water-bar diverts rain and meltwater off the trails that otheriwise erode as they form perfect escape routes for the flow.

Have a muddy good time.

Water, water everywhere...

If all else fails, it's time to push.

As far as grip is concerned, clear running water is a good surface cleaner, so you may get more grip in the rain riding in the stream-let of a track on greaseless rock, than at the slimy edges or verge, even if your feet get more splashed.

Streams and river-crossings

Crossing rivers that are too deep to ford is one of the few times off the bike when it is an aid not a hindrance. Think of yourself as one leg of a tripod with the wheels forming the other two legs. Put the bike in the river, hold on to the handlebar and saddle and step on to the first foothold. Move the bike a little further, first one wheel then the

other, then yourself on to the next foothold. The bike may get wet however, you stay dry.

Fording shallow water-splashes can be done at high speed with an enormous plume of water. But you need to use your judgement to avoid dabbing and getting a wet foot if the water anywhere in the stream is likely to exceed 12 cm (6 in). If that's the case, not only is the bottom likely to be loose and slippery, but the water slows you down so much that just the slight-est loss of momentum means a dab. In freezing temperatures, ride through slowly for the sake of keep-ing the spray to a minimum.

so you want to race

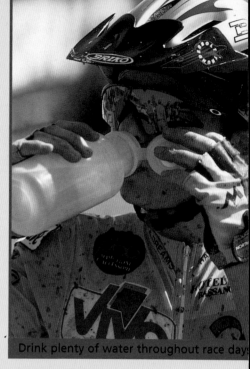
Drink plenty of water throughout race day

Your first race

After you have gained in fitness, stamina and confidence you may feel ready to start competition mountain biking. There are certain procedures and tips that are useful to remeber before you race. After a few events, these preparations will become habitual. Remember to have fun and good luck!

RACE KIT LIST

Helmet – always essential

WARM-UP KIT
Jacket, spare jersey, tights

RACE KIT
Jersey, shorts
Race shoes and socks
Gloves or mitts
Bottle(s)
Pump and tools
Towel and cleaning water
Food – bananas and cake
Water or another drink
such as juice or
an energy drink
Complete set of clothes to
change into, including wet
and cold weather gear
Race number and licence
if necessary

Entering a race

Choose an event that isn't too far from your home, or perhaps combine the race with a weekend's mountain biking and camping. Ideally, being a green sport, you would travel by train, but in low temperatures, a car provides shelter and allows you to carry more clothing to wear after the event.

Scour the specialist press or contact local clubs for dates and venues of forthcoming events. Enter beforehand if you can. The more important the event, the more likely there is to be an entry deadline, although many local races will take entries on the line.

■ **On the day** – make a mental plan of when to sign-on, warm-up, and the start time. Leave nothing to the last minute – allow for changes of times to be made on the day, due to weather or accidents.

■ **Signing on** – even if you've entered in advance you still need to sign on to pick up your number and pins or zip ties.

■ **Pre-ride the course** – in cross-country events, ride the circuit once or twice beforehand to practice the tricky bits and enjoy yourself. In downhill races try to do the run as many times as possible.

PREPARING THE BIKE

Follow the principles of the pre-ride check (see p. 36). Never fix major parts the day or the morning before the race in case they don't work properly, or you have brought the wrong tools. Allow new cables to bed-in before a race. This is particularly important for the gear cables – mis-changes can lose

you places and temper. Set the tyre pressure between 35–55 psi, to suit the softness or hardness of the surface.

In case of punctures during the race, carry a spare tube, tyre levers and a gas cartridge inflator. Take a chain tool too. Practise fixing punctures at home, trying to get the time down to about 2 minutes

RULES

Rules in mountain bike racing are notable by their virtual absence. The main one is that there should be no outside assistance – the mountain bike race must be mechanically self-sufficient throughout the race. This encourages riders to learn to fix their own machines, and creates an open and level playing field between those who have spare machines and those who do not.

Different categories race at the same time, so riders show each other mutual respect. Overtaking riders should announce when they are "coming through". Slower riders should hang back and let the leaders go down ahead over difficult descents.

Riders are largely trusted to choose the appropriate category, although some ranking systems do exist to move riders up and down. Racing licences are optional but recommended for committed racers.

EATING AND DRINKING

Carbo-loading is relevant to races over 90 minutes long. For most riders, it is sufficient to eat a high-carbohydrate meal the evening before and again for breakfast, don't skip breakfast. Don't eat for the 2

hours before a race. Start nibbling dried fruit or pieces of energy bar 45 minutes into a race, and keep nibbling to the finish.

As always water is essential. Sip water for a few hours beforehand and drink small amounts frequently throughout the race. You can exchange empty bottles with full ones

from supporters. In the heat, take plenty of cold water to keep you hydrated

ON THE START LINE

If you are serious about your finishing position, arrive early on the start line. Pick a

A good start is essential for a good finish.

middle ring, middle sprocket gear to start in. The pack will set off at a very fast pace as riders race to the point where the wide opening track narrows down.

HOW TO BE WORLD CHAMPION

- **Start to race in your teens**
- **Train full time from around 18–20 years old.**
- **Have ambition, tenacity, patience – neither too much nor too little ego.**
- **Stay fit, have a good power to weight ratio and handling skill.**
- **Support from family, friends and partner.**
- **Have a healthy diet.**

cross-country and downhilling

Downhilling

Flying down descents is the great attraction in mountain biking – a piece of adrenalin-filled escapism open to anyone with the guts to do it. Small wonder that downhill racing has become a wealthy part of the sport with its own stars and technology.

Top downhillers have proved that you don't need to be fit to be fast – but you do to win. The best in the world are currently the French and Americans, with Team *Sunn Chipie*'s Anne-Caroline Chausson and Francois Gachet at the top, alongside *Cannondale*'s Missy Giove and Myles Rockwell. There are always packs of other riders just a tenth of a second off their times. Cross-country riders who want to improve their handling benefit from entering downhill competitions, even if they're no good at them. Most mountain biking countries have local and national downhill events. This allows amateurs to improve their skill and nerve, and climb steadily up the rankings.

Good all-round skills are required for success at downhill events, particularly, great nerve and balance, rapid acceleration, unshakeable determination and good legs! The runs are short, anaerobic bursts – the longest lasts about 7 minutes – and the effort can bring riders sobbing to their knees once over the line.

John Tomac at his best – going downhill.

Crashing is an occupational hazard. Spaceage jackets with bizarre spine protection, Kevlar chest, knee and elbow pads, and full face helmets are the flesh and brain savers essential to enable you to get up and fight another day.

Naturally, downhill bikes are the juiciest in the business – front suspension is essential, full suspension is preferable. The greed for speed and need for strength has created the stimulus for significant advances in MTB design and technology. The developers are going for bigger bounce with less wobble. Fork stanchions are made thicker with more overlap with the sliders, and the rear suspension bikes are configured to grip the ground during pedalling, which otherwise works against the shock absorption. The vogue is currently for cutaway seat tubes so that the shock unit can be better positioned inside the front triangle. This is evident in models like the *Trek Y33*, *Cannondale*'s *Super V* series and *ProFlex*'s *Animal*.

Cross-country

Cross-country is the largest branch of competitive mountain biking. An individual endurance challenge, it may be taken lightly or seriously. A thrilling self-awareness results from pushing yourself harder than at any other time and, while racing is a natural way to lose weight and get fit, it is also a great way to make friends. The people, drawn together by a love for bikes, the excitement and the land, are unusually friendly. Many cross-country racers have no background in any other endurance sport, and a minority were formerly not even sporty.

The aim is to get yourself and the bike to the finish in one piece, preferably in the top half of the field. After a crunching, bustling mass start, the bunch will thin out over the length of the race, with riders moving up and down places according to whether they went too fast at the beginning or they are warming up. As with all mountain biking crashing is an occupational hazard, so be prepared for impressive scars, although the cuts are rarely more than skin-deep.

There are categories for men and women, from 10 years upward, that take account of existing ability. A good first year goal for a beginner is to finish a "Fun/Novice" race which lasts 30—50 minutes. After that they can build up to the next category "Sports" where races can last between 45 minutes and 2 hours. Many amateurs are content never to advance further, but those with the time, freedom, skill and competitive ambition may rise gradually over a couple of years to "Expert". This is the category for committed amateurs and top former juniors, where part equipment sponsorship deals are sometimes available. The top category is the "Elite", where the races last between 2–3 hours. It generally comprises full-time cyclists, usually with sponsorship and may even feature a world champion or two.

For children, miniature circuits are organized at many of the larger events, with large juvenile (14–16) and junior (16–18) categories for the oldest. The men's "Veteran" and "Master" categories, which race for 45–90 minutes, are large and highly competitive at the front. Although the numbers are smaller, women's racing is well-established and more highly regarded

What beats the thrill of a downhill?

Cross-country racing is a test of all-round skill

than it is in road racing, with a number of professional riders.

Professional salaries on a par with the Continental peloton are confined to a very few riders. Despite its athleticism, cross-country is deemed less televisual, hence less attractive to outside sponsorship money than downhilling and dual slalom. This leaves it largely supported by the faithful bike factories. The amateur grassroots end of the sport is just about self-financing.

The Olympics

Cross-country racing participated in the Olympics for the first time in 1996. Downhill racing may do so in the future.

racing around the world

Stimulate your competitive juices with a look at racing two continents apart.

The desert is the backdrop to the Cactus Cup.

The Cactus Cup

The opening professional race of the US season, March's Cactus Cup in the parched Arizona desert, is famous for the headlining vegetation that gives the event its identity. Spectators and photographers trying to get close to the action have also sighted coyotes and rattlesnakes, and even claim to have been chased out into the wilderness by ravenous insects.

Where the rest of the world see cacti in trim botanical gardens, racers at the Cactus Cup experience the giant three-metre specimens in their natural habitat. A century ago they marked stage-coach trails. Now it is mountain bikes who use them as corner and track markers on this otherwise straightforward single-track, cross-country race course without long climbs or tricky descents.

As long as things go well on the golden, sandy circuit, the lycra-clad riders are oblivious to their silent, prickly hosts. With spines more than 15 cm (6 in) long, it's an unhappy landing for anyone who goes over the handlebars, or is bounced off the trail by a badly timed two-way sprint for a bottleneck. Pursuing – and being pursued – uses up all the concentration, leaving no spare energy to worry about it.

The Cactus Cup is the first round in one of the leading race series that take place in the USA, and it is sponsored by *Specialized*. The four on- and off-road stages take place in and around the town of Scotsdale. The winners are the man and woman with the lowest overall time.

In 1995, the opening stage was a 5-mile time trial, followed by the Fat Boy and Dirt criteriums – the two multiple-lap stages – and finally the cross-country.

The event is held early in the year to catch the lower spring temperatures, so it doubles as a debut for new teams and gives the perennial teams the opportunity to show off their new colours. Riders target the event to test their fitness after the winter and to assess the form of their rivals. A decent result is a good omen of success to come later in the summer, while this is also where young upstarts start their campaign to unnerve the old hacks.

New bikes and components, the products of the winter workshops are also launched at this event, and you can spot *Shimano* prototypes that will grace next year's component ranges.

The prickly US race season opens with the Cactus Cup in Arizona.

The Alpine challenges

The European Alpinists have devilishly high expectations of amateur racers, and tend to set them far tougher challenges than in other countries – challenges which may at first seem impossible. If the rider isn't fit at the beginning of the event, they certainly will be by the end. In Alpine competitions in France, Italy and Switzerland ordinary people cover extraordinary distances and scale extraordinary heights; dazed and battered by the time they reach the finish but ultimately thrilled and skilled. With the Alps as the arena, the challenge is irresistible.

THE TRANS-ALP ADVENTURE IN ITALY

One of the best examples of amateur MTB Alpinism is the annual Trans-Alp Adventure, which takes place in the Italian Piedmontese mountains around Sestriere near the French border. It is a 450-km (280-mile) stage race over 7 consecutive days – a mathematical average of 64 km (40 miles) each day. The altitude shifts between the valley towns at around 1200 metres (around 4,000 feet) and the high passes at 2800 metres (9,000 feet).

These are steep, hot, rocky mountains and there is no easy way through them. The enormous daily ascent totals top 3,000 metres (10,000 feet) and include tracks which are too steep or stepped to ride. The organizers have no shame about

Carry on pedalling.

including bike-carrying sections, and one such piece of portage lasts nearly an hour. The bicep-buzzing, jaw-rattling descents in this event last as long as 45 minutes. The tracks are strewn with boulders and fraught with cavities ready to swallow a front wheel at any moment. A single drop can start just below the snowy peaks and descend down through the lush Alpine pastures, finishing beneath huge "welcome" banners at the host town.

Each team of two goes off at intervals in the reverse order of the previous day's finishing positions. They must stick together through each check-point for about four hours a day for a week before they reach the final finish line. It makes the professionals' Cactus Cup seem like kids' stuff!

THE GRAND RAID CRISTALP IN SWITZERLAND

The Grand Raid Cristalp, an epic one-day race from Verbier to Grimentz in Switzerland, is another typical Alpine terror. The full 130-km (80-mile) version takes the fast men over 7 hours to complete and has 5,000 metres (16,500 feet) of climbing and descending over the mountains. The shorter 5 hour, 75 km (47 mile) version, which starts at Heremence and finishes at Grimentz, has 1,900 metres (6,000 feet) of height difference and is tackled by several hundred amateurs and a small number of professional women.

chapter three classic r

On a bike, as Greg Yeoman of the Trans-Soviet ride sums up, "You have everything around you – the sights, the sounds, the smells of flowers and trees. It's not just a moving display witnessed from the window of a car, train or plane. And you can stop anywhere you want to."

Travellers tell of being offered scant pennies for their bikes, and of welders able to execute tricky frame repairs in the most unlikely corners of the world. Journeying bikers enjoy a status somewhere between hero and weirdo. The sight of an approaching bike helps win the trust of local people, who are often more welcoming to strangers when they pass through under their own steam.

On the downside, you are exposed to unpredictable traffic and you are at the mercy of the terrain and bad weather. It's all part of the improvization. The bike traveller must sit back in the saddle and let experience and self-knowledge unroll like the trail before them. As Western culture is left behind, the bike fades into the background to become an essential part of the backstage rig while the land and the cultures come to the fore.

Much of the globe is mapped for mountain bikes. Numerous tour companies, usually small, personable and competent, run tours to most of the rugged destinations you choose to name. These tours are no soft option, although they are simpler than independent travel and suit those cyclists who are tied to 4 weeks holiday a year.

This chapter celebrates contrasting journeys and pleasure trips throughout the planet's more mountain bike-worthy areas. The journey begins in Pakistan, where the Karakoram Highway climbs through the world's greatest mountain range. What then follows is the account of a remarkable journey that emcompassed over 13,000 km (8,000 miles) across the full width of the former Soviet Union, from Moscow to Vladivostok. In Morocco, North Africa, rocky tracks and peasant villages dot the foothills of the high Atlas mountains. In France, in the shadow of Mont Blanc, the highest Alp, graded tourist MTB trails offer a pure bike blow-out. At Moab, in Utah, USA, enjoy the outrageously bikable red gorges and pinnacles of Canyonlands National Park and the Slickrock trail – the destination that is the heaven to mountain bikers that Hawaii is to surfers.

Before you start packing, here are some names to look out for in the bookshop, who may provide both ideas and inspiration. Historically, accounts of cycling journeys start in 1886 with "Round the World on a Bicycle", an account of the first world circumnavigation on a penny farthing by Thomas Stevens. Walter Stolle ended up living on his bike from 1959 to 1976, as he covered 640,000 km (400,000 miles) through 159 countries. Women are also proven cycle travellers, and among names to look out for are Dervla Murphy, Josie Dew and Bettina Selby.

THE Trans-Siberian Tour

" Be careful, six bears have just gone that way", warned the friendly Siberian, concerned for the two cyclists passing through his patch on a journey that took them 13,000 km (8,000 miles) across the former Soviet Union.

"We saw paw prints, but never actually the beasts", says the British biologist Greg Yeoman, about one of their countless brushes with adventure on the trans-continental trip. It took Yeoman and his fellow traveller, Australian fitness instructor Kate Leeming, 5 months to pedal along the only road across a country that begins in Europe and finishes at the Sea of Japan, and includes large stretches of land that until recently were closed to Russians, let alone Westerners. Contrary to the image of dour Soviet existence, this is a land of inhabited by warm, resourceful people. It was this hospitality that boosted the couple's determination to overcome daily difficulties – including walking 160 km (100 miles) along the Siberian railway track itself.

147

Enjoying a picnic lunch near Novgorod.

FACTS AND FIGURES
Dates – May 1 to
September 30, 1993.
153 days or 722 hours,
30 minutes in the saddle.
Total distance travelled –
13,286 km (8304 miles)
Daily average – 117 km
(73 miles), 6 hours 24 minutes
in the saddle.

Kate and Greg's trip lasted a whole season during which the leaves budded, came out and fell off. "You become used to the daily pedalling, just as you become used to a 9–5pm. We did several days of more than 160 km (100 miles). 80 km (50 miles) felt like a short day." says Greg. The couple's timing was impressive, "We arrived in Vladivostock 12 hours behind schedule."

Cycling for a cause

Greg and Kate's trip raised £2,500 sterling for Childrens' Aid International. April 1996 was the 10th anniversary of the Chernobyl accident and this US charity aims to help the disaster's child victims, many of whom have thryroid cancer. Greg found that understanding of the cause and effect of radiation is low.

"One area had a very high number of sick children, but the local people said it could not be related to an 'old' nuclear accident, which occurred 36 years earlier," he said. "The money raised has provided a valuable English-Russian computerized translation system, and also helped to establish summer camps in Byelorussia.

This is so that children can enjoy cheap holidays in non-contaminated areas, without the sometimes disastrous culture shock of sending them to other countries. The advice and close cooperation of the local people is actively sought for these projects."

The cyclists

■ Greg Yeoman, a British biologist and irregular cyclist, had done a little cycle-touring in Europe, but hankered after travelling across the former Soviet Union.

■ An Australian fitness instructor who is resident in the UK, Kate Leeming had the idea of adding the Baltic–Pacific odyssey to 16, 000 km (10, 000 miles) of cycling in Europe.

The bicycle karma

Greg sums up his philosophy thus: "Cycling is a non-threatening way of travelling, so people trust you. It is also the best way to see the country which you are visiting, because you can ride all the way into the heart of the cities and all the way out into the countryside. You have everything around you, the sights, the sounds, the smells of flowers and trees. It's not just a moving display witnessed from the window of a car, train or plane. And you can stop anywhere where you want to."

The Russian escorts

Although the days are gone when foreigners had to be accompanied by officials on every step of their visit to the Soviet Union, Greg and Kate knew they could not do the trip unsupported. They needed help with the lan-

Trans-Siberian

carried for 13,000 km (8,000 miles), without the right tools for it. Also I carried a pair of new boots for thousands of kilometres, in anticipation of the final section of the route where there is virtually no track. Before that I was using a pair of old touring shoes, which night after night I glued back together. When these finally gave up … I put on the new boots – and within a few days one lost an eyelet. They weren't very good."

<table>
<tr><td>DISTANCES TRAVELLED</td></tr>
</table>

DISTANCES TRAVELLED

St Petersburg, May 1, 1993
The journey begins

Moscow, May 7
802 km (501 miles)

Yekaterinburg, June 2
3,422 km (2,139 miles)

Krasnoyarsk, July 13
7,245 km (4,528 miles)

Irktsuk, July 28
8,398 km (5,249 miles)

Chita, August 16
9,616 km (6,010 miles)

Blagoveshensk, September 13
11,686 km (7,304 miles)

Vladivostok, September 29
13,286 km (8,304 miles)
The journey reaches its end.

guage, with customs, to get food and for security. Getting a visa is no problem, but it is still necessary to have some form of invitation. So they invited and paid members of a Russian cycling club to escort them eastward. Five cyclists helped during the journey: Vladimir, George, Yuri, Eugene and Sasha. Greg and Yuri had little language in common, as both happened to be biologists and managed to discuss the flora using its Latin nomenclature.

Before they set off the travellers established a base HQ, at the office of Centre Pole, an expedition-organizing company run by Polar explorer Misha Malakhov at the westerly town of Ryazan. From here, supplies and funds were despatched with each new escort. They also kept a spare bike there in case the Russians should need it.

Where they stayed

The couple found they could rely on villagers to put them up.

"The hospitality was fantastic," says

Greg. "Many times we spent the night in people's houses, rather than camping. On arrival we would find out where the mayor of a village lived. They would always be thrilled to put us up and to enjoy a communal photo. Or we would arrive at a village and cycle around, asking people for hot water or milk, and hope to be offered shelter."

EQUIPMENT
- 3 *Scott Windrivers*
- 1 *Specialized Stumpjumper*
- *Karrimor* panniers
- *North Face* tents
- *North Face* waterproofs
- Sleeping bags
- Russian petrol stove

Judging what to take and what to risk leaving behind is one of the skills of travelling.

"In all we carried about 30 kg (66 lb) of equipment, which was far too much." says Greg. "We should have taken more first aid, but we could easily have left behind some clothes, and the new bottom bracket I

The great 160 km (100 mile) push.

choked with plants. "First the tarmac stops, and then the dirt track stops." explains Greg. "In places we were down to following single-track. When that finally disappeared we had no choice but to climb on to the ballast of the railway track itself and get walking. We covered 160 km (100 miles) of the railway on foot, pushing the bikes the whole way, after failing to invent a way of keeping the wheels on the rails."

The Trans-Siberian trains are a summer-time lifeline – the only connection then between the east and west of the country.

"We could hear the trains early enough to get out of the way, although if we were between the lines it was nerve-racking standing for minutes between these monsters as they thundered by in each direction. The wheels finish above head-height, they are very long and carry all sorts of cargo; cars, lumber, foodstuffs, coal. The drivers whistled at us, and must have carried the news of our journey down the line, for people seemed to expect our arrival."

Mechanical hitches

No trip of such length and daring could be trouble free, and this one suffered several setbacks.

- 20 punctures.
- 6 broken spokes.
- 1 broken saddle, which was easily fixed.
- 11 worn out tyres, replaced with ones brought out by the next new escort.
- 1 broken chain.
- 2 broken computers.
- 1 broken water bottle cage.
- Greg's steel pannier rack, chosen because it could be re-welded, broke seven times and was twice rebuilt. Kate's alloy *Blackburn* rack did not break the whole trip.
- Kate broke a rib when she slipped off the bike where the road was just mud track. She rode on it for the remaining 3 months of the trip – luckily it knitted.
- 78 days into the trip one rear rim split with wear. The wheel from the spare at HQ was requested, despatched and luckily it fitted. The lesson learned is to start a trip of this length with new, bedded-in wheels.

Crossing the Steppes

Crossing the Russian Steppes involved a two-week 1,760 km- (1,100 mile) pedal along a stretch of flat road heading for a flat horizon. Greg and Kate found the challenge was to find distraction from the saddle soreness they suffered because of never shifting position, the way you would normally as the road rises and falls. During these dreary days Kate actually worked out the total number of pedalstrokes they would make on the journey.

Pushing along the railway

The last third of the trip was the most difficult. Here the road, which is the only way across Russia and yet is unsurfaced throughout much of its length, runs for hundreds of kilometres parallel to the Trans-Siberian railway. During the winter the hard-packed snow makes it easily passable for vehicles. During the summer, being mud track, it progressively deteriorates and eventually becomes impassable, and completely

Unforgettable cuisine

Food while you are travelling by bike is so very important – it's what fuels the trip, but Kate and Greg enjoyed few culinary delights on their trip. They made picnics of bread, cucumbers, nuts and raisins, but most of what was available was appalling. Greg says he will never forget the worst thing they ate – garlic sandwiches.

"There is little fresh fruit or vegetables – and what there is costs a lot of money, but we did enjoy the seasonal food. The people know how to make the most of the wild harvest. When mushrooms came into season the woods we passed were crawling with people, bags in hands, collecting as many as they could find. That went some way toward enlivening our staple nightly diet of Russian packet soup, which we bulked out with rice, then pasta, then rice... Fresh carrots, presented to us by a hospitable local towards the end of the trip, were a delicacy and our first in 4 months. Luckily we rode through Siberia as the wild salmon season began." After the solitude of the wilderness they hoped that towns along the way would bring relief.

"The towns were about 2 weeks apart," says Greg, "and we wanted to get some rest at them, but re-supplying and tracking down food in the different shops was just as tiring as travelling. And because of a currency crisis [in Russia] the price of bread rose by approximately ten times during the five-month period of the trip."

NAVIGATION

"Further, straight on," was the persistently incorrect response to most of the travellers enquiries about the way. Sense of direction, they concluded thousands of kilometres and many misdirections later, is not a strong national characteristic. The journey had started as it meant to go on, explains Greg.

"We were on the outskirts of St Petersburg, our starting point, on our way to Moscow, when we came across a vast roundabout. Vladimir, our first escort, ignored the big sign for Moscow, claiming he knew a better route. However, Within the first 15 minutes of the trip we were hopelessly lost."

Wisely, rather than relying on local help, the pair furnished themselves with American military maps. However these didn't provide much more help.

"Even they were hopelessly wrong about the status and location of the road in places," says Greg.

The pair averaged 6½ hours in the saddle a day.

Cycling through idyllic Sayan in July.

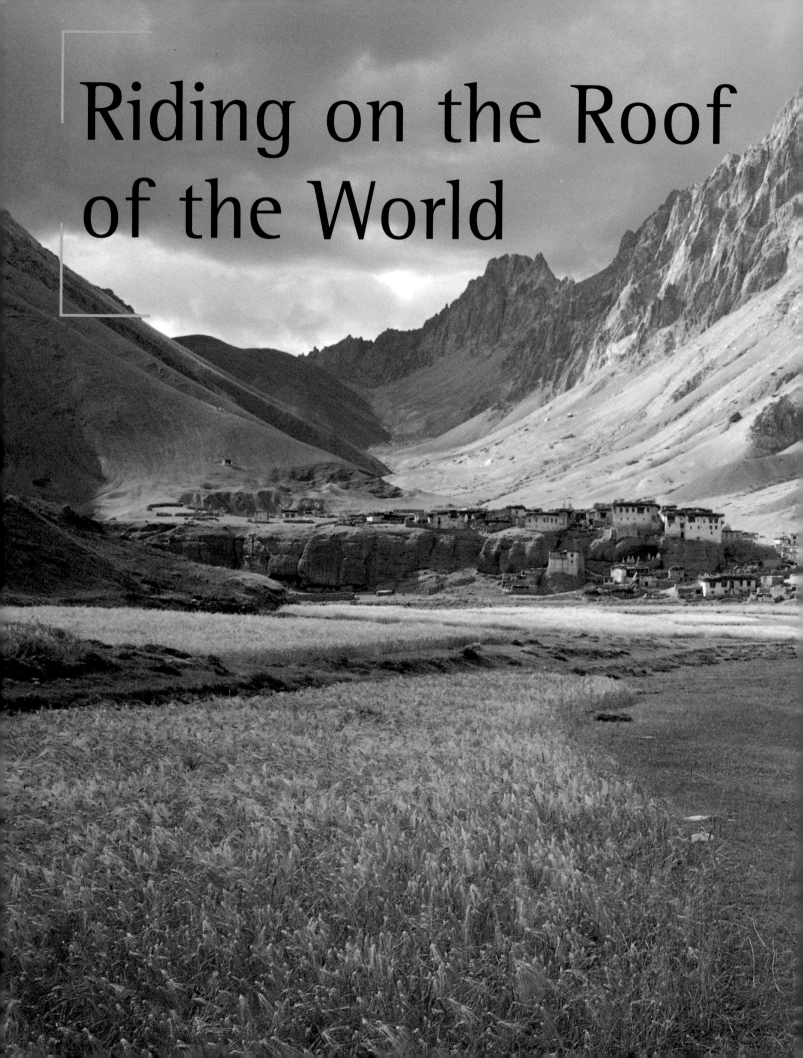

Riding on the Roof
of the World

t he Karakoram Highway has been referred to as the eighth wonder of the world. For 1,300 mountainous km (800 miles), the route runs through Pakistan into China via what is claimed to be the highest surfaced pass yet constructed.

On the way the highway passes between two of the world's mightiest mountain ranges, the western end of the Himalayas and the eastern edge of the Pamirs. The highpoint comes as it crosses the Karakoram range, which, with 33 peaks over 7,300 m (12,950 ft) is unsurprisingly known as "the roof of the world".

Cycling the Karokoram Highway is a tough business, full of physical and cultural challenges – the air is thin, the rockfalls regular and the road in places too high and narrow for comfort. Small wonder that the Hunza kingdom halfway along survived as an autonomy for nine centuries speaking a language that has no known relatives.

Anyone anywhere can enjoy the pleasure a mountain bike brings.

The Karakoram Highway

The landscape that divides Pakistan and China is the kind of terrain that many mountain bikers dream of, but few are able to touch. Above in the Karakoram range soar 12 of the world's 30 highest mountains, with glittering snow-capped peaks, massive shoulders and vast screes of unstable boulders that permanently litter the roads. Below are steely meltwater torrents that flow into the upper reaches of the great river Indus, which gathers strength in the mountains and flows south along the entire length of Pakistan to freedom at the Arabian Sea.

The Silk Road

At varying heights between the snow and the water lies the Karakoram Highway. Even in the narrowest, deepest gorges the road

finds a way through – clinging on to the river-banks or forming a precarious groove along a sheer perpendicular cliff-face 400 m (1,300 ft) above the torrent. Fully surfaced as recently as the 1970s, the Highway is part of the ancient Silk Road, a major trading route since time immemorial by which goods were transported from east to west.

THE LONESOME ROAD

Known in backpack-speak as the KKH, the road is still the only motorable link between Pakistan and China, and it is also a unique and demanding experience by bike. The greater 860 km (540 mile) Pakistani section is more accessible, better supplied and more spectacular, starting at Islamabad and finishing at the Khunjerab Pass after a height gain of over 3,500 m (11,375 ft). The truly adventurous rider on a tour of empires, can do the full 1,280 km (800 miles)

distance across the plainer grassy Central Asian plateau to Kashgar in China.

The Khunjerab pass, opened in 1982, is the top of the Highway and the border between the Pakistan and China. At 4,733 m (15,528 ft) it is supposedly the highest surfaced crossing in the world, cutting across the Karakoram range of mountains that form an otherwise impenetrable barrier between the two countries for about 640 km (400 miles). It is only open during the summer from May until November. Remember if you are travelling on into China, to inform yourself fully of the visa and crossing conditions before arrival.

The High Life

Life along the Highway is changing, with the improved road bringing more goods exchange, tourism and rule from central Pakistan. However, the traditions of the native cultures are largely surviving – for the nature of their land remains more powerful than anything mankind can throw at it. Outside the main towns, the people still inhabit tiny villages, living from what they can grow on the terraces built on any slopes which are less than sheer and can be irrigated. In the spring months the valleys are bright with blooming fruit trees, making this a good time to travel. The summer is baking hot, and as it is outside the monsoon belt, the region has little rain – a sixth of the average for London and a tenth of what falls on New York. Many of the people are the descendants of mountain races which were isolated until the Highway's expansion. The Hunza people, for example, have European colouring and speak Burushaski, a language that has no known linguistic relation.

The Karakoram Highway is a place of massive geological forces. The frequent rockfalls are caused by by the mountains growing taller slightly more slowly than a teenager, as the Indian continental plate shoves against the Asian plate.

Although the Highway's surface is good, it is broken in places and constantly needs repair as it fights a losing battle against frost and debris. The vehicles that ply their trade up and down – the route is well-served by buses – squeeze past each other hub-to-hub in places along the restricted road and charge around blind corners, oblivious to the nil margin of error above the chasms, so cyclists have to keep their wits about them.

Cycling the Highway can be achieved in a number of ways. There is the option of riding independently, but advisedly not alone, up the Highway from Islamabad in Pakistan to the Khunjerab Pass (and back), which will take between 10 days and 2 weeks, or travelling on to China. With hotels and rest-houses along the way this method will suit people already au fait with travelling outside Western cultures. You need to be prepared to deal with the culture, the food and the accommodation. You must be able to adapt to the unexpected, such as trying to get a pannier-rack fixed in Urdu – and bear in mind that the language changes several times along the Highway.

ORGANIZED TOURS

Those who do not have the time or energy necessary to enjoy independent travel, can go on organized trips which are offered by a handful of specialists. These provide back-

The highway's surface is generally good, but watch out for the odd pothole.

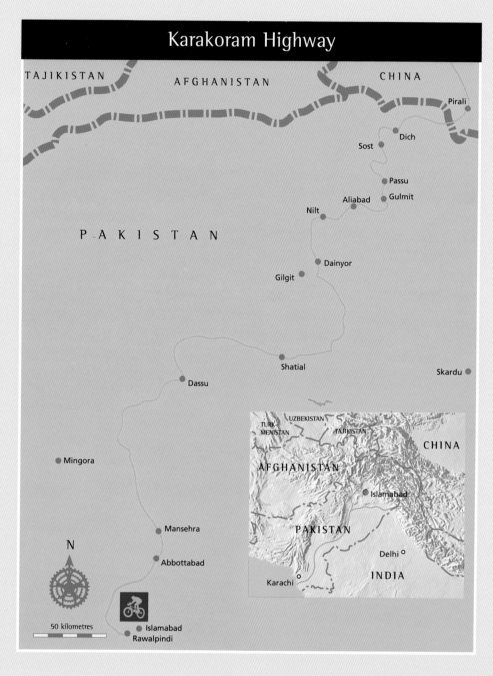

Karakoram Highway

TAJIKISTAN

AFGHANISTAN

CHINA

Pirali

Dich

Sost

Passu

Aliabad   Gulmit

Nilt

PAKISTAN

Dainyor

Gilgit

Shatial

Skardu

Dassu

Mingora

UZBEKISTAN

TURK-
MENISTAN   TAJIKISTAN

CHINA

AFGHANISTAN

Islamabad

Mansehra

N

PAKISTAN

Abbottabad

Delhi

INDIA

Karachi

50 kilometres

Islamabad
Rawalpindi

this isn't a strenuous option — there is enough climbing to keep the fittest cyclists fully occupied.

Highlights of the journey

NANGA PARBAT

For 48 km (30 miles), although not in the direct line of sight, the Highway travels at a height of about 1,200 m (3,900 ft) in the glowering presence of 8,125 m (26,660 ft) Nanga Parbat, the ninth highest mountain in the world and the suitably imposing western-most point of the Himalayan range. The name means "naked mountain", because its faces are too steep for snow to cling to for long. German mountaineers have a more sinister name for the peak, calling it "murder moun-tain", because of the number of lives lost on it during climbing expeditions.

The Nanga Parbat massif is so large that it takes the daily scheduled planes that fly from Islamabad below to Gilgit above 10 minutes to contour around its slopes. It will take the average mountain biker up to 3 hours to complete the route, but the reward, if travelling up the Highway through what at this point is a barren river gorge, is a stunning view back to the massif a few kilometres to the north.

up vehicles and accommodation and may rent you bikes, although it is better to pro-vide your own. There are several choices, including a tour that flies and drives you to the top of the Highway at the Khunjerab Pass, from where you descend back southward through Pakistan, with diversions off the Highway up the neighbouring valleys to visit glaciers and villages. Do not be fooled by the starting point into thinking that

Cyclist take a well earned, high-altitude break.

HUNZA VALLEY

The Hunza valley lies in the upper part of the Highway to the north of Gilgit before the road turns up the Khunjerab river valley to the Khunjerab Pass.

With so much of the Highway an inhospitable desertscape of rock, mud and alluvial detritus, it is easy to understand how life in Hunza was presented by the first European visitors in the early twentieth century as a mountain nirvana, and even claimed, to be the home of people who knew no illness.

For cyclists it is a relief to be out of the the barren jaws of the pressing cliffs for a while and on to Hunza's fertile plateau, which in April and May is full of blossom from the terraced fruit trees. The fruits of the valley can be found on sale at the roadside stalls and in the market at the valley's main town Karimabad, and include delicious nutty tasting apricots and other orchard fruits – all delightful and refreshing to the palate after spending many parched hours in the saddle.

The guardians of the Hunza plain, which lies at 2,500 m (7,700 ft) are the three towering peaks of Rakaposhi, Ultar and Distaghil, which typify Hunza's dramatic history. Ruled by the same family since the eleventh century it was a tiny, virtually impregnable kingdom of great strategic importance to the imperial forces that surrounded it. Control Hunza and you controlled passes leading to Afghanistan and Russia in the west, China to the north, and India to southeast. The British controlled the area from the end of the nineteenth century until partition and independence of India and Pakistan in 1947. Pakistan and China agreed their border during the 1960s, and the Highway is a joint effort between the two nations. The last vestiges of the dynastic rule in Hunza evaporated, although perhaps only for the time being, in 1994 when the current heir lost his elected seat in the administration.

Take time to stop cycling and seek out local landmarks.

The end of the road

The final 150 km (100 miles) from the haven of Hunza to the zenith of the Karakoram Highway at the Khunjerab Pass has both the most dramatic landscape and, if going north, the greatest amount of strenuous climbing. This is where even the fittest bikers could begin to feel breathless with the altitude, although independent travellers who have ridden all the way from Islamabad will probably have adapted to the situation at least to a degree.

A little way on from the plateau village of Gulmit you get the dramatic thrill of steering your wheels right over the nose of the glistening Ghulkin glacier, which bears down on a piece of the Highway already squeezed hard against the river. A little further still and there is the sight of the Passu glacier, pushing down from the Passu peaks above that rise to over 7,000 m (22,750 ft) in height.

From here the biker has just another 2,200 m (7,400 ft) to climb over a good 100 km (60 miles) to the top, where Pakistan finishes with a venerable flourish of a dozen hairpin bends – great descending fodder – the final rungs in a ladder to the high Chinese plateau.

Watch out for the local wildlife!

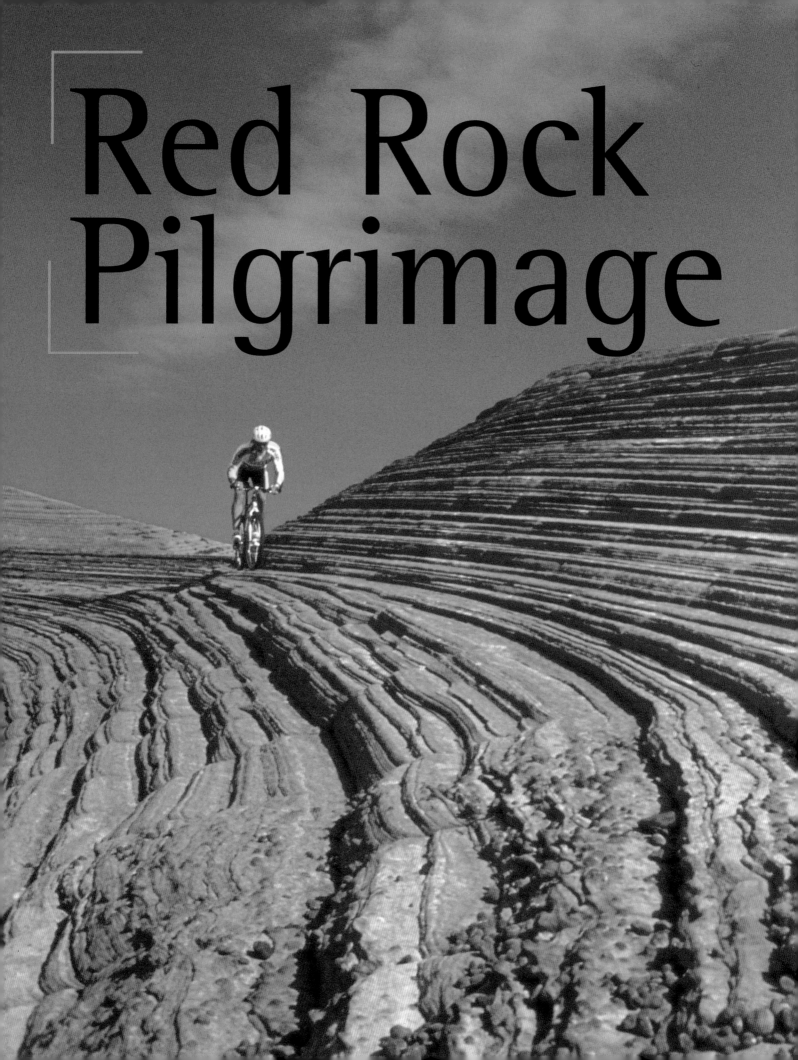

Red Rock Pilgrimage

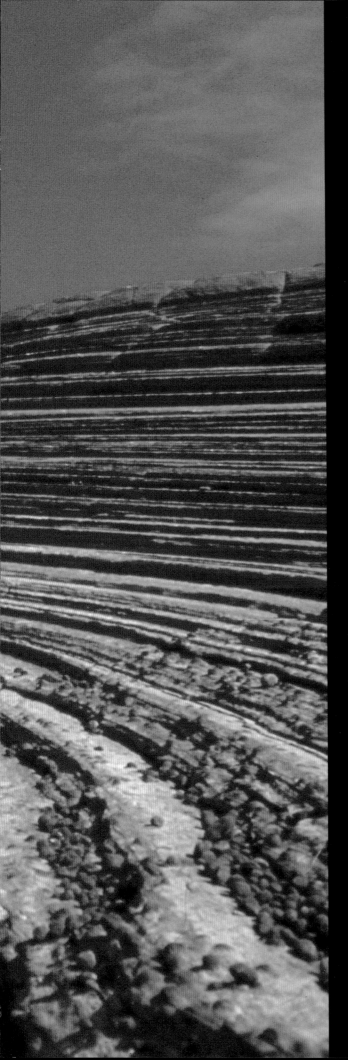

for a reminder that the real world will always be stranger than any virtual experience, go and ride the primitive, bare red rock of Moab in Utah, USA. Its most famous mountain bike trips, the Slickrock Loop and White Rim Tour in the neighbouring Canyonlands national park, draw cyclists from all over the world into an area of breathtaking sandstone formations that are supremely bikeworthy.

Situated on a high, empty plateau above the canyons of the Colorado River, the surface of the bulging rock has been eroded to its slick surface by wind and water, resulting in miraculous tyre-gripping properties. This means that you can stay in the saddle on the steep slopes of the natural half-pipes long after the gradient should have forced you off. The eeriness, heat and drama of these desert trails and the bike-loving atmosphere of Moab, an old uranium-mining settlement, attracts thousands of fat-tyre pilgrims. Riding here is without doubt one of the world's most exciting biking destination.

Extraordinary natural monuments abound.

The natural world – a crash course for bikers

Putting rubber to the extraordinary rock spires, arches and canyons of the high altitude desert of Utah, USA, means putting all former off-road experience into storage and letting your imagination loose once more. Forget the details etched into your consciousness by long hours anywhere else in the saddle as this weird, wonderful landscape delivers a unique sensory experience. There is sight – the air seems coloured red as you gaze at the soaring heights and plummeting depths of majestic sandstone canyons. There feel – the tyres on the smooth rock, sticky, yet bone dry, as found across the area. The sound, on a still day, is of timeless silence. Even when it comes to smell, the hot, red rock exudes a sweet, pungent odour.

There is virtually no vegetation to pollinate the air, to shelter behind or to headbut – only rock. There is no mud, none of that rich, brown life-giving humus that many mountain bikers know too well. Instead in the cracks and crannies of the overbearing rock there is found just a little sand and dust. In this precarious environment damage takes decades to repair. The 50-year-old tracks of the uranium prospectors who graded the trails in the name of the the US nuclear capacity are still at the beginning of nature's slow recycling service.

No water, only rock ...

There is little water, other than the tomato soup-coloured flow of the Colorado River on its way from the Rockies to the watercourses of Los Angeles and the sea on the Gulf of California. With summer-time temperatures averaging between 25–40°C (80–100°F), the priority is water-preservation, not waterproofing. This is desert with an average annual rainfall of 25.4 cm (10 in), where the US Department of the Interior insists you drink a 4.5 litres (8 pints) of water a day.

The rains that do fall come at the summer's end and early autumn, when thunderstorms carry a risk of being struck by lightning and flash floods on the parched sandstone can fill up a creek or gully within seconds. The seeds awaken, and so do innocent campers. Bearing in mind the delicate ecology that strives for life in this high, bare habitat, bikers are requested to leave their "cool" behind, and to see themselves as crusaders who protect a delicate and barely perceptible eco-system. For life finds a toe-hold in the most unlikely places – an apparently infertile grit is held in place and protected from the elements by what is called a cryptobiotic crust. Far from barren, the crust is an ecological niche, a mixture of lichen, algae, fungi and cyanobacteria that forms a living seal against the sand being blown or washed away. In the sand sleep the seeds of the high desert, awaiting the rainstorms, Nature's sign above these precarious plant nurseries says, "do not disturb".

The First People

Ancient and more recent Anasazi Indian wall art peppers the area. Many of the sites are easily visited by the bike, and feature on the bike tours organized by Moab's five licensed companies. Scenes of people hunting and living are shown in petroglyphs (etchings) and pictographs (paintings) on walls of many of the canyons of the area. They date back to a time when this advanced society was growing corn and hunting the Bighorn sheep of the area, and before that too, to more primitive societies. Petroglyphs exist on the surfaced road from Moab towards the White Rim trail and are found at other points such as Newspaper Rock. One of the most famous arrangements is the Harvest Scene pictograph in the Maze, the southwest portion of the Canyonlands park, with its veritable labyrinth of canyons.

Having viewed this evidence that the ancients expressed themselves in colour and form much the same way as we do today, it becomes understandable that Columbus Day, one of the USA's national holidays, is mooted by some to be better known as "Indigenous Peoples Day".

Loose your juice on the Slickrock Trail

Claimed to be "the world's most popular trail" the Moab Slickrock has entered mountain bike folklore. Described as a giant, natural skateboard park, it has spectacular scenery and fabulous riding. Bikes get a big welcome in the town of Moab a couple of kilometres back on Highway 191, with its established bike shops and hospitality.

The 19-km (12-mile) circuit hovering between 1,220–1,500 km (4,000–5,000 ft) altitude, was first laid out in 1969 by local motorcyclists – the outback miners who knew the country like the back of their hands. Mountain bikers stumbled across the trail in the 1980s.

And what about riding the trail? Nothing is straight, nor flat, but it is elevated. Every time you pop up out of a gulch you can see way into the distance across lines of red rock humps formed from petrified sand dunes. More distant to the east are the

There are hundreds of miles of exciting riding in the high desert.

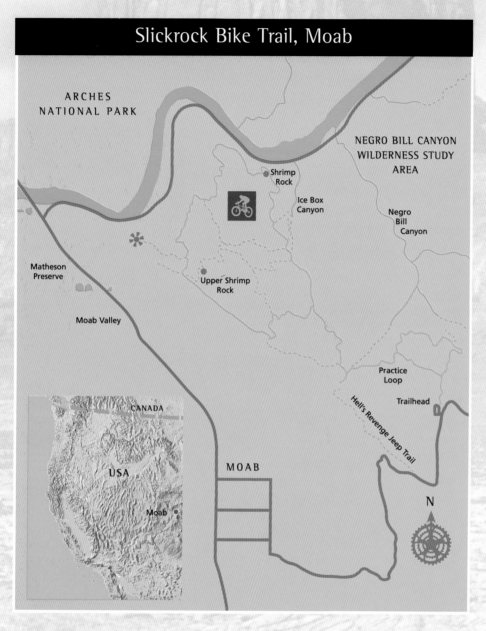

Slickrock Bike Trail, Moab

ARCHES
NATIONAL PARK

Shrimp
Rock

NEGRO BILL CANYON
WILDERNESS STUDY
AREA

Ice Box
Canyon

Negro
Bill
Canyon

Matheson
Preserve

Upper Shrimp
Rock

Moab Valley

CANADA

USA

Moab

MOAB

Practice
Loop

Trailhead

Hell's Revenge Jeep Trail

N

Slickrock Trail as a warm-up for longer, more varied tours, such as the White Rim trail and any of another dozen mapped tracks in Canyonlands and cross-country to Colorado. Slickrock takes between 90 minutes and 8 hours to ride, depending on ability and looking time. Every piece of the trail has been christened and given a two-figure sweat and skill grading. For example, one section called "Interval Straining'" has a 2/8 grading, meaning 2/10 for technical difficulty and 8/10 for effort. Another climb, "Staircase" rates 8/8, which means it is both mentally and physically hard. "Loose the Juice" is a sweet drop marked 3/5 and there is aptly-named "Baby Bottom Bowl". The viewpoints include "Natural Selection" at the far end of the trail which overlooks the Colorado river gorge towards the aforementioned Arches Park, some of whose treasures can be spotted.

Heading for a fall

The words "Danger (stop or die)" occur a couple of times and need no explanation. Falling down cliff edges and getting lost are two good reasons for sticking to the trail, and you are advised not to ride alone. For regulars – there are citizens of Moab to whom Slickrock is the backyard – new spurs and sections of trail were added in 1989, and are distinguished with dots, as opposed to dashes. One bisects the loop via the Black Hole, where caution is advised.

Autumn and spring are the best times to go to Utah. There is no water up on the Trail plateau, not even at the vehicle park at the start. In the cooking summer temperatures you should carry as many as three water-bottles, and drink before you are thirsty. Wear full sun-burn protection and good sun-shades. If riding in a party, make sure everyone is keeping up and can cope. Winter-time brings a chance of snow.

snowy foothills of the Rocky Mountains, and to the north is the awesome Arches National Park, named after its hundreds of natural red rock arches and holes.

White dashes, like road markings, show you the way to go, over huge rock "pillows" and slopes. Extreme slopes become rid-able. both up and down, sometimes over perfectly smooth rock and other times across the close-contoured lines of strata. There are wonderful easy swooping down-hills and half-pipes, and also uphill gradi-ents which will test any rider to their limit. Riding the loop is, for many riders, a feat in itself, and despite its easy surface, Slickrock begins with a 4 km (2.5 mile) prac-tice loop, as the rest of the trail is desig-nated as technically difficult. But that should not put off beginners, as you can easily walk with the bike anywhere that you cannot ride as long as you stay on the marked trail.

Experienced riders will not believe what has hit them. Nevertheless, they can use the

Blazing rubber on the White Rim Trail

With the relatively busy Slickrock Trail in the bum-bag, the neighbouring Canyonlands National Park offers remoter adventure.

Out there the awaits the 160 km (100 mile) White Rim Trail, an epic circuit with 4 days riding and camping. The route runs along what is the seat of a massive white sandstone bench. Below are the 518 km (1,700 ft) walls of the Colorado and Green river gorges. Above, is the seat back, an extraordinary upper plateau called the "Island in the Sky" with its highest point at 1,828 m (6,000 ft).

Overwhelming vistas of sky and rock make this canyon country trip a must. You can either ride it independently, in which case you must stay in the official simple campsites. Firewood must be brought in, and waste must be taken out. Have someone else see to it by joining one of the guided bike trips.

DOWNTOWN MOAB

A little town with a big name, Moab is home to several cult bike shops and the centre of information on guided bike tours in the area and where to stay.

The unforgettable scenery around Moab – a mountain bikers paradise.

THE Chamonix experience

t he mountain resort of Chamonix, directly below Mont Blanc in the French Alps, is famous in all walks of alpinism. The place is revered in mountaineering for its concentration of glaciers and sharp, soaring peaks and in skiing for its high-quality slopes. So, naturally, it has also become a superb summertime mountain bike destination. Halfway between the world of the exposed climber above, and the holidaymaker on the below, a cyclist can test his bike's "mountain" pedigree on a an abundance of great tracks that pass along the mountainsides, through beautiful valleys and over high passes, using the spectacular cable-car network to link trails and mountain cafés.

Chamonix has some sign-posted local mountain bike trails. These are colour graded like the ski slopes and are mostly suitable for gentle rides, beginners or as a warm up for more strenuous rides. For more experienced cyclists, specialist tour companies offer more adventurous trips.

Chamonix history

Chamonix has long been a fashionable winter sports resort. At the end of the last century the town hosted one of the first ever package tours, run by Mr Thomas Cook, and the first Winter Olympics in 1924. As well as being a mountaineering base, busy ski resort and hard-core hiking centre, it has developed a reputation as a location for extreme stunts such as ultimate ski-ing.

Chamonix – peaks and glaciers

The town's main attraction is the highest Alpine peak Mont Blanc, which, at 4,807 m (15,771 ft), looms directly above it. The valley also features no fewer than six major glaciers, the most famous of which, the Mer de Glace, finishes just 200 m (650 ft) away from the town boundary, as well as more than 20 smaller ones. Lying in an Alpine corner where France, Switzerland and Italy meet, just an hour's drive from Geneva airport, Chamonix is also the location of the northern entrance of the 12-km (8-mile) Mont Blanc tunnel, which carries heavy freight in and out of Italy. The closest open-air border crossing is the 2,469-m (8,100-ft) Grand St Bernard Pass between Switzerland and Italy, which is 80 km (50 miles) to the east.

The uniquely spectacular character of the European Alps over some of the world's other higher mountain ranges is the absolutely breathtaking height difference between the valleys and the mountain tops. The beautiful snowy Monts, Dents and Aiguilles dwarf the mere smudges of civilization below. Chamonix itself sits at a height of 1,035 m (3,360 ft), a full 3,772 m (12,260 ft) below the tip of Mont Blanc, which measures a mere 10 km (6 miles) away from the town centre on the map.

With smart shops and dozens of cafés, Chamonix is a magnet for mountain bikers.

Mountain biking in the Mont Blanc area

Chamonix is a good place to get a taste of biking the Alps, where you can ride in the three countries in as many days, without any sense of making a border crossing. Like many of the alpine ski resorts the town switches between summer and winter sports. The mountain biking season lasts from May to September, with visitors attracted by the fact that the town is geared around holidaymakers, with plenty of restaurants and clothing stores. You can arrange accommodation independently and follow your own routes, or use the services of an MTB tour company, which also offers full-board chalet accommodation.

The tourist board has produced a starter map showing several easy sign-posted routes – using the symbol of a triangle with

Basking at an *auberge* is one of many delights of the Alps.

two circles to the left. The guided tours take bikers of all standards on more adventurous routes, lasting anything between one and seven days, over some of the area's hundreds of kilometres of tracks.

One ride guided by Mont Blanc Mountain Biking (a specialist cycling tour operator see acknowledgements for details) holidays uses the cable car to climb up to 1,850 m (6,000 ft), for a pure descent of 1,250 m (4,050 ft) back down to the valley – the height, their brochure points out, of Ben Nevis, the United Kingdom's highest peak. Another ride has a 1,000 m (3,250 ft) climb to a mountaintop cafe.

The soaring peaks and the deep valleys of the European Alps.

The Tour du Mont Blanc

The classic MTB route of the area is the 5-day circumnavigation of the Mont Blanc massif. The trip takes in four cols above 2,000 m (6,500 ft), meaning lots of climbing and descending, and is only suitable for fit bikers who are either already experienced, or who are on the fast-track to MTB wisdom. Staying in mountain refuges, the trip is irregular.

Supported 7-day tour

On this trip you spend 7 days in the saddle. In the Mont Blanc area, the accommodation is in *gites* high in the high mountain villages, with the luxury of full baggage support.

Sample rides

30KM INTERMEDIATE RIDE

Starting from the Foyer de Ski de Fond on the main road, follow the tourist office map along the trail marked No. 1. Follow this until you reach the "Pont de Corrua". From here follow the signs for Lavancher (route No. 5). When you arrive in Lavancher descend on the road. A hairpin right, a hairpin left then look out for the MTB trail sign on the right (route No. 7). Take this trail (Petit Balcon Nord) to Argentiere. Follow the Petit Balcon to Le Tour (good luck on the "Le Planet" climb). Go to the cable car station and take the lift to Charamillion. Once out of the cable car, ride towards the Col Des Possettes (2,000 m/6,500 ft). Over the

The Mont Blanc tour – not for softies.

Col des Possettes, ride downhill toward Vallorcine. The track is a logging trail and is quite fast and stony, but great fun.

Once you've got your breath back, in Vallorcine ride in the direction of Le Buet on the trail on the left side of the valley. Go through Le Buet and follow the trail until it meets the road on the Col Des Montets. Join the road and pass the Col des Montets. Start the descent after the Col but after about 500 m (1,600 ft) take a left to a

Chamonix, France

SWITZERLAND

Geneva

Chamonix

F R A N C E   I T A L Y

Argentiere

La Joux

7

7

7

7

Les Tines

Les Praz

2 Les Bossons

Chamonix

1

6 5   Le Lavancher

4

3

11

F R A N C E

hamlet called Trelechamp. Take the gravel track through Trelechamp and just before it meets the road again take a little single-track to the left, for some great hairpins. Go through Argentiere on the road but just before the railway bridge, take a right and pick up a trail called the "Petit Balcon Sud". You will arrive at "Paradis Des Praz" where you can get back to Chamonix via the details in ride 1 and the Tourist Office Map.

40KM HARD RIDE VIA THE "CORKSCREW"

This is a tough one. Pick up the road out of Chamonix to Les Gaillands. At the climbing wall in Les Gaillands pick up the trail leading to Les Bossons. Using signs and your map go to Les Bossons, Les Montquarts, Les Roches to the train station in Les Houches

(Gare SNCF). Cross the main road and ride to the Bellevue cable car station in Les Houches and take the cable car to the top.

When you get out of the cable car, descend to Col de Voza. Follow the trail that leads to "Prarion", but not all the way. After four hairpins take the trail on the left to La Charme. Follow this trail for at least 4 km (10 miles). You arrive at a T-junction where you will see a tarmac road descending to the left and a trail going right. Take the right and follow the trail for about 1 km (⅔ mile) until you reach a small hamlet called Montfort.

There is a turning left that is tricky to find, but you will if you look. This is the start of the legendary "corkscrew", a trail known only to a handful of the local mountain bikers. This brings you out on to the main road connecting Le Fayet and St Gervais. Descend to Le Fayet.

Take the D43 road toward Chedde. When you arrive at Chedde by the hang-glider landing field. You see a sign left, "Servoz par D13". Take this road and after the first sharp left hairpin you see a trail on the right marked "Chemin du Butteaux". This 15-minute climb will bring you to the D13 road to Servoz. Go through Servoz on the road, following road signs to Chamonix. When you

meet the main road (Route Blanche) head towards Chamonix. After only about 700 m (2,300 ft) on this Route Blanche you will see a turn off right that appears to go nowhere. Take this but don't follow the road to the house. Go straight on following a trail under the railway bridge and on to Les Houches. Go through Les Houches and you will come to the Bellevue cable car that you took earlier. From here you go back to Chamonix via Taconnaz, Les Bossons and Les Gaillands on the road. Alternatively, you can return along the trail you rode in the morning.

CLOTHING

These are high mountains where the weather can change drastically in a short period of time. During the winter the slopes are snowbound, and in the spring and autumn take clothing ready for cold wind and snow or rain. If you are going high, remember that the temperature drops a degree for every 100 m (300 ft) climbed, and that the air can be much cooler than the sunshine might suggest. By contrast, summer is warm, and carrying drinking water is the priority. Most of the rides in the Chamonix valley pass water butts with a constant supply of running spring water that is safe to drink.

[10]

[9] Le Tour

[8]

Key

■— Cable Car

mountain biking in
Morocco

tracks formed over thousands of years by the Berber people and their animals, linking fortified villages through gorges and over barren mountains which shimmer with the heat from the Sahara below. That's the riding that draws mountain bikers to the High Atlas range in Morocco.

The Atlas mountains have become one of the favourite destinations among the sort of wanderlusting mountain bikers who enjoy experiencing other cultures as much as they enjoy the views, effort and highs of a sporting adventure.

Morocco is well-served by flights from Europe, speaks French and cooks a mean colourful cuisine, which makes a visit here relatively practical and accessible. Alternatively, specialist mountain bike tour companies offer a selection of supported trips that also take in the Atlas beauty spots. This means that all you need to do is push round the pedals and enjoy the sights and smells.

The glorious Atlas mountains of Morocco.

"The mountains that time forgot", is the description used by Moroccan tour guides seeking business in the High Atlas. The sentiment is one of cultural rather than geographical accuracy. The ancient and remote Berber villages, which wring a living from the high, dramatic slopes of the Atlas range are way above the reaches of power and plumbed water. But they are not beyond the reach of the knobbly tyre and a determined driver – as long as she or he is happy with the idea of living simply while exploring the rich network of tracks.

The Atlas mountains are made up of a quartet of roughly parallel ranges that form the southern edge of the Mediterranean bowl. All together the four ranges, the Anti Atlas, High Atlas and Mid Atlas in Morocco and the Algerian Atlas run for 2,250 km (1,400 miles) from the Atlantic coast almost to Tunisia. Much of the guided mountain biking takes place in the 320-km (200-mile) High Atlas range, which rises well over 12,000 feet in places, with some in the Anti Atlas to the south. The highest point is Mount Toubkal at 4,165 m (13,665 ft) – the fourth highest peak in Africa.

Despite being a neighbour of the Saharan desert and having "Africa" in its address, the ice-capped High Atlas range is an example of how dependent temperature is on altitude. Although warm during the day most of the year round, the sun deserts the steep upper valleys early in the day, and night-time frosts are common. So travellers cannot pack as lightly as they might expect. Recommended equipment includes a three-season sleeping bag and thermals.

When Nick Crane and colleagues made their end-to-end trip in 1989, they were travelling in the age-old explorers' tradition – to

Why take the bridge?

see whether the range was at all navigable by MTB. It is, and since then the area has become a destination for more far-sighted European mountain bikers, keen to experience the Arab and Berber cultures and itching for hundreds of kilometres of rock and dung trails. For them, Morocco is relatively close – just 5 hours flight from the UK – with a choice of travel options courtesy of the boom in rough travel and the young, keen tour companies.

Visiting the High Atlas independently is quite feasible if you are confident outside Western culture, or if you would like to become so, and hardy enough either to camp or to seek simple shelter with the people on a day-by-day basis. After flying either to Agadir at the western tip, or to Marrakech, the former Berber capital, inland to the north of the range, the mountains are a day's ride, or less if you travel by bus. from there you are then free to roam using hiking maps, your nose and local knowledge.

The alternative, for people who want the riding and culture without the unpredictability that comes with being self-sufficient, is an all-in tour. On these, let experienced guides and a support team take care of the MTB routes, travel, food, camping and local logistics.

The descent from Mount Toubkal.

The mountain biking scores highly in this land, where the rock is the colour of tarnished copper. The number of trails is huge in what is, to remind you, a 320-km (200-mile) mountain range. You never get to the end of them. These are working tracks; unpaved, extremely rough under-tyre but well packed down by thousands of years of hooves and feet. Barring the mule trains and tour landrovers, there are very few vehicles – another reason for the "forgotten by time" tag. As long as you don't disturb the local people or the flocks of animals they depend upon to survive, you can enjoy a rare biking treat – untrammeled riding according to your energy, ability to stay in one piece and the hours of daylight.

The tracks run through the valleys and along the mountainsides, linking village with pasture, village with village, and village with town. The lower valleys are fertile but goat-nibbled, but the upper plains are barren with tough desert scrub and trees the only flora. Up there, above the rain-clouds, the water source is melt-water fed springs. Mud, the Europeans will be glad to know, plays no role in MTBing Moroccan-style. The mud and stone set-tlements are built of the same material as the surrounding rock and so well camouflaged that from a distance they melt into the background. The more significant villages are dominated by crumbling fortresses, or kasbahs, which are worth a detour and which feature on the itineraries of the tour companies. Another Atlas speciality is the dozens of spectacular gorges; deep, still clefts, perhaps with a stream at the bottom, but more likely a dried stream-bed.

There is little problem finding food in the foothills, but the higher the altitude and more remote the hamlet, the fewer supplies there may be, particularly during Ramadam. Highly recommended is *tagine*, a delicious meat and vegetable stew and staple of the Moroccan diet. Berber hospitality, as is often the norm in undisturbed cultures, is warm and friendly, and the Berber people are no strangers to Europeans, apart, again, from those who inhabit extremely remote hamlets.

MTB tours are organized and take place all year round, except in July as the heat is too intense. Such tours are suitable for anyone of any age, as long as you are averagely fit. The trips involve several hours of biking a day, usually between 30–50 km (20–30 miles), and vary between a tour of "the valley of a thousand kasbahs" and a special winter-sun trip, which is 70% downhill – a Landrover does the uphill work.

Mutually curious, an intrepid explorer and Berber meet during the 1989 Atlas Biker expedition.

Atlas Biker Route-Sahara to the Sea

Morocco

AFRICA

Malaga

SPAIN

Gibraltar

MEDITERRANEAN SEA

Tangier

ATLANTIC
OCEAN

Rabat

Casablanca

Fes

ALGERIA

M O R O C C O

Marrakesh

Imilchil

Rich

Oudeddi

Tabant

Zaouia
Ahansal

Er Rachidia

Telouet

Erfoud

N

Jbel Toubkal

Rissani

Quazazarte

Chebbi Sand Sea

Agadir

Taroudant

250 Kilometers

SAHARA   DESERT

Highlights of the Atlas range

■ **Ait Benhaddou** – a pretty fortified village used for location filming of the epic movies "Lawrence of Arabia" and "Jesus of Nazareth", this makes it a tourist trap.

■ **The Cascades d'Ouzoud** – a 35 m (100 ft) waterfall within a fertile cauldron.

■ **The Dades Gorge** – one of the most handsome in the area

■ **The Tizi**, or passes, for memorable climbing and descending:

■ **Tizi n'Tazzazert** –2,200 m (7,000 feet)

■ **Tizi n'Tichka** – 2,260 m (7,350 ft), on the road from Marrakech on the north side, to Ouarzazate on the south side.

■ **Tizi n'Ouano** – 3,300 m (10,700 ft), near Imilchil towards the eastern end of the Atlas range.

NICK CRANE'S ATLAS TRAVERSE

What first drew mountain biking attention to the High Atlas was adventurer Nick Crane's "Atlas Biker" trip in 1989. Inspired by traveller Wilfried Thesiger, he and Matt Dickinson successfully completed a 1,200-km (750-mile) continuous MTB traverse of the range from the Sahara to the sea, conquering the icebound summit of Mount Toubkal at 4,165 m (13,665 ft) on the way. The purpose was to see if the mountains were navigable by MTB using the most direct route possible from east to west. The pair stuck to the high route, even when it meant carrying the bikes for hours, and using difficult, even foolhardy tracks over outcrops and along the sides of steep gorges, to save dropping in height to go around them. Their bikes, rigid *Ridgeback 501s*, were not sophisticated by current standards, but they proved that it is not necessary to have a supercharged bike to perform a supercharged feat – you just have to be crazy enough.

As the trip was filmed the bikers had the advantage of vehicle support, but rode every inch of the trek themselves. The film was broadcast on TV in the UK in June 1989 as a half-hour programme, "Blazing Pedals". No fewer than 6 million people tuned in, which unexpectedly brought Nick closer than any other mountain biker to household name status, meanwhile putting High Atlas mountain biking firmly on the map.

Starting at the east end of the range on top of the highest dunes in Morocco at the Chebbi sand sea, the trekkers averaged 60 km (38 miles) every day, before finishing at the Atlantic in Agadir, three bruised and bumped weeks later. Their elevation averaged between 1,000 and 2,500 m (3,250–8,125 ft) with a high diversion up Mount Toubkal.

Conditions were often tricky, as the men froze by night and boiled by day. The bikers split off from the landrovers whenever the route cross-country became unmotorable, which usually indicated slow progress. For example, the 70 barely mapped kilometres to the Berber sanctuary of Zaioua Ahansal ended up taking them three days, delayed by several factors. They had to do their own filming and carry the equipment themselves in backpacks wrapped up in sleeping backs. Chris Bradley the third rider went over the handlebars, damaged his knee and had to hobble on painfully for the next 2 days before quitting the continuous biking attempt. Also the map that these highly experienced men was using was a 1:100 000 general of North Africa, and the directions given them by the rare goatherd or whoever crossed their path, were flawed.

The ascent of the peak Djebel Toubkal took 2 days, most of which was spent carrying the bikes, through steep, deep snow and ice. But the trek had to be done to maintain the image that cyclists and explorers share for heroism and eccentricity.

When the bicycle fails, the mule keeps plodding along.

chapter four stunt

riding

representing the circus ring of mountain biking, trick riding is a highly skilled and spectacular branch of the sport. Here it is acceptable for full-grown women and men to fool around on bikes and perform feats beyond the comprehension of most mountain bikers – however many times they have circumnavigated the world or however many gold medals clutter up the mantelpiece.

These are acrobats doing the things on bikes that you are supposed to grow out of in your teens – grown men and women behaving badly, and who should know better, but who are desperate to explore to the limits what they and their bike are capable of, and give the onlookers a thrill into the bargain.

The list of tricks is always growing, as new riders choreograph their own repertoires. Stunt riding is an individual thing. Look at Hans Rey, the king of the MTB entertainers, giving the graffitied wall on California's Venice Beach a glancing blow from his wheels, 2 metres up, or jumping from car roof to car roof in an LA traffic jam as part of a *Swatch* promotion, or giving a feisty young woman lying on her back a front-wheel kiss in the middle of London's Piccadilly Circus.

In Britain, the mysteriously named "Switzerland Squeaker" was a trick unique to Jez Avery, who could balance on his front wheel while the rear one was whisked away by his lovely assistant, Paul – just one in a bag of improvized, personalized tricks. Everyone likes to develop their bike-handling skills, and stunt riding is a way of improving your overall off-road control. There's also a sense of peak satisfaction when you start getting a trick right after practising it over and over again, whether it is your first bunny-hop or lengthy wheelie, or red phase-long trackstand at the lights. Trick riding is a great leveller for MTB riders who are never going to be particularly fast or have the levels of endurance needed to shine in the cross-country pack. Check your equipment and ride with care, for if you land awkwardly and bend the fork, or wrap the frame around a tree, do not expect the manufacturer to sympathize.

This chapter features some great examples of flamboyant MTB riding to entertain and inspire you. Take a look at trials competitions, which are few and far between despite their great crowd appeal and the balletic balance displayed by the professionals. Then there is downhill duelling, the athletic end of trick riding, as featured in pieces on the fastest event in the world, the *Reebok* Dual Eliminator in the US, and a popular new test of control and mettle in the British *Coors* Dual Descender. And finally, get ready to duck as the air bandits get jumping and lake leaping.

A word of warning – many of the stunts shown here are done by professional riders with years of practice and should not be attempted by inexperienced riders

mountain bike trials

Fun, skilled and spectacular – that's trial riding.

Almost a part of the biking underground, trials competitions are thin on the ground, but very popular with bikers who possess the light touch. They are the competitive expression of the self-testing that all bikers, particularly urban cowboys, practice when they do track-stands at red lights, or wheelies, when they hop crates or ride see-saws. Most competitions have ability and/or age bands, so anyone can have a go, although teenage boys seem to shine especially. A world championship exists, but has virtual sideshow status beside the downhill and cross-country championships. The situation undervalues the incredible skill of the riders and the visual appeal of "balance and suss" mountain biking.

So what is it? The trials course has a number of different obstacle stations, each obstacle being more or less within sight of the next and no two trials arenas are alike. The obstacles vary from carefully constructed works of art to natural features, such as found in a piece of woodland. Woods are rich in trials opportunities; you can try and get over fallen logs, or hop 180° round a tree-trunk on a slope, or see who can hop highest up a slope sideways.

World championship courses are extremely difficult, designed so that only experts stand even a slim chance of a avoiding failure. The favourites are head-high log-piles, that might take the competitor anything up to 5 minutes of continual hopping to complete. Other artful obstacles include

Practice lifting up the front wheel.

and the riders concentrate on getting it right. The reward is successfully clearing an obstacle, and a big cheer goes up as the tension is released. There is frustration when you make a mistake accompanied by a ripple of sympathetic applause. Many of them can dream of one day toppling professional stunt rider Hans "No Way" Rey, his famous quote being: "just don't say 'no way'" as he performs another impossible trick. A man who can hypnotize his bike, Rey relocated from his native Austria to the USA to hone his MTB skills after starting in BMX. Rey has pulled off stunts such as riding *up* the cascade of the Dunn River Falls in Jamaica, holding a front wheel end in the face of some unamused guards outside Buckingham Palace, and careering off the roof of his house into the swimming pool.

Like downhilling and dual slalom, MTB trials have grown from BMX, where the smaller bikes are more malleable but the bigger you grow, the more oversized you look on one.

You can use your rigid mountain bike for trialling – although a badly timed jump or hop can spell curtains for the front fork, and you should note that the damage will not be covered by the warranty. To increase the clearance above the ground, experts use just the little front ring, and trials frames are built around a high 12-inch-plus bottom bracket.

All-purpose MTB riders, whose bikes have to double up for cross-country and downhilling, might just add a chain-guard to stop the big ring losing its teeth on the obstacles.

Of all MTB disciplines, trials is the one that improves most with practice. Timing and balance are the key qualities, alongside upper body strength. The techniques you can practice are continuous hopping with turning, lifting the front wheel under perfect control to mount an obstacle, and pivoting on the front wheel to change direction. Scour local trails for obstacles, or build your own progressively more difficult versions, and always wear helmet, elbow and knee pads. Trials are great for sharpening off-road skills and are lots of fun, but do not attempt them until you know what you are doing.

Hans Rey in action.

burnt-out wrecks, where you have to jump up into the back of a rusting van, and come out through one of the rear doors.

Each station has its own dedicated marshall to do the scoring. You tackle the stations in whatever order you fancy. The aim is to get through the station without putting down your foot, known as a "dab". Every dab scores one penalty point on your scorecard, and the winner at the end of the show is whoever has the lowest score, perhaps even a clear round. You've blown the section if you dab three times, while even worse is if you put down both feet, which scores five penalty points. Expert riders practice damage limitation with tactical dabs when they find themselves in an impossible spot, which is better than total failure.

The atmosphere is calm and controlled, as the spectators concentrate on the riders

the reebok
dual eliminator

California 1992. The sunshine state and the birthplace of mountain biking. A new event, the *Reebok* Dual Eliminator was born which, like the 1970s' Repack Downhill, will set new levels of off-road adrenalin and media coverage. The course and the nail-biting format draw a speeds to match the Tour de France swooping down the Alps.

Commissioned by television, with an opulent US$5,000 prize purse for the winner in both women's and men's competitions, the *Reebok* has gone down in history as the mother of downhill duels. Unlikely to be surpassed in scale or speed it has been an unforgettable triumph for the un-Eliminated: Missy Giove and Dave Cullinan in 1992; Kim Sonier and Myles Rockwell in 1993, Regina Stiefl and Jürgen Benecke in 1994 and in 1995 Myles Rockwell and Giovanna Bonazzi.

Mammoth Mountain

The dual eliminator is run on the slopes of Mammoth Mountain – a high-altitude ski resort. The course, which begins at a height of 3,000 m (10,000 ft), was already notorious as the home of the "Kamikaze Downhill", an open national championship event. Any competitor in this regular Kamikaze, hurling their body out of ski-gates down the track with Californian magma rocketing out from under the wheels knew they were riding for their lives. A fact attested to by a video made of the event that focused in gruesome detail on the sliding crashes.

Devoid of technical trials the course is a wide, plain piste that curves around the mountain and descends a total of 630 m (2,050 ft) over 5.6 km (3½ miles). The surface is gravel with small rocks and a couple of dustbowl corners. The top half of the course overhangs huge drops and is above the vegetation line. It is very exposed, with the Californian sun glaring down summer and winter, and surrounded by a fabulous vista of peaks covered with lingering snow.

With so few obstacles to slow the riders down, the Kamikaze handlebar computers told a scary story. The course speed record had gradually risen in these open events past 72–80 km/h (45–50 mph), as technology introduced full suspension bikes and life-preserving body armour. The speeds were unheard of on any other mountain bike course, even the notorious European runs designed and hammered by riders born and bred in the traditions of Alpine downhill ski-ing.

The Reebok goes one step further. From the first year, the involvement of big bucks American *ESPN TV* and *Reebok* as sponsor threw more petrol on the fire. The organizers, facing the task of satisfying the demands of televisuality, announced a new format for the competition. The Dual Eliminator would be an invitational pairs knock-out. While the Kamikaze event is one rider at a time against the clock, the Eliminator is a head-to-head, which means unwelcome consequences if either duellist loses control too close to the other or to the edge.

The first year, the fastest downhillers in the world, 32 men and 8 women, were selected on their results. Each pair would have two tries the difference between total run times deciding who would go through to the next round. The final would be decided the same way, and, with the exception of a couple of small changes, this remains the format to today.

The action that first year was watched by hundreds of spectators as the pairs shot by a total of 76 times in about 5 hours. As they completed each run, there was no quiet moment for the riders to contemplate how good it felt to be alive. As one commentator put it, they had to stay, "smiling brightly for ... the television soundbites".

The men's finalists managed to complete an exhausting total of 10 chicken runs; the women finalists, without particular regret, 6. To keep the pace high, a helicopter picked up the riders who had qualified for the next round and choppered them back to the top of Mammoth Mountain – skinning 10 minutes off the gondola's best uphill run.

Competitors feel the thrill of the downhill.

Faster and faster

The Dual Eliminator has always been a showcase for the latest downhill bikes. Full suspension and chain tensioners are universal, sometimes with booming disc wheels and usually with single chainrings as big as 60 T. The first year, the fastest time was less than 5 minutes, with an average speed over 48 km/h (30 mph). Top speeds now reach 88 km /h (55 mph), and, it is rumoured, even higher, as the world's fastest and most colourful mountain bikers open the throttle into each other's faces.

In the first year excitement and curiosity overcame doubts about the recklessness of elbowing for dusty corners at 72 km/h (45 mph). Although no-one has been badly hurt, John Tomac, the darling of US racing, has declined his invitations to subsequent events ever since, because of the risks.

On the Dual Eliminator riders have perhaps come closest to discovering the absolute limits of downhilling, limits that still thrive today.

And they're off – the start of the Dual Eliminator.

the coors
dual descender

A new action competition has sprung up in the UK which looks a trend-setter. The thrilling Dual Descender, sponsored by *Coors* lager, combines the pacing of a downhill knock-out with the technical challenge of a dual slalom. Like the *Reebok Dual Eliminator*, the Descender is a head-to-head race on one lane, but features dozens of zig-zags marked by ski-gates. The first rider over the line qualifies for the next round, the loser is out. The finalists can conceivably be the only contestants left with working bikes and bodies.

There are no rules to govern the sporting behaviour between the start and finish. You cannot commit a foul, nor cry foul on your opponent. The action starts the second the riders burst from the starting gate in an anaerobic charge for the first corner. The strategy is to get there in the lead and hold the advantage down the zig-zags, blocking counter-attacks from your opponent. Sharp riders win the advantage with a neat pivot not their sprints. Whoever comes out in front from the final turn is odds-on favourite to win the sprint for the finish line.

Lasting less than 5 minutes, the entry is dominated by stunt masters from BMX, MTB downhilling and motorbike trials. These gals and guys and have the fastest 0–50 km/h (0–30 mph) times, rely on their feet for braking and balance and can manipulate a bike beneath them as if it were made of rubber. They either feel no fear, or they don't show it, or, most likely, they forget fear in the excitement of the duel. Contestants wh are used to more genteel cross-country racing have to shift attitude and accept the rough and ready.

It's fast and furious over the zig zags.

Make some air and please the crowds.

Spectators get a treat when a pair of equally matched riders do the Descender and each turn is a struggle for control. The ground shakes and the dust rises as two *Kevlar*-clad warriors with precious little sense of personal safety rip at top speed for the first right-hand flag. At the last moment, they slam on the brakes and skid to grab the tightest angle into the corner. One rider gets ahead, forcing the other on to the wider line, or to wait for the next corner to pounce. The most exciting contests come when the riders barge each other all the way down the course – as if locked together in a fairy elephant waltz. Like a chicken run, if neither rider backs down for a turn you have impact. Occasionally the individuals disappear into an indistinguishable cartoon cloud of wheels, arms and legs – you half-expect to see bang! crash! flash up in a superimposed bubble. Or they both oversteer and end up going nowhere uphill. Then there's a scoot with one leg, the weight on the cross-bar to get the bike back under control and charge back downhill.

Collisions are shrugged off as part of the game, and there are surprisingly few serious breakages of people or parts. Any damage done is more likely to result from the corner clashes than the speed, which never gets high. The amount of minor frame dinks and snapped-off bits of bike, however, explains why most of the regular competitors are sponsored riders with a bottomless pool of equipment.

The bikes used in the Dual Descender are the same as for downhilling, built to be bomb-proof and to withstand crashes at higher velocities than dashing from pole to pole. The favourite suspension fork is the beefy *RockShox Judy* and most bikes have full suspension. High action mountain biking being the depository of technological development, there is a ready sprinkling of the latest colourful components and an utter absence of pannier racks and reflectors.

Body armour is a must. Some riders favour full-face helmets, or BMX lids with chin-straps. Full-length *Kevlar* arm and body padding is everywhere, even when the temperature is high, with the professionals wearing protective skin-suits. Because there are wildly swinging legs on every corner, the downhill-only riders use platform pedals devoid of straps or springs. SPDs are chosen by women and men who use their pedalling fitness to supplement their technical prowess, or whose bikes double up for cross-country, often also held sometime during a weekend event.

The *Coors* Dual Descender gets the crowds cheering and the competitors think it's great fun. Many of them welcome a break from the earnest, intense business of downhilling and cross-country. The event undoubtedly a winner with an assured future in action mountain biking

Its a fierce contest for the lead on the finishing straight.

big-time air

Air bandits are singularly awesome among bikers. No other skill in the mountain bike's repertoire is as dramatic or as much pure fun as high-jumping. A little goes a long way and anyone who can even jump a few inches, possesses the key to respect from their posse. And what better way is there to chat up the object of your desires, than to let the bike make the introduction.

So how does mankind go about flying without wings? When building up for some ethereal action, the first thing to do is buy air-time. Build up your speed and launch yourself off a lip, heading for a landing point which is preferably lower than the take-off point. Every mountain biker should be able to make a fistful of air on any old off-road track, using even little ripples and momentum. Then there are proper launch pads, for example the bumps and flat-tops, abundant on BMX tracks, which have long run-offs. Or, as in trials, seek out the local disused quarry or woodland for bomb-holes and drops.

The bigger the lip, the closer the sky, so start low and work up to greater height. Approach the launch-pad fast, and either let momentum drive you upward, or help it by pulling up on the pedals on take-off. Rule number one is to land with the front and

Jason McRoy carves up the air.

back wheels level.

Once airborne, it is time to start styling. Most bikers who can jump grew up in BMX, and have applied the tricks to the faster if less manoeuvrable mountain bike. Hence the crossover in airborne positions. Try the "pointer", where you point at your desirable individual, or the camera or the spectators with one hand, or cross it over your heart in a prayer for deliverance.

There's the "cross-up", where you steer the wheel round an invisible corner in the air until the brake levers go plink on the top tube, then try to get pointing straight ahead again before touch-down. The "table-top" is a bigger version of the cross-up, where you pull the whole bike up flat in the air ahead of you perpendicular to the trail, and then re-align in time for landing. Sticking one or both legs out is only part-way to the most outrageous position, the fabled "nothing"

where nothing is in contact with the bike, arms, legs or bum. Catching the bike again is the trick, or getting a big mattress in place quickly.

Wear the gear. A helmet, elbow and knee-pads will take the brunt of a bad landing, as will the bike, which cannot be protected the way you can. Apart from a stack of new pairs of forks, the best equipment aid is a pair of spring-clip SPD pedals. Particularly helpful for beginners, they make it much easier to boost the bike's upward motion.

This goes no way

toward explaining why great jumpers get high wearing trainers. Maybe their coordination is better simply because the air up there is cleaner. Take it easy, bike birds.

The crossover – turning the bars until they face the top tube.

The softer the landing, the bigger the air.

making a splash

The trigger for the UK's annual lake-leaping spectacle – at the Malverns Classic festival a few years back – was spontaneity. A handful of splash-loving bikers, a ramp, a waist-deep landscaped pond and some rapidly withdrawing ducks is all it took. Like a Hollywood musical number, hurling your bike and body into water off a ramp should not look rehearsed, but there is inevitably some forethought involved somewhere. However, although these guys could build jump ramps in their sleep, what they were not so used to was the soft, wet, and for once warm, landing. They saw Malvern's muddy waters, felt the 35°C (95°F) heat, remembered their ram-ant BMX education and got launching.

First there were two, then three, then five. The multi-coloured crowds gathered to join in the outburst of fun and the discovery of another crazy new bike thing. Forget off-road, the MTB could now go off-land, confirming its legendary versatility. Guys and a single girl who fancied having a go tentatively peered into the murky shallows, observed the guy who had just bobbed back up grinning, with hos arms aloft in triumph, flinging his hair out of his eyes, and very much not drowned. One by one, the intrepid bikers committed themselves to the Malvern baptism and took their place a short distance back from the ramp until 20 bikers had leapt.

The crowd loved it. Each sprint for the boards was accompanied by a crescendo of cheers. The cheerleader, and likely ringleader of the affair, was concealed beneath the ramp, just like a prompter at the theatre, supporting the plywood with his back, as he spurred the crowd on.

The styles fluctuated wildly from the high trajectory short-distance splashdown, to the low trajectory, long-distance splashdown. Lots of favourite jumping styles were on display, such as table-tops and cross-ups, neither of which really left enough time to get rid of the bike before hitting the water. But what are a few more bruises when the sun is shining?

For lake leaping in shallow waters the only safety rule is to let go of the bike – even better to eject it forcibly – the minute you leave the ramp. The two of you can then go your separate ways. The worst leap was where one of the guys, apparently scared rigid, held firmly on to the bike, hands on the handlebars, bum on the seat and feet on the pedals, all the way into the water.

The best leap that first year was a single front somersault with unbelievable height, perhaps 6 m (20 ft) into the air. The guy rapidly threw the bike aside while he tumbled about in the ether and eventually hit the water near the far bank after what seemed to be a full 20 minutes in the air.

Since those heady days of 1990, the Malverns festival has remained one of the biggest summer MTB events in Britain. There have been attempts to recapture the spontaneity of the first lake leaping bonanza, but, everyone agreed, by making the event official, and even includ-

Dive! Dive! Dive!

ing it on the timetable, the spirit of the moment was somewhat lost.

A group of British bikers based in the Lake District have since claimed to have pre-empted that occasion – in the chilly and much deeper waters of Lake Windermere. No ramp needed here, just a jetty or a quayside, a lifebelt and a mug of cocoa. In winter if you are submerged in the waters of the northern lakes for more than a minute or so, the chill can quickly lead to hypothermia. Another wild and crazy crew has since exploited the waterski jump ramp at Britain's national water sports centre for a bit of big leaping.

Of course, you can drown playing about in water hanging on to items that sink like stones. So, do not do it unless you can find shallows to leap into or have the watchful eye of a fully qualified lifeboat crew.

Rule number 1 – rapidly let go of the bike.

187

glossary

Aheadset An improved style of headset steering bearings, which clamps rather than screws on to the special steerer tube. It can be adjusted using a single Allen key, rather than a pair of bulky headset spanners.

Allen keys The hexagonal-head tools that fix the majority of bolts around the mountain bike.

Aluminium In its pure form, a soft, light material, which, with added alloys becomes strong and stiff enough for bicycle frames. It is used in oversize dimensions for strength, allowing the tube walls to be made extremely thin, giving an overall weight advantage.

Bar ends Add-ons for the handlebars to give more hand positions.

Barrel adjuster The initial, tool-free method of adjusting brakes and gears. To adjust the brakes, turn the barrels – placed where the cables come out of the levers – anti-clockwise to bring the brake blocks closer to the rim. To adjust the accuracy of the pre-set in the rear gearing, turn the barrel – where the cable exits the rear changer (derailleur) – clockwise to pull the changer away from the wheel.

Bearing A part which allows two pieces of the bike to turn independently of each other, while remaining firmly attached. Bikes generally have five sets of bearings; the headset for steering; the bottom bracketfor pedalling; in the pedals themselves; the hubs (the wheels) and in the freewheel or freehub for freewheeling and back-pedalling. All bearings must be maintained.

Brake types The cantilever rim brake is the most common MTB brake for its accessibility, although disc brakes, which clamp to a disc at the hub are more powerful. Coaster brakes, which work by stopping the pedals spinning, were found on the early klunkers. Hub brakes are sealed from the elements and are operated from the levers.

Brazing (fillet brazing) A method of joining steel tubes using a secondary molten material, such as silver or brass.

Bottom bracket or pedal spindle The axle bearing around which the pedals and cranks turn to operate the chain.

Butting Where tubing has been made with a variable wall thickness for strength and lightweight appropriately. Double butting means that the tubing is thicker, but not necessarily doubled, at the ends near the joins, and thinner in the central section.

Carbon fibre A material derived from crude oil, carbon fibre is light and strong, has a grain like timber and can be used directionally for strength and light weight.

Cartridge bearings Enclosed bearing units that are theoretically maintenance-free (see bearings).

Chainrings On MTBS, the triple front gears. Chains wear together with chainrings, so change the chain frequently to save money on replacing the rings.

Chainset The cranks, crank spider (to which the chainrings attach) and the chainrings.

Chain stay The tubing that runs from the rear hub to the bottom of the seat tube at the bottom bracket. Usually around 40.5–43 cm (16–17 in) long. A shorter chain stay gives better grip at the rear of the bike when climbing, but is more difficult to control downhill.

CNC (computer numerically controlled) Cut or carved from a billet of material, usually aluminium, by a robot blade or laser directed by computer.

Componentry One of the two main constituents of a bicycle, the other being the frame. You can either choose an almost complete set of componentry (groupset) from one manufacturer, or mix-and-match your choice of parts to include those from specialists, according to budget and performance.

Crank A simple part with a pedal at one end and the bottom bracket at the other.

Cromoly (chromium-molybdenum) A steel alloy that comes in different price and performance grades, from basic to top class.

Derailleur The French word for de-railer, or front and rear gear changers.

Down tube The strongest tube in the frame, running diagonally from the head tube to the bottom bracket.

Dropouts The slots at the back of the frame and bottom of the fork into which the wheels slip and do up. In road riding, horizontal dropouts allow you to set the fore and aft position of the wheel, but MTBS almost universally have easier, pre-set vertical dropouts.

End-stop screw The little cross-head screws on the front and rear changers that set how far the changers can move. These are adjusted to prevent the chain falling off either side.

Fork Holds the front wheel on, forks are manufactured with or without suspension.

Frame materials The skeletal structure of an MTB can be made from steel, aluminium, titanium, carbon-fibre and magnesium.

Gear ratio The relationship between the number of teeth in the chainring (front) and sprocket (rear) engaged. If equal, the gear ratio is 1:1 – the rear wheel turns at the same speed as the pedals. On fast ground, if the chainring has 48 teeth and the sprocket 24, the ratio is 2:1 – the rear wheel turns at double the speed of the pedals, twice for every pedal revolution.

Gear shifter types Three main versions include barrel (GripShift) changers, underbar (*Shimano RapidFire*) levers and overbar thumb levers.

Groupset A set of compatible componentry from one maker, usually *Shimano* or *Sachs*, found on the majority of shop bikes. Groupsets are made at different prices and quality.

Gussets Individual reinforcing plates placed at tube junctions, particularly the head tube, such as on *Bontrager* bikes.

Headset The steering bearing.

Head tube The short length of tubing that forms the front apex of the frame.

Hi-tensile steel The grade of steel below cromoly, found either in part or in full on cheaper bikes.

Hub The bearings on which the wheels turn.

Indexing (index shifting) Pre-set "click-click" gears.

Jockey wheel The two wheels in the rear changer which align the chain across the sprockets.

Kevlar A branded, highly-resistant carbon material layered in tyres to prevent punctures.

Lubricant The grease, oils and lubes that keep a bike turning and prolong its life. All moving surfaces should be kept lubed, so lubrication is an essential part of pre- and post-ride maintenance.

Lugging (lugwork) Reinforcing sleeves that may be used in the brazing process in making steel frames. On aluminium frames, the tubing may be bonded inside aluminium lugs at low temperatures.

Main triangle The front half of a regular diamond-shaped frame, containing the top, seat, head and down tubes. On cheaper steel bikes, often the rear triangle, or the secondary tubes in the front triangle, such as the seat tube, will be made of high-tensile rather than cromoly steel.

Microdrive The original *SunTour* name for close MTB gearing (smaller chainrings and sprockets) that has the same ratios as former wider gearing with less bulk, more clearance and, in theory, more wear. The *Shimano* equivalent, *Hyperdrive*, is commonplace.

Play The looseness that needs to be eliminated in bearings and brake cables.

Quick release One-lever ties for the wheels and seat post.

Rear triangle In a conventionally-shaped diamond frame, the back tubes, the chain and seat stays. They may be of a lower grade steel on cheaper bikes.

Rim The structural outer edge of the wheel, the rim is made of aluminium alloy, and provides the braking surface, hooks the tyre and tube in place, and anchors the spokes. Its size is measured in millimetres according to the diameter of the inside edge that holds the bead of the tyre. The average for an MTB is 559 mm.

Seat cluster The tube junction of the seat tubes and the seat stays at the saddle. It is often reinforced when using a long seat post with lugging, a gusset or butting.

Seat stay The double tubes that run from the rear hub to the seat cluster below the saddle. The two configurations are "wishbone" – where the stays come together above the wheel and a single tube connects them to the seat cluster – and the standard "dual" – where the two tubes run all the way to the seat cluster, usually with a reinforcing bridge for rigidity.

Seat tube The central vertical tube that runs from the bottom of the bike at the bottom bracket to the seat post.

Single-butting No butting, where a tube has the same wall thickness throughout its length (see also butting).

Single-track Where the trail is only wide enough for a single bike, or person, or horse. Great fun.

Sprockets The seven or eight rear gears.

SPD pedals (Shimano pedalling dynamics) The standard clipless/spring binding pedal (and compatible shoe cleat and shoe) made under licence by other manufacturers. Essential for racing, helpful for fun riding and touring, but clogs up in bad mud.

Spokes The tensioned wires in the wheel that spread the load and keep the rim circular under compression from the ground. Butted spokes are thinner in the middle than at the edge.

Spoke nipple The little nut used to put tension into the spokes with a spoke key.

Standover height Measured from the ground to the top of the top tube where you would stand over it. It is the key measurement in getting the right size mountain bike, and should be 5–7 cm (2–3 in) shorter than your inside leg measurement.

Stem The section that attaches the handlebars to the head tube.

Straddle cable The brake wire that bridges the two arms. In conventional cantilever brakes it should hold the arms at 45° at rest. Other versions do away with a single straddle cable, by running the main cable all the way to one brake arm and having a shorter wire for the other arm.

Suspension Allows either the front or both wheels to move independently of the frame and rider for better control and higher speeds. For comfort, secondary suspension in the seat post or stem is also available.

Titanium An abundant element, used extensively in the aerospace industry. It is lighter than steel, stronger than aluminium and expensive to work.

Toeclips and straps Simple, effective, versatile way of keeping the feet attached to the pedals. Recommended for touring, but not for racing.

Top tube The horizontal tube that connects the head tube with the seat cluster.

Tungsten Inert Gas (TIG) welding A method of welding steel and aluminium tubing without oxygen or a secondary welding material.

Tyre types MTB tyres are 26 in (650 mm) in diameter, with a variety of patterns, from slick for tarmac, to spiky for deep mud. They come in different widths, averaging 1.95 in, with a minimum 1.5 in permissible in MTB racing. Much is talked about tyres for different conditions – dry, wet, muddy – with the fundamental proviso that they are knobbly and wide.

Tyre pressures MTB tyres should be run at 35–55 psi, according to the softness of the ground – this information will be written on the sidewall of the tyre. Lower pressure means better grip; higher pressure mean less comfort – no problem if the bike has suspension.

Valves The most popular type is the thin Presta. Less common is the wider Schraeder, also found on car tyres, which needs a wider-drilled hole in the rim.

Wheel size Everyone calls the standard MTB wheel, a 26-inch (650 mm) wheel, referring to the size of the tyre (the outside diameter). However, according to the standard metric Systeme Internationale (SI), wheels are actually measured in millimetres, using the diameter of the inside edge of the rim where the tyre beading sits. This is generally 559 mm (22 in).

index

index

further reading

Nick Crane, *Atlas Biker – Mountain Biking in Morocco*,
The Oxford Illustrated Press, 1990

Judy Ridgeway, *Food for Sport*,
Boxtree, 1994

Bicycling Science,
The MIT Press, 1993

Douglas Hayduk,
Bicycle Metallurgy for the Cyclist,
Johnson Publishing Co, 1987

Edmund R Burke,
Cycling Health and Physiology,
Vitesse Press, 1992

acknowledgements

With thanks to the following for their help:
Brixton Cycles, London for their loan of equipment and mechanic Mel Allwood; *Exodus MTB Travel* for their help with the section on Morrocco; Carole Bauer-Romanil, curator of the Mountain Bike Hall of Fame; Crested Butte, Colorado for information on the history of Mountain Biking; *Rim Tours*, Moab, Utah, for their help with the Slickrock section; Greg Yeoman for the Trans-Siberian Ride; *Mont Blanc Mountain Biking*, for help with the Chamonix section (Tel: UK – 01462 43786 for further details); Colin Farmer, *CTC Off-Road* for all his good work; Richard Hemington, *Specialized UK*, for UK reminiscences, Geoff Apps, *Cleland MTBs* for his tales, *Kona*, *Gt* and *Cannondale* MTBS for bike photos and specifications, Madison for *Shimano* information. Also John and Sarah Crowther and Perry Bellisario for their support and inspiration.

This book is dedicated to Jason McRoy.

picture acknowledgements

The publishers would like to thank the following sources for their kind permission to reproduce the photographs in this book.

Actionsnaps/Dave Stewart 178cl, 179br, 180cl, 181bl, 186tc; **ATB Sales** 66; **Jules Bellier** 6, 57c, 62, 43, 143; **Bliss/M.Fearon** 12br, 14, 25, 29, 41c, 58r, 66, 77, 80, 85, 91br, 91bl, 93br, 101tr, 102, 103bl, 106, 110c, 132tr, 138, 139tr, 141tr, 142br, 142tl, 160tl, 161bl, 162, 163, 181tr, 185tc; **Cannondale USA** 26, 27; **Caratti Sport Ltd** 28; **Nick Crane** 170, 172cl, 173tr, 173bl, 174tc, 175tr; **Nicky Crowther** 24, 158; **C. Hultner/MTB Action**.78; **David Epperson** 8tc, 9bl, 10tr, 11tr, 86, 133bc; **Image Bank/JKelly** 158; **Madison Cycles** 10bl; **John Schwelm** 152, 154tc, 155bc, 156cr, 157bl, 157tr; **Schwinn Cycles** 11bl; **Science Photo Library** 20,21; **Stockfile/S.Behr** 4, 11tr, 12tl, 13tl, 16, 20, 21, 26, 34c, 60c, 64, 65, 66, 67, 70, 72, 73, 75, 76, 79, 81, 83, 85, 88, 90, 92bl, 93tl, 100, 104tl, 105tl, 105br, 109c, 110 tcr, 111br, 112cr, 113r, 114tc, 117tl, 117l, 118, 121bl, 121tr, 123tr, 124br, 125tc, 126, 128bc, 129r, 129tl, 130, 134tc, 135cr, 135bl, 136bl, 137tc, 137br, 138b, 140tr, 141bl, 164, 166tl, 167bc, 167tr, 168tr, 169, 179tl, 182bc, 183br, 183tl, 184cl, 185br, 187cl, 187tr, 190; **X-Lite** 82; **Dave Yates** 13; **Greg Yeoman** 38l, 146, 148tr, 148tl, 150tl, 151tr, 151bc.